MUSCLE CARS

An Illustrated Guide

MUSCLE CARS
An Illustrated Guide

CHARTWELL
BOOKS

This edition published in 2015 by CHARTWELL BOOKS, an imprint of Book Sales,
a division of Quarto Publishing Group USA Inc.
142 West 36th Street, New York, New York 10018 USA

Printed with permission of and by arrangement with Amber Books Ltd.

ISBN: 978-0-7858-3228-7

Produced by
Amber Books Ltd
Bradley's Close
74-77 White Lion Street
London N1 9PF
United Kingdom
www.amberbooks.co.uk

Printed in China

CONTENTS

Introduction

WHILE THE 1950s saw the American auto industry undergo a period of colossal growth, the 1960s were the decade that saw it really diversify. America was witnessing huge changes, on both a social and an economic scale. The Cuban missile crisis was a warning that even the world's newest superpower wasn't invincible, John F Kennedy was assassinated, Martin Luther King led the Selma March, there was violence building in Vietnam and rock 'n' roll was giving way to newer types of progressive rock, experimental music and an era of free love. For car fans, the late 1960s were rebellious times. Gone were the glitz, glamour and outrageous fins of the '50s, a driver's status no longer dictated by the amount of chrome on the car. And if you did not want to join the hippies in their VW Buses and Bugs, or make an environmentally-conscious decision to downsize to a bland and boring compact sedan, there was only one way to go – the muscle car.

Muscle Car Revolution

It is impossible to say where it all started, as different people have different opinions about when precisely the muscle car revolution began. Some say it was 1964, with the launch of the Ford Thunderbird – a car that brought sports styling and affordable power to the masses. This, after all, was Thunderbird-style for the working man. But others believe the DNA of a muscle car to be such that the original cannot a sports model – and if you accept that definition, then there is only one place if could have all started, and that was with the Pontiac GTO.

Based on a stock Pontiac Tempest saloon, the 'Goat' came with a 6374cc (389ci) V8 engine under its hood and neat styling touches, including

With a top speed of 194km/h (121mph), the Ford Mustang Mach 1 was an immediate hit with muscle car lovers when it was introduced in 1969.

stacked front headlamps, polished magnesium alloy wheels, white-banded tyres and vinyl-covered roof. It was astonishingly fast, reaching 96km/h (60mph) from standstill in less than six seconds – a performance that many of today's brand new cars would struggle to beat. It is impossible to imagine the impact the GTO had over 40 years ago, when it first appeared in showrooms.

But if proof were needed that its impact was huge, you have only to look at what followed. Iconic models such as the Dodge Charger, Plymouth Roadrunner, Chevy Chevelle SS396 and Plymouth Hemi 'Cuda all owe a debt to the original Pontiac, and even more so to the hardcore of young American car enthusiasts who wanted wheels that could still make a stand against authority – without having to dig too deep into their pockets to afford them. It is ironic, then, that on the crest of a wave of damning media articles, GM stopped officially selling GTOs shortly after launch because of concerns over its public image. Luckily, the Pontiac dealer network was a little less nervous, and continued to build up GTOs from stock Tempests.

American Icon
This book celebrates the muscle car as an American icon. A four-wheeled breed of hero, it has been popularized in film and in song, from the silver screen classic *Two Lane Blacktop,* to Bruce

The Oldsmobile 4-4-2 W30 had plenty of power with its massive 6554cc (400ci) engine. This model features hood-mounted air-intakes.

Springsteen *Racing in the Street* in his '69 Chevy. This book charts the social impact, iconoclastic style and sheer boldness of cars that were so brave that some policy makers and safety panels tried to get them banned.

Ultimate Muscle Cars aims to put you behind the wheel. As well as charting the key dates, technological developments and under-hood data of America's finest muscle machines, the book is packed with stunning studio photography in a unique five-view format, coupled to detailed driving impressions and expert trivia. Given the trend towards rising prices on the muscle car scene in recent years, this is the closest that you will probably come to owning some of the true greats. These cars redefined the American car market, gave head to the street racing scene and did not so much break as completely shatter the performance car mould.

In *Ultimate Muscle Cars*, our aim is to show just how stunning these cars really were, and also to convey the thrill and exhilaration of driving them, with their incredible power outputs, stock drum brakes and wayward steering all adding to the appeal of cars that required skill just as much as brawn to drive.

AMC **AMX**

American Motors struggled to establish the sort of market identity that the other manufacturers had gained. Its 'character' car, possibly aimed at the Chevrolet Corvette, was the curious AMX two-seat coupe.

'...serious performance.'

'Turn the V8's starter motor and your senses awaken – this really sounds like a muscle machine. The deep reserves of torque make driving very easy, and there is plenty of power for fast takeoffs. Add in the optional quick-rack power steering, front disc brakes and limited-slip differential, and you have a serious performance machine that is just as capable of tackling twisty mountain roads as taking part in a traffic light drag race.'

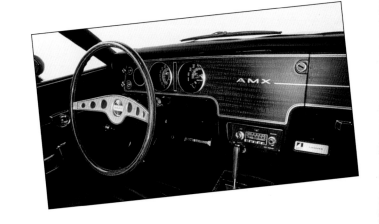

The dashboard is trimmed with wood grain trim, which was very stylish in the late 1960s.

Milestones

1968 Mid-season, AMC launches its new compact sports coupe with a choice of three V8 engines.

Another of AMC's compact muscle cars of the period was the Hurst SC Rambler.

1969 This year the AMX remains very much as the previous year.

1970 A mild restyle includes moving the spotlights to the front grill and adding a prominent hump to the bonnet. The standard engine expands to 6391cc (390ci) and power outputs rise. This is the last year of AMX sales.

Due to its design, many thought the AMX was supposed to compete with the Corvette.

1971 The AMX name is reduced to an option package on a larger and curvier Javelin. After 1973, it is more show than go.

UNDER THE SKIN

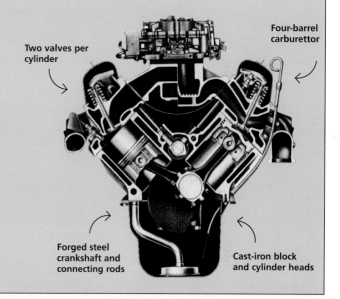

Independent front suspension

Live rear axle

Power front disc brakes

Unitary construction

Big-block V8

A classic Detroiter

Basically a shortened Javelin, the AMX is surprisingly usable and has an independent wishbone front suspension, with coil springs, shocks and an anti-roll bar. At the rear are semi-elliptic leaf springs and a rigid axle, plus telescopic shocks. Quick-ratio power-assisted steering options aid driveability.

THE POWER PACK

Muscle car V8

The standard engine in the AMX is a 225bhp, 4752cc (290ci) V8, although larger 343 and 390-V8s were optional. The 390 has a forged steel crankshaft and connecting rods, and a Carter AFB four-barrel carburettor. Its 315bhp power output is more than adequate, and the 425lb-ft of torque gives it pulling power which modern cars can only dream of. Though very underrated, this two-seat machine is one of the most potent cars ever to have seen action on American pavement.

Two valves per cylinder

Four-barrel carburettor

Forged steel crankshaft and connecting rods

Cast-iron block and cylinder heads

Super rare

Few changes occurred in 1969, but the 1970 AMX received a new grill with air vents, plus an improved interior, revised graphics and optional 38.1cm (15in) wheels. Just 4116 of the 1970 model were built, making it the rarest and most desirable of all AMXs.

The 1970 AMC AMX muscle cars are the most sought-after by collectors.

AMC **AMX**

By shortening the Javelin, AMC produced a cheap all-American two-seater sports coupe. Just 19,134 AMXs were built, making it a highly desirable muscle car today.

Bulging hood

A popular and sporty option on the AMX was the performance bonnet complete with dual air scoops. In 1968 the bonnet bulge was only decorative, but in 1970 the 'Go' package included a fully functional ram air system.

Sporty rear styling

The rear end is styled to give the car a smooth side profile but a ridged-out appearance from behind.

Chrome sills

With AMC's move toward flashier styling, the AMX featured chrome-plated sill covers. Later, these sills gained mock vents, mimicking a side-mounted exhaust.

Short wheelbase

Riding on a 246cm (97in) wheelbase, the AMX is 30.5cm (12in) shorter than the Javelin. This is even shorter than the Corvette, and qualified the AMX as one of the most compact American cars on the market at the time.

Two-seat interior

Shortening the bodyshell of the 2+2 Javelin means the AMX has room for just two passengers sitting on bucket seats, although there is a large space behind the seats for extra luggage.

Racing paintwork

The typical paint scheme for the AMX in its first two years was twin racing stripes running down the centre. Late 1970 models lose the bonnet stripes but have side stripes instead.

V8 power

Emphasizing its sporty role, the AMX was only ever sold with V8 engines. It was the only AMC at the time not to be offered with a straight-six engine as standard.

Specifications
1968 AMC AMX

ENGINE

Type: V8

Construction: Cast-iron block and cylinder heads

Valve gear: Two valves per cylinder operated by a single camshaft, pushrods and rockers

Bore and stroke: 106mm (4.16in) x 91mm (3.57in)

Displacement: 6391cc (390ci)

Compression ratio: 10.2:1

Induction system: Single four-barrel carburettor

Maximum power: 315bhp at 4600rpm

Maximum torque: 425lb-ft at 3200rpm

Top speed: 208km/h (129mph)

0–96km/h (0–60mph): 5.9 sec

TRANSMISSION

Three-speed automatic or four-speed manual

BODY/CHASSIS

Integral with two-door steel coupe body

SPECIAL FEATURES

AMX meant something special after AMC showed a stunning mid-engined sports car with the AMX badge.

The 6391cc (390ci) V8 was AMC's biggest engine in the late 1960s.

RUNNING GEAR

Steering: Recirculating ball

Front suspension: Wishbones with coil springs and shocks

Rear suspension: Rigid axle with leaf springs and shocks

Brakes: Drums (front and rear)

Wheels: Steel, 35.6cm (14in) dia.

Tyres: E70 x 35.6cm (14in)

DIMENSIONS

Length: 4.5m (177in)

Width: 1.82m (71.5in)

Height: 1.31m (51.7in)

Wheelbase: 246cm (97in)

Track: 149cm (58.8in) (front), 145cm (57in) (rear)

Weight: 1542kg (3400lb)

AMC REBEL MACHINE

After the overachieving little SC/Rambler of 1969, AMC returned to the muscle car market with the Rebel Machine. It still sported loud graphics, but thanks to a 6391cc (390ci), 340bhp V8, it was more than capable of outshining the competition and backing up its flashy appearance.

'...built to be a performer.'

'It may have a horizontal-sweep speedometer, but a four-on-the-floor and bucket seats assure you that this car was built to be a performer. The 6391cc (390ci) V8 is a lot more tractable than some others in everyday driving, and although throttle control is required to really get the Machine moving, the end result is worth it. Through corners, the AMC feels quite nimble for its size, with much less understeer than you would expect.'

A four-speed transmission with a cue-ball shifter is nestled between the front seats.

Milestones

1968 American Motors releases

photographs of a menacing mid-size Rebel. It has semi-gloss dark paint with matching bumpers and wheels. Called the Machine, it is intended for production in 1969, but none are actually sold.

The SC/Rambler was American Motors' first serious muscle car.

1969 With help

from Hurst Performance, AMC puts its biggest engine in the Rogue, resulting in the Hurst SC/Rambler. Packing 315bhp and capable of 14.3-second quarter miles, 1512 of these patriotic-looking cars are built.

The two-seater AMX could also get the big 390-c.i. V8.

1970 Replacing the

SC/Rambler is a new, larger Rebel Machine. Packing 340bhp from a 390 V8, it is a potent performer too, but lasts for only one model year.

UNDER THE SKIN

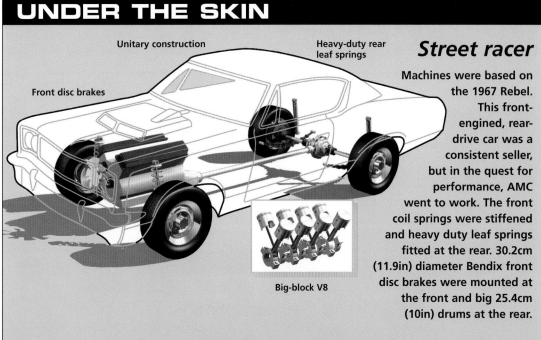

Unitary construction

Heavy-duty rear leaf springs

Front disc brakes

Big-block V8

Street racer

Machines were based on the 1967 Rebel. This front-engined, rear-drive car was a consistent seller, but in the quest for performance, AMC went to work. The front coil springs were stiffened and heavy duty leaf springs fitted at the rear. 30.2cm (11.9in) diameter Bendix front disc brakes were mounted at the front and big 25.4cm (10in) drums at the rear.

THE POWER PACK

AMC's biggest

In order to compete with the big three, American Motors realized that the best way was to stuff its largest engine in a mid size car. The 6391cc (390ci) mill that powered all Machines is an enlarged version of the 343 unit. It followed customary practice with a cast-iron block and heads, plus two valves per cylinder. Where the 343 has cast-iron rods and crankshaft, the 390 has forged-steel items and larger bearings. The 390 is a moderate performer, producing its 340bhp at 5100rpm.

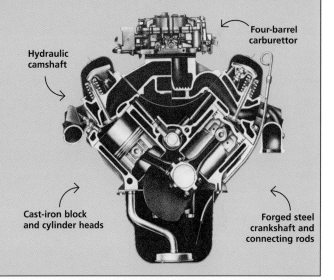

Four-barrel carburettor

Hydraulic camshaft

Cast-iron block and cylinder heads

Forged steel crankshaft and connecting rods

Patriotic

Rebel Machines were offered for only one year, and with a production total of 2326 are not exactly common. The first 1000 cars built had a special white, blue and red colour scheme, making them particularly sought-after in AMC circles.

Later Machines could be ordered in any Rebel factory colour.

AMC **REBEL MACHINE**

Although AMC stated 'The Machine is not that fast,' the car could give many muscle cars from the big three a run for their money, particularly with an experienced driver behind the wheel.

King of the cubes

In 1970, the 6391cc (390ci) V8 was the biggest engine offered by American Motors. With a big four-barrel carburetor and functional bonnet scoop, it produces a credible 340bhp and 430lb-ft of torque, good enough for mid-14-second $1/4$-mile ETs.

Strong transmission

Like the AMX and Javelin, the Machine was offered with a Borg-Warner T-10 four-speed manual transmission and a Hurst shifter. This enabled lightning-quick getaways from the lights.

Twin-Grip

Transmitting power to the rear tyres is a Twin-Grip differential with standard 3.54:1 final drive. Steeper gearing was offered over the counter – up to an incredible 5.00:1 for hardcore drag-racer types.

Power steering

Manual steering was standard, but many buyers considered it too heavy and thus ordered the optional power setup. It was, however, boosted and contemporary road testers wrote that it was 'grossly over-assisted.'

Stiff suspension

Rebel Machines rode on some of the stiffest suspension from Detroit. Fitting the Rebel wagon's heavy-duty rear leaf springs gave a street racer stance, and although handling is good for a muscle car, the jacked-up rear results in severe wheel hop if the pedal is floored from a standing start.

Hood scoop

Besides having an interesting look, the vacuum-operated bonnet scoop is functional too, forcing cooler, denser air into the engine. The scoop assembly also contains an integrated 8000rpm tachometer, which can be difficult to read in harsh sunlight or rain.

Specifications

1970 AMC Rebel Machine

ENGINE

Type: V8

Construction: Cast-iron block and heads

Valve gear: Two valves per cylinder operated by pushrods and rockers

Bore and stroke: 106mm (4.17in) x 91mm (3.57in)

Displacement: 6391cc (390ci)

Compression ratio: 10.0:1

Induction system: Four-barrel carburetor

Maximum power: 340bhp at 5100rpm

Maximum torque: 430lb-ft at 3600rpm

Top speed: 204km/h (127mph)

0–96km/h (0–60mph): 6 sec

TRANSMISSION

Borg-Warner T-10 four-speed manual

BODY/CHASSIS

Steel unitary chassis with two-door coupe body

SPECIAL FEATURES

In 1970, the 390 was the largest engine in AMC's inventory.

The functional bonnet scoop houses an integrated tachometer.

RUNNING GEAR

Steering: Recirculating ball

Front suspension: Unequal-length A-arms with coil springs, telescopic shock absorbers and stabilizer bar

Rear suspension: Live axle with semi-elliptic leaf-springs, telescopic shock absorbers and stabilizer bar

Brakes: Discs front, drums rear

Wheels: 17.8cm (7in) x 38.1cm (15in) pressed steel

Tyres: Goodyear Polyglas E60-15

DIMENSIONS

Length: 5.05m (199.0in)

Width: 1.96m (77.2in)

Height: 1.43m (56.2in)

Wheelbase: 290cm (114.0in)

Track: 151.6cm (59.7in) (front), 152cm (60.0in) (rear)

Weight: 1656kg (3650lb)

Buick **GNX**

The basic idea of the GNX was to mimic what Buick did with the GSX™ project in 1970. Because 1987 marked the end of the rear-wheel drive Regal™, Buick wanted to build a killer limited edition performance car using its turbo V6 engine.

'...B-B-Bad to the Bone."

"The caption on the 1987 Buick GNX poster read: "The Grand National™ to end all Grand Nationals." When the V6 is fired up, it sounds docile. With one foot on the brake and the other on the pedal, the boost needle rises to 1 psi. Release the brake and drop the accelerator and the 3.8l (232ci) engine makes 15 psi of boost rocketing the car down the ¼ mile in 13.43 seconds at 167km/h (104mph). Another Turbo Buick promotion labelled the car as 'B-B-Bad to the Bone' – and it lives up to this reputation.'

The standard GN gauges were scrapped in favour of analogue instruments from Stewart-Warner.

Milestones

1978 A downsized Buick Regal is launched with a turbo 3.8l (232ci) V6 engine that kicks out 150bhp.

The turbo V6 was also offered in Regal T-Types.

1982 215 Grand Nationals and 2022 T-Types are built.

1984 GNs return with an all-black exterior and a 200-bhp turbo V6 engine. Grand Nationals are nothing more than an appearance package on the Buick T-Type.

1986 The Grand National and T-Types get an air-to-air intercooler revised fuel management system and relocated turbocharger. The engine makes 235bhp.

Buick sold 20,193 GNs in 1987.

1987 Stock turbo Buicks make 345bhp. Buick and ASC/Mclaren build 547 GNX cars to commemorate the final year of the turbocharged cars.

UNDER THE SKIN

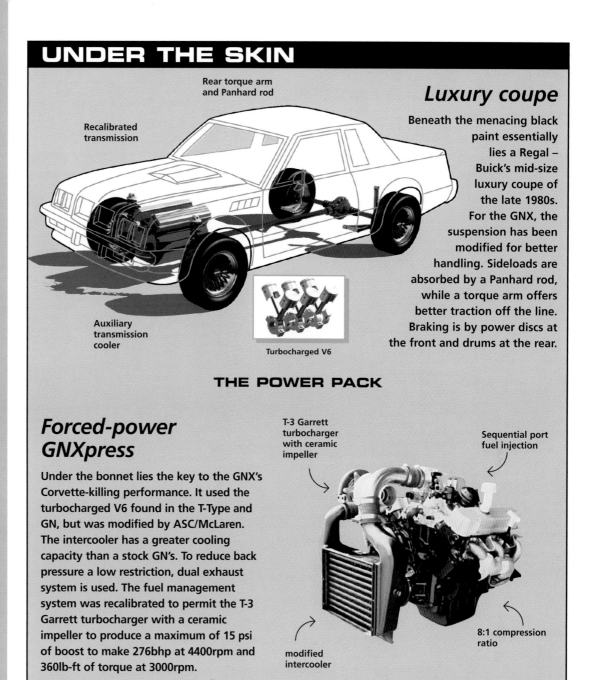

Rear torque arm and Panhard rod

Recalibrated transmission

Auxiliary transmission cooler

Turbocharged V6

Luxury coupe

Beneath the menacing black paint essentially lies a Regal – Buick's mid-size luxury coupe of the late 1980s. For the GNX, the suspension has been modified for better handling. Sideloads are absorbed by a Panhard rod, while a torque arm offers better traction off the line. Braking is by power discs at the front and drums at the rear.

THE POWER PACK

Forced-power GNXpress

Under the bonnet lies the key to the GNX's Corvette-killing performance. It used the turbocharged V6 found in the T-Type and GN, but was modified by ASC/McLaren. The intercooler has a greater cooling capacity than a stock GN's. To reduce back pressure a low restriction, dual exhaust system is used. The fuel management system was recalibrated to permit the T-3 Garrett turbocharger with a ceramic impeller to produce a maximum of 15 psi of boost to make 276bhp at 4400rpm and 360lb-ft of torque at 3000rpm.

T-3 Garrett turbocharger with ceramic impeller

Sequential port fuel injection

8:1 compression ratio

modified intercooler

Modern Muscle

During the 1980s late-model muscle cars were beginning to resurface. It was the first time since the 1960s that American cars were running the S/S ¼ mile in under 14 seconds. The Buick GNX was the fastest production car in 1987 and is a landmark car for collectors.

Surprisingly, the 1987 GNX was faster than the new Corvette that year.

Buick GNX 🇺🇸

Buick had three objectives with the GNX; to drop its 0-96km/h (0–60mph) by almost a second over a stock GN, to revise the body and interior in functional areas, and to build a limited number to create exclusivity and collectability. It met them all.

Flared wheel arches
Because of the larger and wider wheels and tyres, the front and rear wheel well openings had to be modified and fitted with composite fender flares. They blend in nicely with the rest of the GNX's styling.

Upgraded turbocharged engine
The 3.8l (232ci) SFI turbocharged engines are refitted with a better turbo, improved intercooler, recalibrated fuel management system and a low restriction exhaust system.

Ceramic impeller
The ceramic impeller in the turbocharger greatly reduces turbo lag.

Live axle
The same 8.5-inch rear that is found in the GN and T-Type is retained in the GNX. It also uses the same 3.42:1 axle ratio. All GNX cars came equipped with aluminium rear brake drums to help save weight.

Powermaster brakes
A unique braking system was used on all turbocharged Buicks. Instead of a vacuum-assisted system, it uses a hydraulic system that works off the power steering pump.

Modified transmission
A stock GN 200-4R transmission with a 2.74:1 first-gear ratio and an increased stall speed torque converter was used in the GNX. It was recalibrated for increased line pressure, resulting in firmer shifts.

40.6cm (16in) x 203cm (8in) alloy wheels
Larger 40.6cm (16in) x 20.3cm (8in) BBS style black mesh wheels were used on all GNXs. It's a very similar wheel used on the Trans Am GTA, but with a different offset.

Stiffer suspension
The GNX has a unique rear suspension. It uses a Panhard rod and torque arm. It also uses the same 19mm (0.75in) anti-roll bar and Delco shocks found on GNs and T-Types.

Black out
Like all 1984–1987 Grand Nationals, the GNX was only available in black. Tinted glass, black wheel centres and a complete lack of exterior chrome further enhanced its menacing appearance. It did receive special 'GNX' badging on the front fenders, grill and rear boot lid.

Stewart-Warner gauges

A special Stewart-Warner analog instrument cluster replaces the stock gauges. It includes a 225km/h (140mph) speedometer, 8000rpm tachometer, turbo boost gauge, amp meter, oil pressure and water temperature gauge.

Fender vents

Vents were incorporated into the fenders to reduce engine bay heat.

Specifications

1987 Buick Regal GNX

ENGINE
Type: V6

Construction: Cast-iron block and heads

Valve gear: Two valves per cylinder operated by a camshaft with .389/.411 inch lift and 294/290 degrees of duration

Bore and stroke: 97mm (3.80in) x 86mm (3.40in)

Displacement: 3785cc (231ci)

Compression ratio: 8.0:1

Induction system: SFI with modified intercooler and Garrett T-3 turbocharger

Maximum power: 276bhp at 4400rpm

Maximum torque: 360lb-ft at 3000rpm

Top speed: 200km/h (124mph)

0–96km/h (0–60mph): 5.5 sec

TRANSMISSION
Modified GM 200-4R four-speed automatic

BODY/CHASSIS
Steel two-door four-seater

SPECIAL FEATURES

GNXs have special fender vents which release hot air from the engine compartment.

RUNNING GEAR
Steering: Recirculating ball

Front suspension: Double wishbones with shocks and anti-roll bar

Rear suspension: Live axle with Panhard rod, torque arm, trailing links, coil springs, and anti-roll bar

Brakes: Discs, 26.7cm (10.5in) dia. (front), drums, 24.1cm (9.5in) dia. (rear)

Wheels: Alloy, 20.3cm (8in) x 40.6cm (16in)

Tires: Goodyear Gatorbacks, 245/50 VR16 (front), 255/50 VR16 (rear)

DIMENSIONS
Length: 5.1m (200.6in)

Width: 1.82m (71.6in)

Height: 1.42m (56.0in)

Wheelbase: 275cm (108.1in)

Track: 150.9cm (59.4in) (front), 150.6cm (59.3in) (rear)

Weight: 1608kg (3545lb)

Buick **GS400**

While the competition offered bare-knuckled street fighters, Buick loaded its GS 400 with luxury features. It may have looked like an overstuffed luxury coupe, but with 6555cc (400ci) it was not to be taken lightly.

'...few can rival its power.'

It is hard to judge the GS 400 when you slide behind the wheel, but its character soon becomes clear. The big-block engine has enough torque to light the back tyres up on even the driest pavement, yet unlike some other hi-po mills it's turbine smooth. The Buick is more at home on the straights than through corners – push it too hard, and it begins to understeer. But for its intended purpose – a stop-light racer – few can rival its power."

A modest-looking sweep speedometer belies this car's searing performance.

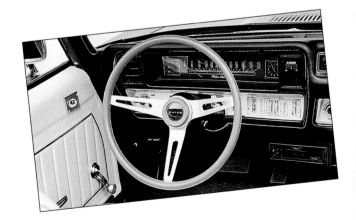

Milestones

1965 Buick jumps into the muscle car fray by dropping its 'nailhead' V8 into the intermediate Skylark™, creating the Gran Sport™.

1967 The Gran Sport gets a new 6555cc (400ci) engine and is renamed GS 400.

The 6555cc (400ci) engine was first seen in the 1967 GS 400 sport coupe.

1968 All GM A body intermediates get new two-door bodies and ride on a shorter, 284cm (112in) wheelbase. The GS 400 returns with a standard 340-bhp, 6555cc (400ci) V8.

The successor to the GS 400 was the 1970 GS 455™ sport coupe.

1969 Functioning bonnet scoops are made standard and a new Stage 1 option boosts power to 345 bhp. A Stage 2 package is also offered with 360bhp.

1970 The GS 400 is replaced by the GS 455.

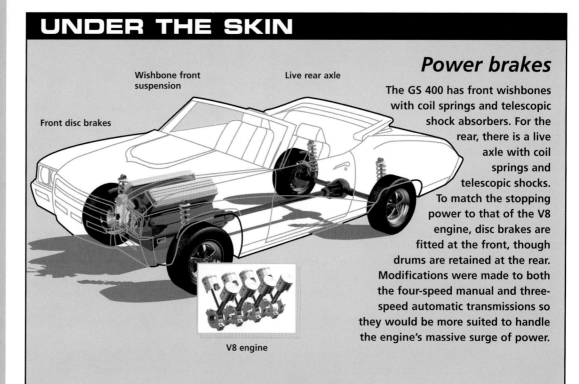

Wishbone front suspension

Live rear axle

Front disc brakes

V8 engine

Power brakes

The GS 400 has front wishbones with coil springs and telescopic shock absorbers. For the rear, there is a live axle with coil springs and telescopic shocks. To match the stopping power to that of the V8 engine, disc brakes are fitted at the front, though drums are retained at the rear. Modifications were made to both the four-speed manual and three-speed automatic transmissions so they would be more suited to handle the engine's massive surge of power.

THE POWER PACK

Nasty nailhead

The 6555cc (400ci) 'nailhead' engine in the GS 400 is a bored and stroked version of the 340, the extra power supplied to match the car's sporty image. It has a special 'Cool Air' induction system fitted to increase the power output. The two scoops in the bonnet feed a system which features a twin-snorkel air cleaner with two foam muffs that seal the hood's air inlets. Buick claimed that the system increased horsepower by 8 per cent. Two optional power packages were also available. Stage 1 used specially tuned carbs to reach 345bhp, and the rare Stage 2 increased power to 360bhp.

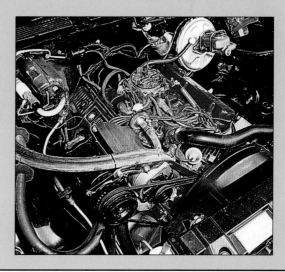

Rare treat

If there is a choice to be made between the 1968-1969 GS models, it is arguably the convertible. Just 1776 were built, making them hard to track down. Find one with the hot Stage 1 setup and you have one of the finest muscle cars of the 1960s.

The 1969 convertible models are among the most desirable for collectors.

21

Buick **GS400**

Although it wasn't the best selling muscle car, the GS 400 certainly did not take a back seat when it came to performance. With 440lb-ft of torque on tap, the GS400 Stage 1 was the perfect weapon to shut down the competition with.

Large bore V8
The 6555cc (400ci) engine in Stage 1 trim received a higher lift cam, 11.0:1 compression pistons, a special Quadrajet carburetor, plus low-restriction exhaust pipes. The result was a 0–96km/h (0–60mph) time in the high 5-second range.

Subtle changes
GM's Astro Ventilation system dispensed with the need for vent windows, and the grill and taillights were also mildly altered.

Power disc brakes
By 1969, engineers were beginning to pay more attention to making cars stop as well as they accelerated. Therefore, power front disc brakes were standard on the GS 400, though drums were still fitted at the rear.

Shorter wheelbase
For 1968, all GM A-body intermediates received revised styling and split wheel-bases – two-door models were 7.6cm (3in) shorter than the 4-door versions.

Functional bonnet scoops

Buick stole a lead, not only on rival manufacturers but on other GM divisions too, by offering a standard 'Cold Air' package. It uses a twin-snorkel air cleaner to increase power.

Live rear axle

Like most muscle cars, the GS put power to the pavement through a live axle. With the Stage 1 package, a set of 3.64:1 gears and a Positraction limited-slip differential were standard – the latter helping the skinny, bias-ply tires to hook up under fierce acceleration.

Specifications

1969 Buick GS 400

ENGINE

Type: V8

Construction: Cast-iron block and heads

Valve gear: Two valves per cylinder operated by a single block-mounted camshaft with pushrods and rockers

Bore and stroke: 103mm (4.04in) x 99mm (3.90in)

Displacement: 6555cc (400ci)

Compression ratio: 11.0:1

Induction system: Single Rochester Quadrajet four-barrel downdraft carburetor

Maximum power: 345bhp at 4800rpm

Maximum torque: 440lb-ft at 3200rpm

Top speed: 201km/h (125mph)

0–96km/h (0–60mph): 5.8 sec

TRANSMISSION

TurboHydramatic three-speed automatic

BODY/CHASSIS

Separate steel chassis with two-door convertible body

SPECIAL FEATURES

The 'Cold Air' induction system helps to boost engine power.

The Turbo-Hydramatic transmission was fortified to handle the engine's massive torque output.

RUNNING GEAR

Steering: Recirculating ball

Front suspension: Unequal length wishbones with coil springs, telescopic shock absorbers and anti-roll bar

Rear suspension: Live axle with coil springs and telescopic shock absorbers

Brakes: Discs (front), drums (rear)

Wheels: Magnum 500 steel, 15.2cm (6in) x 35.6cm (14in)

Tires: G-70 14

DIMENSIONS

Length: 5.1m (200.7in)

Width: 2.95m (81.0in)

Height: 1.37m (54.0in)

Wheelbase: 284cm (112.0in)

Track: 150cm (59.0in) (front and rear)

Weight: 1630kg (3594lb)

Buick GSX

If the 1970 mid-size GS™ 455 wasn't wild enough, Buick raised the muscle car ante with the fearsome GSX. It had all the power of the regular GS 455, but included a better suspension and wild appearance package. When ordered with the optional 455 Stage I engine, the GSX became lethal.

'...the Velvet Hammer.'

'Unlike most other muscle cars of the era, Buick's GSX offered creature comforts that were mostly associated with luxury cars. Included in the package was a brutal 455 V8. The GSX combined luxury with high performance, earning it the nickname the "Velvet Hammer." With more than 510lb-ft of torque, its low-end power was nothing short of insanity. Thanks to its heavy duty suspension and 38.1cm (15in) wheels, the GSX handled great for such a heavy car."

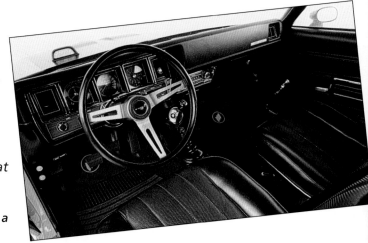

Although one of the quickest muscle cars built, the GSX is definitely not a stripped-out racer.

Milestones

1970 Buick unveils

a restyled Skylark™. The Gran Sport (GS) model receives a 455-V8. The GSX option package also appears, but the cars are only available painted in Apollo White or Saturn Yellow. Production for the model year is just 687 units.

Although overshadowed by the GSX, regular GS models continued into 1972.

1971 The GS and the GSX option continue.

A wider assortment of colours is now available. GM drops the compression ratio in the 455 engines down to 8.5:1 to meet stricter emission standards. The regular 455 now makes 315bhp while the Stage 1 engine makes 345bhp.

When Buick launched the GN™ in the 1980s, it made one of the fastest late model street cars.

1972 The GS reverts

to an option package on the Skylark models. The GSX package is still available, but only 44 cars are ordered. The Stage 1 455 only makes 270bhp.

UNDER THE SKIN

Beefed up

Like rival GM intermediates of the era, the GSX has independent wishbone front suspension and a live rear axle with coil springs. For improved handling, the shocks and springs are stiffened and large front and rear anti-roll bars are installed. Stopping power is provided by big 27.9cm (11in) discs up front and finned 24.1cm (9.5in) drum brakes at the rear.

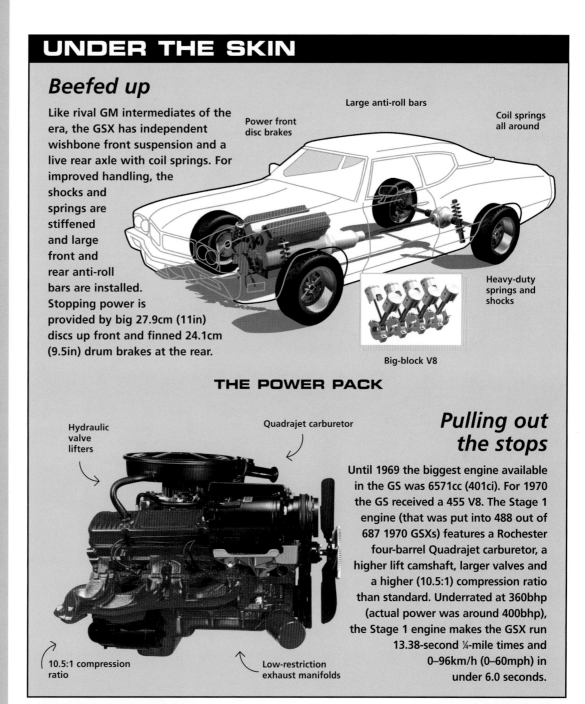

Power front disc brakes

Large anti-roll bars

Coil springs all around

Heavy-duty springs and shocks

Big-block V8

THE POWER PACK

Pulling out the stops

Hydraulic valve lifters

Quadrajet carburetor

10.5:1 compression ratio

Low-restriction exhaust manifolds

Until 1969 the biggest engine available in the GS was 6571cc (401ci). For 1970 the GS received a 455 V8. The Stage 1 engine (that was put into 488 out of 687 1970 GSXs) features a Rochester four-barrel Quadrajet carburetor, a higher lift camshaft, larger valves and a higher (10.5:1) compression ratio than standard. Underrated at 360bhp (actual power was around 400bhp), the Stage 1 engine makes the GSX run 13.38-second ¼-mile times and 0–96km/h (0–60mph) in under 6.0 seconds.

Still potent

Although the GSX was Buick's muscle flagship for 1970, regular GS models were just as powerful and could also be ordered with the 360-bhp, 7456cc (455ci) Stage 1 V8. Only 1416 GS convertibles with this package were built for the 1970 model year.

Standard GS 455s may have a more subtle appearance, but they are still fast.

Buick **GSX**

With its loud paintwork, spoilers, scoops and graphics, plus a monstrous 455 engine, the GSX is Buick's finest muscle car and comes complete with all the trimmings.

Front disc brakes

With so much performance just a stab of the throttle away, the GSX needs powerful brakes. It uses 27.9cm (11in) diameter disc brakes at the front, but made do with finned drum brakes at the rear.

Awesome power

1970 marked the introduction of 7456cc (455ci) engines in GM intermediates. A standard Buick GS 455 churns out 350bhp, but the optional Stage 1 produces 360bhp due to a more aggressive cam and a higher compression ratio.

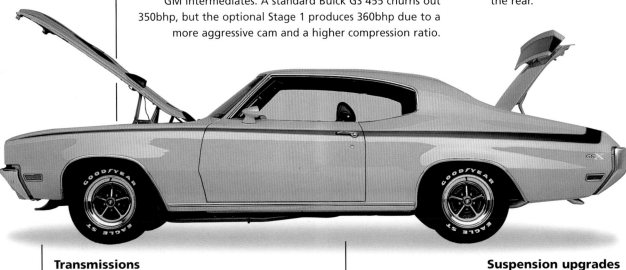

Transmissions

Three different transmissions were available: three- or four-speed manual, or a TurboHydramatic 400 automatic transmission with a Hurst gear shifter.

Suspension upgrades

The GSX has heavy-duty suspension and powered front disc brakes, plus uprated shock absorbers and stiffer springs for better handling.

Color availability

Introduced halfway through the model year, the 1970 GSX was available in only two colours: Apollo White or Saturn Yellow.

Chrome wheels

The GSX package included handsome 17.7cm (7in) wide Magnum 500 chrome-plated steel wheels and Goodyear Polyglas GT series tyres.

Restyled body

Some people criticized the 1968-1969 GS for looking out of proportion. For the 1970 model year, the Skylark received an attractive facelift and full rear wheel cut-outs.

Specifications
1970 Buick GSX

ENGINE

Type: V8

Construction: Cast-iron block and heads

Valve gear: Two valves per cylinder operated by pushrods and rockers

Bore and stroke: 110mm (4.33in) x 99mm (3.9in)

Displacement: 7456cc (455ci)

Compression ratio: 10.5:1

Induction system: Rochester four-barrel Quadrajet carburetor

Maximum power: 360bhp at 4600rpm

Maximum torque: 510lb-ft at 2800rpm

Top speed: 201km/h (125mph)

0–96km/h (0–60mph): 7 sec

TRANSMISSION

Four-speed close-ratio manual

BODY/CHASSIS

Steel coupe body on separate chassis

SPECIAL FEATURES

A bonnet-mounted tachometer came standard on all GSX models.

The rear spoiler and black accent stripes are some of the GSX's styling features.

RUNNING GEAR

Steering: Power-assisted recirculating ball

Front suspension: Independent wishbones with coil springs, telescopic shocks and heavy-duty roll bar

Rear suspension: Live axle fitted with 3.64:1 axle gears, heavy-duty coil springs, telescopic shocks and anti-roll bar

Brakes: Vented discs, 27.9cm (11in) dia. (front), finned drums, 24.1cm (9.5in) dia. (rear)

Wheels: Magnum 500, 17.8cm (7in) x 38.1cm (15in)

Tires: Goodyear Polyglas GT G60-15

DIMENSIONS

Length: 5.13m (202in)

Width: 1.93m (75.9in)

Height: 1.35m (53in)

Wheelbase: 284cm (112in)

Track: 153cm (60.1in) (front), 150cm (58.9in) (rear)

Weight: 1615kg (3561lb)

Chevrolet II

Chevrolet equipped their Chevy II compact with a hot small-block 5359cc (327ci) V8 in Corvette® tune. The resulting Chevy II Super Sport became an instant classic and was one of Detroit's best kept secrets during the whole muscle car scene.

'...a wolf in sheep's clothing.'

'A "sleeper" is a fast car with mild styling and simple trim. The 1966 Chevy II SS is exactly this type of car – a real wolf in sheep's clothing. What looks like a typical vehicle that someone's grandmother might drive to church on Sunday came from GM with a hot 5359cc (327ci) V8 in Corvette tune. A Chevy II SS might blend in well in traffic with all the other plain coupes. However, when the light turns green, the 360-lb-ft of torque reveals the car's true intention.

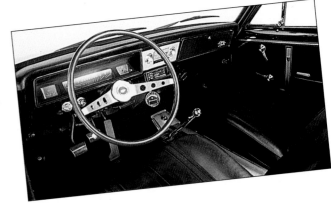

The cabin of the Chevy II SS is plain but functional and ready for action.

Milestones

1962 Chevrolet introduces
the Chevy II, which is designed as a conventional competitor to Ford's very successful Falcon.
It comes with a standard four-cylinder engine or an optional straight-six.

Tuner Don Yenko squeezed a 427 V8 engine into the Nova™.

1964 Enthusiasts are pleased
when GM finally installs a V8 in the humble Chevy II compact. Along with a 220-bhp, 4638cc (283ci) unit, the hot package included dual exhaust and a four-speed transmission.

1966 Crisper styling and more
powerful engines mark this year's Chevy II and Nova SS performance variants.

By 1976 the Nova was a real slug when it came to performance.

1967 The 350bhp engine
was retained for one final year. Disc brakes were available for the first time this year. In 1968, the body style changes and the car becomes known as the Nova.

UNDER THE SKIN

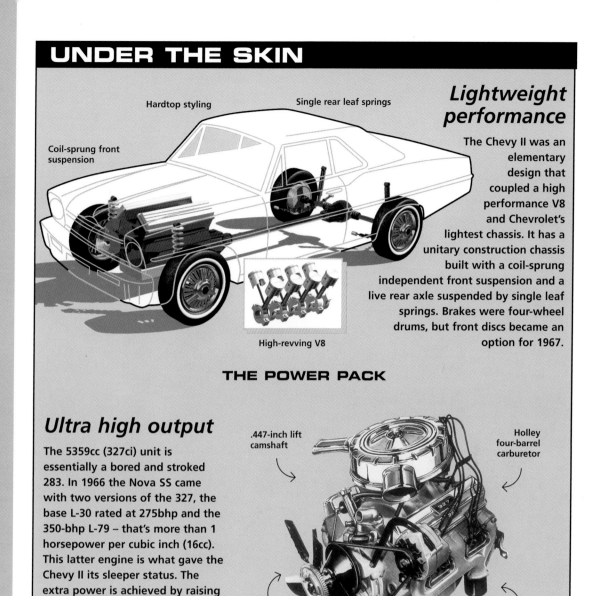

Hardtop styling

Single rear leaf springs

Coil-sprung front suspension

High-revving V8

Lightweight performance

The Chevy II was an elementary design that coupled a high performance V8 and Chevrolet's lightest chassis. It has a unitary construction chassis built with a coil-sprung independent front suspension and a live rear axle suspended by single leaf springs. Brakes were four-wheel drums, but front discs became an option for 1967.

THE POWER PACK

Ultra high output

The 5359cc (327ci) unit is essentially a bored and stroked 283. In 1966 the Nova SS came with two versions of the 327, the base L-30 rated at 275bhp and the 350-bhp L-79 – that's more than 1 horsepower per cubic inch (16cc). This latter engine is what gave the Chevy II its sleeper status. The extra power is achieved by raising the compression to 11:1, using a .447-inch lift single profile cam and 2.02/1.60-inch valve heads.

.447-inch lift camshaft

Holley four-barrel carburetor

2.02/1.60-inch intake and exhaust valves

11:1 compression ratio

Sleeper car

Out of 16,300 Chevy II SS V8 models built for 1966, only 5481 were equipped with the L-79 engine. This low production run, combined with an incredible power-to-weight ratio, makes the L-79-engined Chevy II a contender for the muscle car crown.

The 350-bhp 327 Chevy II was one of the most underrated muscle cars.

Chevrolet II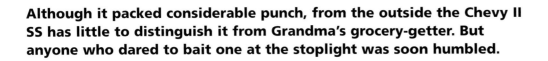

Although it packed considerable punch, from the outside the Chevy II SS has little to distinguish it from Grandma's grocery-getter. But anyone who dared to bait one at the stoplight was soon humbled.

L-79 engine

It was this engine that transformed the peppy little Chevy II into a muscle car legend. With the L-79 engine, 14-second quarter-mile times were common.

Four-wheel drum brakes

Engine technology was far ahead of braking and the Chevy II SS has drums front and rear. As many road testers have discovered, panic stops can often cause the wheels to lock up.

Live axle

Single rear leaf springs can often result in severe wheel hop and loss of traction under hard acceleration. Consequently, many Chevy IIs have been fitted with traction bars to reduce this.

Cleaner styling

The first-generation Chevy IIs and Novas had rather awkward styling, but for 1966 the little compact adopted sharper and more angular lines. Nova SS models were available only as two-door hardtops.

Optional four-speed

Although the Chevy II SS came with a standard three-speed manual transmission, many buyers stepped up to the optional close-ratio four-speed. This was better suited to the high-output small-block V8.

Super Sport

Strangely enough, the Chevy II SS could be ordered with a six-cylinder engine, although most buyers specified V8. The two 327s received a new four-barrel carburettor for 1966.

Specifications

1966 Chevrolet Chevy II SS

ENGINE

Type: V8

Construction: Cast-iron block and heads

Valve gear: Two valves per cylinder operated by a single camshaft via pushrods, rockers and hydraulic lifters

Bore and stroke: 102mm (4.00in) x 83mm (3.25in)

Displacement: 5359cc (327ci)

Compression ratio: 11.0:1

Induction system: Single Holley four-barrel carburettor

Maximum power: 350bhp at 5800rpm

Maximum torque: 360lb-ft at 3600rpm

Top speed: 198km/h (123mph)

0–96km/h (0–60mph): 6.5 sec

TRANSMISSION

Four-speed manual, close ratio

BODY/CHASSIS

Steel monocoque with two-door hardtop body

SPECIAL FEATURES

Super Sport wheel covers are fitted with simulated knock-off spinners.

RUNNING GEAR

Steering: Recirculating ball

Front suspension: Double wishbones with coil springs, telescopic shock absorbers and anti-roll bar

Rear suspension: Live axle with semi-elliptic leaf springs and telescopic shock absorbers

Brakes: Drums (front and rear)

Wheels: Steel discs, 12.7cm (5in) x 35.6cm (14in)

Tyres: 17.7cm (6.95in) x 35.6cm (14in)

DIMENSIONS

Length: 4.65m (183.0in)

Width: 1.81m (71.3in)

Height: 1.37m (53.8in)

Wheelbase: 279cm (110.0in)

Track: 144cm (56.8in) (front), 143cm (56.3in) (rear)

Weight: 1424kg (3140lb)

Chevrolet BEL AIR 409

As the horsepower wars began to heat up in the early 1960s, Chevrolet unleashed its hot 6702cc (409ci) engine, primarily aimed at drag racers. With it, the lightweight Bel Airs cleaned up, both on the track and on the street.

'...legendary racing status.'

'This is the quintessential early-1960s factory hot rod in its purest form. Take your place behind the wheel – everything about the car is plain and boring, but once the key is turned, your attitude changes. Grab the shifter and release the clutch. With 420lb-ft of torque, the rear tyres will chirp in every gear. Although strong at low speed, give the 409 a little pedal and it really pulls hard. It is at this point you realize why the 409 has achieved such legendary racing status.'

A column-mounted tach and cue-ball shifter are the only clues to performance inside.

Milestones

1961 Midway through

the year, Chevrolet unleashes its 6702cc (409ci) V8, as a larger, more powerful version of the 348. There is also a Super Sport™ option on the Impala™ series, but by the end of the year, only 142 cars are fitted with the 409.

The 409 debuted in 1961 along with the Impala Super Sport.

1962 In competition, Chevy 409s

do exceedingly well. In the NHRA's Stock Eliminator class, Hayden Proffitt sets a class record at the Nationals at Indy with a 12.83-second ET at 113.92 mph. He also took the Super Stock championship this year.

Only 2828 Chevy 409s were built in its last year, 1965.

1963 Chevrolet offers the Z-11.

It's a bored and stroked version of the 409. This elusive race engine displaces 6997cc (427ci) and is rated at 430bhp.

UNDER THE SKIN

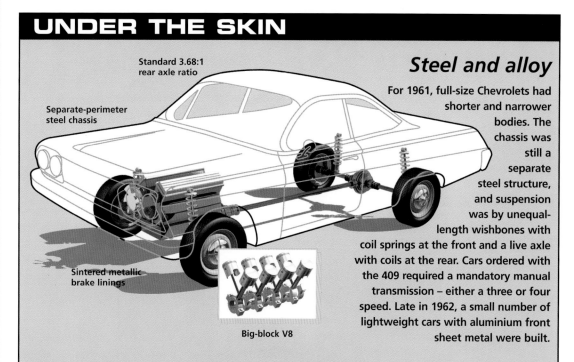

Standard 3.68:1 rear axle ratio

Separate-perimeter steel chassis

Sintered metallic brake linings

Big-block V8

Steel and alloy

For 1961, full-size Chevrolets had shorter and narrower bodies. The chassis was still a separate steel structure, and suspension was by unequal-length wishbones with coil springs at the front and a live axle with coils at the rear. Cars ordered with the 409 required a mandatory manual transmission – either a three or four speed. Late in 1962, a small number of lightweight cars with aluminium front sheet metal were built.

THE POWER PACK

Top flight 409

Having its parentage in the 348 W-series V8, the 409 has few interchangeable parts with the former. It does, however, share the same block, W-shaped cylinder heads and wedge-shaped combustion chambers. The 409's wedge originated from the top of the block, cut at a 74° angle to the cylinder walls. This also required high-compression heads and pistons (11.25:1), making the 409 a handful for the average driver on the street and very difficult to tune. For 1962, a revised cam and 11.0:1 compression heads boosted power from 360 to 380bhp, and a dual-quad intake resulted in 409bhp.

Bold and bubbly

With just 15,019 built, the 409-equipped Chevy is rare today. Aesthetically, the lightweight 1962 Bel Air bubble-top models are perhaps better looking than the Impalas. In fact, they were the best choice for drag racing and won that year's NHRA S/S championship.

Bel Air 409s were strong performers on the street and unbeatable at the strip.

Chevrolet **BEL AIR 409**

When the Beach Boys sang about it, the 1962 Chevy 409 gained a reputation few other engines or cars possessed. But as the competition found out, this reputation was entirely justified.

W-series V8

It may have been derived from a 348 truck engine, but the solid-lifter 409 is a true high-performance motor. In 1962, it was rated at 380bhp with a four-barrel carburettor, or 409bhp with two four barrels – achieving the magical one horsepower per cubic inch (16cc).

Separate chassis

Like most full-size cars of the time, 1962 Chevrolets ride on a separate chassis. Suspension is fairly standard for the day – wishbones at the front and a live axle at the rear. Big GM cars differed from rivals by having rear coil springs for a smoother ride.

Hardtop bodystyle

Full-size Chevrolets were fitted with shorter and narrower bodies for 1961 but retained the 302cm (19in) wheelbase separate chassis. In 1962, the Impala hardtop coupe adopted a more formal roofline, leaving the Bel Air as the sole bubble-top coupe. The 409 could be ordered in any bodystyle, but the majority were fitted in coupes.

Optional rear gearing

A manual transmission was mandatory with the 409, and the standard rear axle ratio was 3.68:1. Dealers could install 4.10:1 or 4.56:1 cogs for better low-end launches.

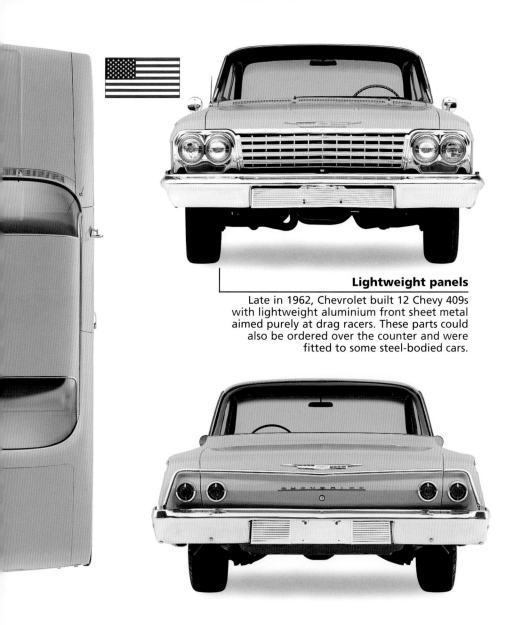

Lightweight panels

Late in 1962, Chevrolet built 12 Chevy 409s with lightweight aluminium front sheet metal aimed purely at drag racers. These parts could also be ordered over the counter and were fitted to some steel-bodied cars.

Spartan interior

Most buyers who ordered 409s were interested only in speed, and thus many Bel Airs had spartan interiors. This one has a meager front bench seat, manual windows and no heater or radio. A column-mounted tachometer was standard, however.

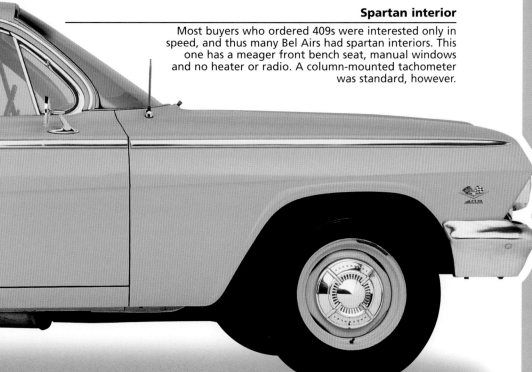

Specifications

1962 Chevrolet Bel Air 409

ENGINE
Type: V8

Construction: Cast-iron block and heads

Valve gear: Two valves per cylinder operated by a single block-mounted camshaft with pushrods and rockers

Bore and stroke: 109mm(4.31in) x 89mm (3.50in)

Displacement: 6702cc (409ci)

Compression ratio: 11.25:1

Induction system: Carter AFB four-barrel downdraft carburettor

Maximum power: 380bhp at 6000rpm

Maximum torque: 420lb-ft at 3200rpm

Top speed: 185km/h (115mph)

0–96km/h (0–60mph): 7.3 sec

TRANSMISSION
Four-speed manual

BODY/CHASSIS
Separate steel chassis with two-door hardtop body

SPECIAL FEATURES

The 409 features a 7000rpm, column-mounted tachometer.

RUNNING GEAR
Steering: Recirculating ball

Front suspension: Unequal-length A-arms with coil springs, telescopic shock absorbers and anti-roll bar

Rear suspension: Live rear axle with coil springs and telescopic shock absorbers

Brakes: Drums (front and rear)

Wheels: Pressed steel, 38.1cm (15in) dia.

Tyres: 20.3cm (8.00in) x 35.6cm (14in)

DIMENSIONS
Length: 5.32m (209.6in)

Width: 2.14m (84.2in)

Height: 1.76m (69.4in)

Wheelbase: 302cm (119.0in)

Track: 153cm (60.3in) (front), 151cm (59.3in) (rear)

Weight: 1579kg (3480lb)

Chevrolet Callaway CAMARO

The Callaway C8 is an almost totally re-engineered Chevrolet® Camaro. The 6.3l (384ci) engine is tuned to produce 404bhp, and the suspension and brakes have been vastly upgraded to cope with its impressive 276km/h (172mph) top speed.

'...phenomenal grip.'

'The big engine revs quickly to 6000rpm and never runs out of breath, hurling the Camaro to 160km/h (100mph) in a staggering 11.5 seconds and reaching over 170 mph. Braking is incredibly strong, and the stiffer suspension eliminates roll. But despite the stiffer settings and lowered suspension, it is never uncomfortably hard. Understeer is nearly eliminated, and the grip from the huge 275/40 ZR17 tyres is phenomenal with the C8 able to pull .94gs in cornering tests.'

One major difference in the cockpit over a stock Camaro is a Hurst shifter.

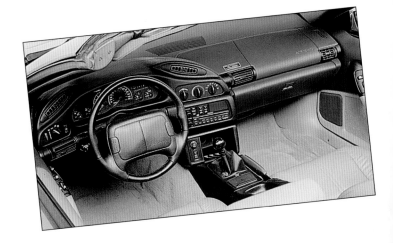

Milestones

1985 Callaway gains recognition by transforming the performance of the Alfa Romeo GTV6 by adding a twin-turbo system and taking power up to 230bhp. This leads to the famous Callaway Twin Turbo Corvette® of which more than 500 are made in five years.

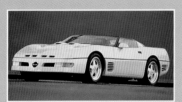

Callaway produced the Corvette Speedster on a limited run.

1989 The 880-bhp Callaway SledgeHammer is introduced. This is followed by the Twin Turbo Speedster in 1991.

The standard Camaro was the basis for the C8.

1993 Production of the Twin Turbo ends. The normally aspirated SuperNatural replaces it.

1994 The Los Angeles Auto Show is chosen to debut the C8. It is a thorough conversion of the latest Chevrolet Camaro. Production lasts from 1993 to 1996.

UNDER THE SKIN

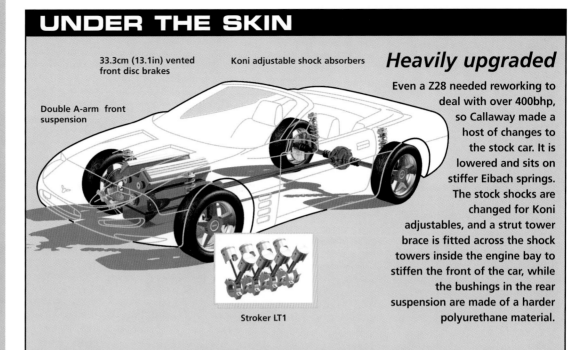

33.3cm (13.1in) vented front disc brakes

Koni adjustable shock absorbers

Double A-arm front suspension

Stroker LT1

Heavily upgraded

Even a Z28 needed reworking to deal with over 400bhp, so Callaway made a host of changes to the stock car. It is lowered and sits on stiffer Eibach springs. The stock shocks are changed for Koni adjustables, and a strut tower brace is fitted across the shock towers inside the engine bay to stiffen the front of the car, while the bushings in the rear suspension are made of a harder polyurethane material.

THE POWER PACK

LT1-based

Callaway totally reworks the Chevrolet LT1 V8 engine. The cast-iron block is overbored by .030 inch. When the longer-stroke, forged-steel crankshaft is added, the displacement is increased from 5.7l (348ci) to 6.3l (384ci). The pistons are forged alloy, and there are forged, four-bolt, main-bearing caps, as well as larger stainless-steel valves in aluminium cylinder heads. These are operated by a roller-lifter camshaft with more lift and duration. The inevitable result is a massive increase in power – output rockets to 404bhp at 5750rpm, while torque increases by a comparable amount to 412lb-ft.

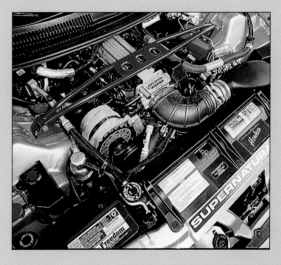

Many options

You can choose the mod-ifications that combine to make the C8. It is possible to have just the Cam Aero bodykit, or the wheels and tyres, or even the uprated engine. It's only when the Cam Aero body is combined with the 6.3l (384ci) engine that the car becomes a C8.

The C8's sporty look is accentuated by its bold performance.

Chevrolet Callaway **CAMARO**

There is no point building a 267km/h (166mph) Camaro if it looks like a standard car. The Callaway Cam Aero bodykit transforms the car's looks, which is just as well, as the fully loaded C8 costs over $60,000.

Bodykit

The C8 is fitted with a bodykit designed by Paul Deutschman. It consists of a long nose section with faired-in headlights as well as different cladding for the doors. It fits all 1993–1997 Camaros and is available separately for $4500. It is aerodynamically efficient as well as distinctive.

V8 engine

As well as making it bigger, Callaway applied the usual tuning tricks to the V8 engine. It was given a three-angle valve job for better airflow, and the combustion chambers and ports were reworked for enhanced performance, with careful matching of all joins between heads and manifolds. In addition, there are stronger dual valve springs and a higher, 10.5:1 compression ratio.

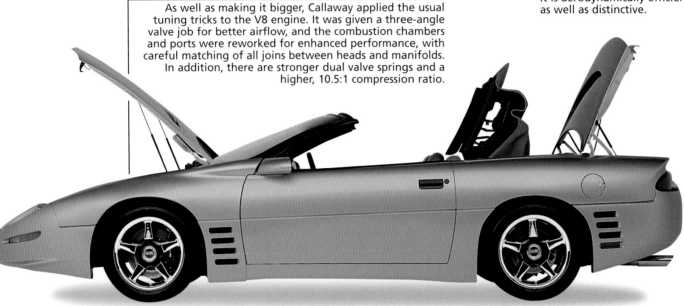

Brembo brakes

The ultimate brake upgrade offered by Callaway consists of four-piston, 33.3cm (13.1in) diameter, front Italian Brembo discs, which are cross drilled, grooved, and vented to prevent fade.

Six-speed transmission

The standard Borg-Warner six-speed transmission is used but the stock shifter is replaced by a heavy duty Hurst shifter. Because Callaway fits a higher final-drive gear ratio, top speed can be reached only in fifth. The engine won't pull enough revs in sixth.

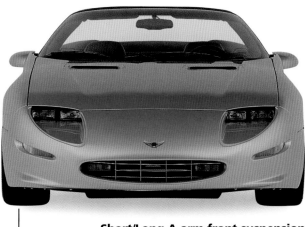

Short/Long A-arm front suspension

The SLA (short/long A-arm) front-suspension system has low Eibach springs and a thicker anti-roll bar. Two different sets of Koni shocks can be ordered: one is recommended for street use, the second should be specified if the car will be raced.

Honker air intake

With so much extra air flow required, Callaway fits a new intake system called the Honker Heavy Breathing System. It consists of a new moulded duct, which flows 46 per cent more air volume than the standard duct and is mated to a superior high-efficiency K&N filter. It is effective enough to increase power on the stock engine by 16bhp.

Specifications

1994 Callaway Camaro C8

ENGINE

Type: V8

Construction: Cast-iron block and alloy cylinder heads

Valve gear: Two valves per cylinder operated by a single block-mounted camshaft with pushrods, roller rockers and roller lifters

Bore and stroke: 102mm (4.03in) x 95mm (3.75in)

Displacement: 6276cc (383ci)

Compression ratio: 10.5:1

Induction system: Delco electronics port fuel injection, 52mm throttle body

Maximum power: 404bhp at 5750rpm

Maximum torque: 412lb-ft at 4750rpm

Top speed: 277km/h (172mph)

0–96km/h (0–60mph): 7.3 sec

TRANSMISSION

Borg-Warner T-56 six-speed manual

BODY/CHASSIS

Unitary steel construction with steel and composite panels

SPECIAL FEATURES

The SuperNatural 400 tag is a sure-fire indication of sensational performance.

RUNNING GEAR

Steering: Rack-and-pinion

Front suspension: Short and long A-arms with coil springs, adjustable telescopic shock absorbers and anti-roll bar

Rear suspension: Live axle with two trailing arms, Panhard rod, torque arm coil springs, adjustable telescopic shock absorbers and anti-roll bar

Brakes: Vented discs, 33.3cm (13.1in) dia. (front), 28.9cm (11.4in) dia. (rear)

Wheels: Alloy, 24.1cm (9.5in) x 43.2cm (17in)

Tyres: 275/40 ZR17

DIMENSIONS

Length: 4.9m (193.2in)

Width: 1.88m (74.1in)

Height: 1.3m (51.3in)

Wheelbase: 257cm (101.1in)

Track: 154cm (60.7in) (front), 153.9cm (60.6in) (rear)

Weight: 1530kg (3373lb)

Chevrolet **CAMARO PACE CAR**

Chevrolet's Mustang fighter debuted in 1967 and, also that year, served as the pace car for the Indianapolis 500. Two years later, the Camaro was again pacing this prestigious race. This time, however, a greater number of replicas were offered for sale – all in white with orange interiors and stripes.

'...unbeatable experience.'

'It's easy to see why this is one of the all-time great American classics. The hound's tooth upholstered seats may have little support and the thin wheel may almost slip through your fingers, but turn the key dangling from the column, put her in gear and hit the road. The V8 has a pure, unadulterated sound and the driving experience soon becomes all-enveloping. The shifter feels good in your hand, and with the top down the experience is unbeatable.'

The Pace Car package added an orange interior with hound's tooth seat inserts.

Milestones

1966 Introduced in September, the Camaro is Chevrolet's answer to the Ford Mustang. It was also selected to pace the Indy 500 race. Four Camaro RS/SS convertibles – all have white with blue stripes and are powered with modified 396 V8s – were used. To give the public a chance to own this pacing legend, Chevrolet built 100 replicas, which were sold through select dealers.

The most fearsome of all 1969 Camaros was the ZL-1™.

1968 After building 220,906 copies for 1967, Chevy makes a few changes to its pony car. V8 models get multi-leaf springs. An Astro ventilation system results in the elimination of the front vent windows.

The second-generation Camaro was only available as a coupe.

1969 Camaros pace the Indy 500 again. The 1969 pace car – like the 1967 – was painted white but has orange instead of blue stripes. 3675 replicas are sold.

UNDER THE SKIN

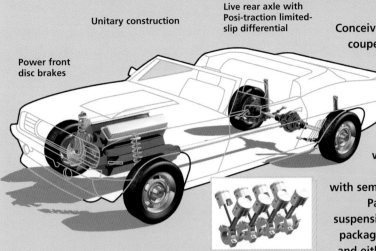

Unitary construction

Live rear axle with Posi-traction limited-slip differential

Power front disc brakes

Small-block V8

Uniframing

Conceived as a budget-wise sports coupe, the Camaro shared many parts with the Nova™. They include its unitary body/chassis design, a front bolt-on subframe carrying the engine and double wishbone front suspension. At the back was a live axle with semi-elliptic multi-leaf springs. Pace Cars have a heavy-duty suspension (which is part of the SS package), power front disc brakes and either a four-speed manual or an automatic transmission.

THE POWER PACK

Mighty mouse, roarin' rat

Camaro entered its third season for 1969 and still the base engine was a 3769cc (230ci), six-cylinder unit. The Z11 Pace Car replicas, however, were only offered with two different V8s. The majority (like this one) came with the 5735cc (350ci) V8 and some came with the stout 396. Sharing many features with the original small-block of 1965, including its cast-iron block and five-main-bearing crankshaft, the 350 put out 300bhp and a credible 380lb-ft of torque. Approximately 100 of the Z11 Pace Cars used the 6489cc (396ci) Turbo Jet V8, which was available in three different states of tune. The top L-78 version thumped out a mighty 375bhp.

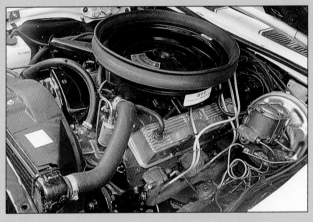

Vintage year

1969 models are possibly the most coveted Camaros of all and the Pace Car replicas are highly desirable machines. Excellent examples trade hands for up to $45,000. A small number of coupes under the code RPO Z10 were also built.

1969 is considered the pinnacle year among Camaro afficionados.

Chevrolet CAMARO PACE CAR

Driven by 1960 Indy 500 winner Jim Rathmann at the Brickyard, the actual Pace Car was powered by a 375bhp, 6489cc (396ci) big-block, but in the interests of driveability most of the replicas had small-block engines.

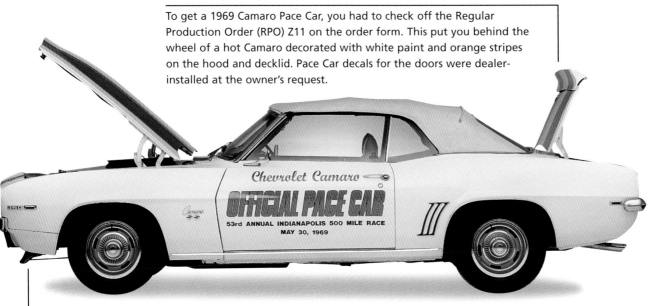

Pace Car package

To get a 1969 Camaro Pace Car, you had to check off the Regular Production Order (RPO) Z11 on the order form. This put you behind the wheel of a hot Camaro decorated with white paint and orange stripes on the hood and decklid. Pace Car decals for the doors were dealer-installed at the owner's request.

One-year wonder

Although they were based on the 1967–1968 cars, the 1969 Camaros received new sheet metal with sweeping fender lines.

RS/SS package

The price of $37 for the Z11 option was deceiving because you also had to order the SS package, Z/28 cowl induction hood and rear spoiler, plus the hidden headlight RS grill.

Automatic transmission

Two different automatic transmissions were available on the Pace Cars, depending upon what engine the car was equipped with. Cars with the 350 V8 were equipped with a TH350, while ones with the big-block 396 used the TH400.

Posi-traction rear end

First-year Camaros came with single rear leaf springs, but severe axle tramp on the more powerful versions caused Chevrolet to fit multi-leaf springs in 1968. A Posi-traction, limited-slip differential also helped increase tyre grip.

Specifications

1969 Chevrolet Camaro Pace Car

ENGINE

Type: V8

Construction: Cast-iron block and heads

Valve gear: Two valves per cylinder operated by a single V-mounted camshaft with pushrods and rockers

Bore and stroke: 102mm (4.00in) x 88mm (3.48in)

Displacement: 5735cc (350ci)

Compression ratio: 10.25:1

Induction system: Rochester Quadrajet four-barrel carburettor

Maximum power: 300bhp at 4800rpm

Maximum torque: 380lb-ft at 3200rpm

Top speed: 208km/h (129mph)

0–96km/h (0–60mph): 6.4 sec

TRANSMISSION

Turbo 350 automatic

BODY/CHASSIS

Steel unitary chassis with two-door convertible body

SPECIAL FEATURES

Convertibles were sold with pace car decals in the trunk ready to stick on.

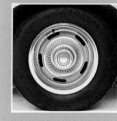

The actual pace car used in the race was fitted with Chevy rally wheels like these.

RUNNING GEAR

Steering: Recirculating ball

Front suspension: Unequal length A-arms with coil springs, telescopic shock absorbers and anti-roll bar

Rear suspension: Live axle with semi-elliptic leaf springs and telescopic shock absorbers

Brakes: Discs (front), drums (rear)

Wheels: Steel Rally, 17.8cm (7in) x 43.2cm (14in)

Tyres: Goodyear Polyglas, G-70 14

DIMENSIONS

Length: 4.72m (186.0in)

Width: 1.88m (74.0in)

Height: 1.3m (51.0in)

Wheelbase: 277cm (108.0in)

Track: 151.4cm (59.6in) (front) 151.1cm (59.5in) (rear)

Weight: 31540kg (395lb)

Chevrolet CAMARO RS/SS

In February 1970, Chevrolet introduced a radical new Camaro. Almost from the start, these cars have begged to be turned into street machines. Unlike most, however, which are built for the drag strip, this hot rod has been modified for street duty.

'...classic and modern blend'

'This Camaro has a nice blend of classic styling and modern mechanicals. It handles like a late-model car, its big tyres stick to the road and the steering is razor sharp, with instant response. The tuned small-block V8 produces power all the way up to the 7000rpm redline. Stopping is no problem either: simply depress the brake pedal and the huge Baer discs slow the car immediately without any hint of fading. Everything about this Camaro is first class.'

Two-tone upholstery and a wood rimmed steering wheel add a modern touch.

Milestones

1967 Chevrolet's Mustang Fighter,

the Camaro, is finally launched in coupe and convertible body styles. The SS model is the mainstream performance variant. A 6489cc (396ci) V8 turns the Camaro into a major league muscle car.

An SS package debuted for 1967. This Camaro is a 1968 model.

1970 Delayed by an

autoworkers strike, a new second generation Camaro is introduced. It is longer, lower and wider, with a smoother ride and improved handling. The SS is still listed and the 396 is bored out to 6588cc (402ci).

Camaro's other performance offering in the early 1970s was the Z28.

1971 The Camaro SS

396 returns, but power is down, from 375bhp to 300bhp. The model enters a decline and after 1973, the performance SS is replaced by a Luxury Touring (LT) model.

UNDER THE SKIN

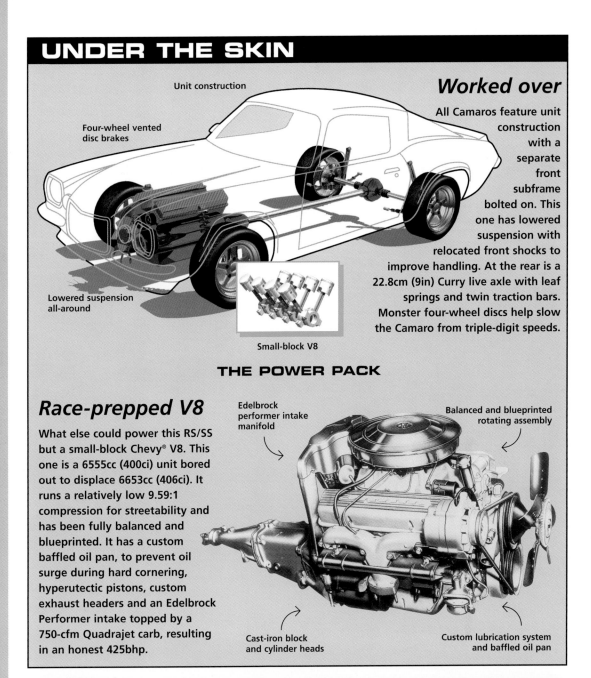

Unit construction

Four-wheel vented disc brakes

Lowered suspension all-around

Small-block V8

Worked over

All Camaros feature unit construction with a separate front subframe bolted on. This one has lowered suspension with relocated front shocks to improve handling. At the rear is a 22.8cm (9in) Curry live axle with leaf springs and twin traction bars. Monster four-wheel discs help slow the Camaro from triple-digit speeds.

THE POWER PACK

Race-prepped V8

What else could power this RS/SS but a small-block Chevy® V8. This one is a 6555cc (400ci) unit bored out to displace 6653cc (406ci). It runs a relatively low 9.59:1 compression for streetability and has been fully balanced and blueprinted. It has a custom baffled oil pan, to prevent oil surge during hard cornering, hyperutectic pistons, custom exhaust headers and an Edelbrock Performer intake topped by a 750-cfm Quadrajet carb, resulting in an honest 425bhp.

Edelbrock performer intake manifold

Balanced and blueprinted rotating assembly

Cast-iron block and cylinder heads

Custom lubrication system and baffled oil pan

1971 RS/SS

As indicated by the front badge this Camaro is an SS (super sport), but since it has a split bumper, it's also a RS (rallye sport). The SS option is a performance package while the RS is an appearance option. So this Camaro RS/SS has the best of both worlds.

Although an SS, this street Camaro behaves more like a modern day racer.

Chevrolet **CAMARO RS/SS**

The second generation Camaro has long been considered a design classic. This example was built to prove that muscle cars from the early 1970s can be made to handle and stop, too.

Modified small-block V8

Taken from a full-size Chevrolet, the 6555cc (400ci) V8 has been fully balanced and blueprinted and now has an output of 425bhp. Other modifications include an aggressive camshaft and an Edelbrock induction system.

Stylish interior

Inside, major changes include Flo Fit sport bucket seats, a wood rimmed steering wheel, plus air conditioning and a premium Clarion sound system with remote CD player.

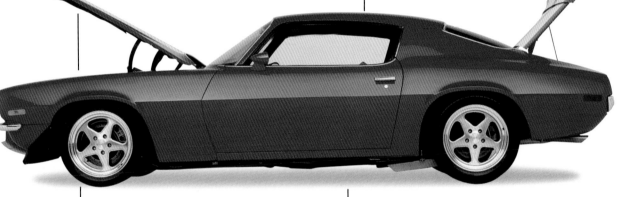

Unique wheels

Large wheels are required in order to fit the monster 33cm (13in) Baer Claw brakes. However, rather than source an existing set, renowned custom car builder Boyd Coddington was commissioned to build a unique set of five-spoke wheels which measure 43.2cm (17in) in diameter. The large slots considerably help cool the brakes.

Stiffened chassis

To reduce body flex, this Camaro benefits from sub frame connectors and a custom welded roll bar.

Nose treatment

If ordered with the RS (Rally Sport) package, 1970–73 Camaros received an endura-covered nose cap, with twin parking lights inboard of the headlights and small bumperettes.

Late model transmission

Many hot rodders rely on GM's 700R4 four-speed automatic transmission, because of its ability to handle so much extra power and torque. For this application, it has been fitted with a Transgo shift kit for shifting at higher rpm and a competition-style B&M ratchet shifter.

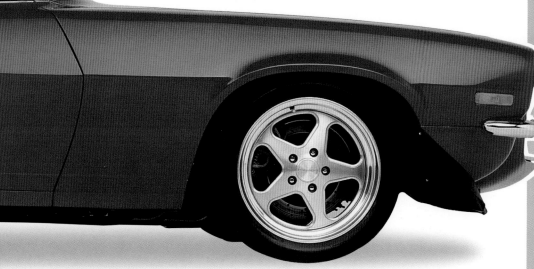

Specifications

1971 Chevrolet Camaro RS/SS

ENGINE

Type: V8

Construction: Cast-iron block and heads

Valve gear: Two valves per cylinder operated by pushrods and rockers

Bore and stroke: 105mm (4.12in) x 95mm (3.75in)

Displacement: 6555cc (400ci)

Compression ratio: 9.59:1

Induction system: Rochester Quadrajet 750-cfm four-barrel carburettor

Maximum power: 425bhp at 4800rpm

Maximum torque: 330lb-ft at 3000rpm

Top speed: 230km/h (143mph)

0–96km/h (0–60mph): 5.4 sec

TRANSMISSION

GM 700R4 four-speed automatic

BODY/CHASSIS

Unitary monocoque with steel two-door coupe body

SPECIAL FEATURES

Housed in the trunk are twin Orion amplifiers for the ultra-loud custom sound system.

RUNNING GEAR

Steering: Recirculating ball

Front suspension: Unequal length wishbones with coil springs, telescopic shock absorbers and an anti-sway bar

Rear suspension: Live rear axle with semi-elliptical leaf springs, telescopic shock absorbers, traction bars and an anti-sway bar

Brakes: Baer Claw 33cm (13in) dia.

Wheels: Boyd's alloy five-spoke 43.2cm (17in) dia.

Tyres: Bridgestone 27540ZR 17

DIMENSIONS

Length: 4.76m (188.0in)

Width: 1.89m (74.4in)

Height: 1.25m (49.5in)

Wheelbase: 275cm (108.1in)

Track: 156cm (61.3in) (front) 152cm (60in) (rear)

Weight: 1506kg (3320lb)

Chevrolet **CAMARO SS 396**

Unveiled in February 1970, the all-new second-generation Camaro was an instant design classic. Benefitting from a smoother ride and better handling, it could still be optioned with a pile-driving 375bhp 6489cc (396ci). Because of the immediate popularity of the then-new 350bhp, 350 LT-1™, few buyers specified the big engine.

'...no ordinary Camaro.'

'If you want a good handler, try the Z28® but if it's outright power that makes your mouth water, slide in and start 'er up. Inside the SS396, you're quickly greeted with a rough-idling engine and a loudly roaring exhaust. That's just one sign that lets you know this is no ordinary Camaro. Coax the shifter into first, bring up therpm and drop the clutch – the tyres spin with ease from the SS396's massive 415lb-ft of torque. Then, powershift into second and hang on – it'll reach 96km/h (60mph) in 6.2 seconds.'

Supportive front bucket seats and a well laid-out instrument panel are Camaro traits.

Milestones

1970 An all-new, second-generation

Camaro makes its debut in February. Offered only as a coupe, it comes in base, SS™ and Z28 versions. A United Auto Workers strike causes production to dip to 124,889 units. The SS gets a new 402 big block during the year but is still badged as a 396.

The Camaro was introduced in September 1966 in both coupe and convertible bodystyles.

1971 Few changes

occur this year, although emissions begin to bite. The 6588cc (402ci) V8 has a lower 8.5:1 compression ratio and power drops from 350bhp to 300bhp.

Second-generation Camaros got their final facelift for 1978.

1972 Power ratings

are switched to SAE net ratings, with all engine ancillaries attached. The SS is still offered with 5735cc (350cin), four-barrel and 6588cc (402ci) engines, but power is down to 200bhp and 240bhp, respectively. The SS is replaced by the LT for 1973.

UNDER THE SKIN

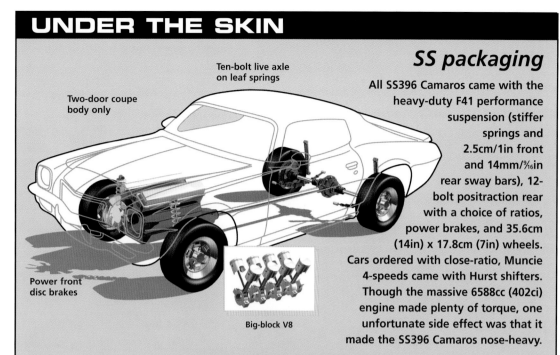

Two-door coupe body only

Ten-bolt live axle on leaf springs

Power front disc brakes

Big-block V8

SS packaging

All SS396 Camaros came with the heavy-duty F41 performance suspension (stiffer springs and 2.5cm/1in front and 14mm/⁹⁄₁₆in rear sway bars), 12-bolt positraction rear with a choice of ratios, power brakes, and 35.6cm (14in) x 17.8cm (7in) wheels. Cars ordered with close-ratio, Muncie 4-speeds came with Hurst shifters. Though the massive 6588cc (402ci) engine made plenty of torque, one unfortunate side effect was that it made the SS396 Camaros nose-heavy.

THE POWER PACK

Is it a 396 or a 402?

Though the popular combination for the Camaro in 1970 was the Z-28 with 360bhp, LT-1 power, customers were still offered the 396 big block. Although its bore was increased to 10.5cm (4.125in), making its actual displacement 6588cc (402ci), GM badged the engine as a 396. If ordered in Camaro SS trim, the motor was available in two states of tune – 350bhp (L-34) or 375bhp (L-78). 350bhp versions had 10.25:1 compression, a cast-iron intake manifold and a Rochester Quadrajet carburetor. 375-bhp versions came with higher compression, an aluminium intake manifold and a Holley four-barrel carburettor.

Rare find

Although the SS was in its prime in 1969, one year later it was eclipsed by the LT-1-powered Z28. The rarest of the 1970 SS396 Camaros have the elusive 375bhp, L78 engines. Only 600 were built. Today, these powerful Camaros are hard to find and have kept their value well.

The original SS leaves the lineup in 1972 due to a changing market.

Chevrolet **CAMARO SS 396**

Overshadowed by the better balanced Z28, the 1970 SS396 was the weapon of choice for drag racers. As the muscle car dynasty of the 1960s began to unfold during the early 1970s, Chevrolet still offered a truly brutal performer.

Standard front

The standard front-end treatment consists of a full-length chrome bumper with turn signals mounted below it. RS-equipped Camaros have an Endura nose and twin bumperettes.

Big-block V8

With more than 6555CC (400ci) and 415lb-ft of torque, the SS396 could run with the best cars the competition had to offer. Improved suspension also gave the factory SS ¼-mile times in the low 14-second range.

Unitary chassis

Camaros retained a unitary body/chassis for 1970, but greater attention was paid to refinement, including greater use of sound-deadening in the body.

Hardtop styling

Two bodystyles were initially planned, although with a growing buyer preference for closed bodystyles, it was decided to drop the convertible early in the development stage.

Small rear window

GM stylists originally intended to give the 1970 Camaro a wraparound rear window, but problems with the installation delayed this until 1975. Thus, all early cars got small back windows, which led to criticism of rearward visibility.

SS equipment group

The SS package included a stiffer suspension and a refreshing appearance package with twin sport mirrors, blacked-out grill and a sporty interior.

External spoilers

Front and rear spoilers were optional on any Camaro. The rear spoilers increased in size later in the 1970 model year.

Specifications
1970 Chevrolet Camaro SS396

ENGINE
Type: V8

Construction: Cast-iron block and heads

Valve gear: Two valves per cylinder operated by pushrods and rocker arms

Bore and stroke: 105mm (4.125in) x 96mm (3.76in)

Displacement: 6489/6588cc (396/402ci)

Compression ratio: 10.25:1

Induction system: Rochester Quadrajet carburettor

Maximum power: 375bhp at 5600rpm

Maximum torque: 415lb-ft at 3200rpm

Top speed: 206km/h (128mph)

0–96km/h (0–60mph): 6.2 sec

TRANSMISSION
Muncie M21 four-speed manual

BODY/CHASSIS
Steel unitary chassis with two-door body

SPECIAL FEATURES

Quad taillights mimic its big brother, the Corvette.

The SS396's transmission, the Muncie M21 four-speed, was named after the town where they were made – Muncie, Indiana.

RUNNING GEAR
Steering: Recirculating ball

Front suspension: Unequal-length A-arms with coil springs, telescopic shock absorbers and anti-roll bar

Rear suspension: Live axle with semi-elliptic leaf springs and telescopic shock absorbers

Brakes: Discs (front), drums (rear)

Wheels: Super Sport, 17.8cm (7in) x 35.6cm (14in)

Tyres: Firestone Wide Oval, F70-14

DIMENSIONS
Length: 4.78m (188.0in)

Width: 1.89m (74.4in)

Height: 1.27m (50.1in)

Wheelbase: 274cm (108.0in)

Track: 156cm (61.3in) (front), 152cm (60.0in) (rear)

Weight: 1610kg (3550lb)

Chevrolet **CAMARO SS**

In 1998 the SS tag was applied to a Camaro for the third year straight. Early versions of this modified Z28® was developed by tuning company SLP (Street Legal Performance), but Chevrolet began building them in 1998.

'...balanced and brutally fast'

'Extremely well balanced and brutally fast, tight handling and braking that exceeds almost anything are some of the characteristics of the newest version of the Camaro SS. Thanks to the new LS1 347 V8, it can reach 0–96km/h (0–60mph) in only 5.2 seconds. The Camaro SS will impress even the most dedicated enthusiasts. Even at speeds as high as 257km/h (160mph), the Camaro's 30.5cm (12in) ABS enhanced brakes will slow the car down in record distance.'

The SS interior screams performance thanks to its large analogue gauges, supportive seats and perfect placement of pedals and shifter.

Milestones

1987 Ed Hamburger forms SLP Engineering,
which is dedicated to making Camaros and Firebirds® go faster and look better.

The SS was the original Camaro performance package from 1967 until 1969. This is a 1968 model.

1996 This year SLP offers
a package on the Chevrolet Camaro Z28. It includes ram-air induction and upgraded suspension. Harking back to the muscle car era, this package is named SS. In this first year 2263 cars are built.

1998 Camaro SS models are based on the Z28.

1998 The Camaro is facelifted
with a new front end and receives the all-alloy LS1 V8. Due to growing demand, SS models are now built in house by General Motors instead of being farmed out to Street Legal Performance.

UNDER THE SKIN

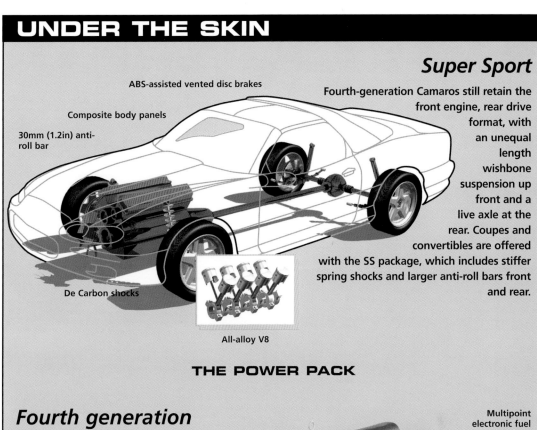

ABS-assisted vented disc brakes

Composite body panels

30mm (1.2in) anti-roll bar

De Carbon shocks

All-alloy V8

Super Sport

Fourth-generation Camaros still retain the front engine, rear drive format, with an unequal length wishbone suspension up front and a live axle at the rear. Coupes and convertibles are offered with the SS package, which includes stiffer spring shocks and larger anti-roll bars front and rear.

THE POWER PACK

Fourth generation

From 1993 through 1997 V8 Camaros were powered by the LT1 350. For 1998, it was replaced by an all-aluminium small-block V8. Known as the LS1, this engine shares the same bore spacing as the LT1, but is shorter and lighter than the old unit. It also features longer intake runners, a winged oil pan, wider camshaft journals and a coil for each cylinder. In the Camaro Z28 it is rated at 305bhp, but with ram-air induction installed, as on the SS, power is boosted to an impressive 320bhp.

Two valves per cylinder

Multipoint electronic fuel injection

Alloy block and cylinder heads

Hydraulic roller camshaft

Future classic

Only a few thousand Camaro SS models are built in 1998. They all offer a 320bhp 5686cc (347ci) LS1 V8 and a limited slip rear axle. With a 0–96km/h (0–60mph) time of 5.2 seconds and a top speed of 259km/h (161mph), the SS is one of the fastest Camaros ever built.

Without doubt, the current SS Camaro will become a collector's car.

Chevrolet **CAMARO SS**

During its 10 years of modifying Pontiac Firebirds and Chevrolet Camaros, SLP Engineering has produced a performance package with outstanding acceleration, braking and handling.

V8 engine

For 1998 the Camaro Z28 and SS get an all-new engine, in the shape of the all-alloy small-block V8. Displacing 5686cc (347ci), it includes a 10:0 compression ratio and a .500-inch lift hydraulic roller camshaft and thumps out 320bhp in more powerful SS trim.

Big wheels and tyres

SS Camaros have larger wheels and tyres than standard Z28s, with meaty P275/40 ZR17 Goodyear Eagle F1s and 22.8cm (9in) x 43.2cm (17in) cast-alloy five-spoke wheels. Huge ABS- assisted vented discs and anti-roll bars front and rear ensure that handling and stopping are also not a problem.

Tuned exhaust

Fitting a freer-flowing exhaust is an established route for releasing more horsepower from an engine. SLP uses it to extract an additional 5bhp from the LS1, bringing the total to 325bhp.

Front-heavy weight distribution

Even though the SS has a front-heavy weight distribution, with almost 57 per cent of its bulk on the front wheels, it still accomplishes .90 gs of lateral acceleration on the skid pad and can slalom at 106km/h (66mph).

Oil cooler

To ensure that the SS can meet the demands of ultra-high performance driving, SLP provides an engine oil cooler as an option. It can be ordered in conjunction with Castrol Syntec oil for driveline components, which are warranted for up to 500,000 miles.

Specifications

1998 Chevrolet Camaro SS

ENGINE

Type: V8

Construction: Cast-iron block and alloy head

Valve gear: Two valves per cylinder operated by pushrods and rockers

Bore and stroke: 102mm (4.0in) x 88mm (3.48in)

Displacement: 5686cc (347ci)

Compression ratio: 10.1:1

Induction system: Sequential multipoint electronic fuel injection

Maximum power: 320bhp at 5200rpm

Maximum torque: 345lb-ft at 4400rpm

Top speed: 259km/h (161mph)

0–96km/h (0–60mph): 5.2 sec

TRANSMISSION

Borg-Warner T56 six-speed manual

BODY/CHASSIS

Unitized stamped steel with composite two-door coupe body.

SPECIAL FEATURES

SS models are fitted with a single tailpipe, although dual pipes are offered as an option.

These smart five-spoke alloy wheels were first seen on the Corvette ZR-1.

RUNNING GEAR

Steering: Rack-and-pinion

Front suspension: Short and long arms with coil springs, telescopic shock absorbers and anti-roll bar

Rear suspension: Live axle with trailing arms, Panhard rod, torque arm, coil springs, telescopic shock absorbers and anti-roll bar

Brakes: Vented discs,30.5cm (12in) dia. (front), 30.2cm (11.9in) dia. (rear)

Wheels: Alloy, 22.9cm (in) x 43.2cm (17in)

Tyres: Goodyear Eagle F1, P275/40 ZR17

DIMENSIONS

Length: 4.9m (193.2in)

Width: 1.88m (74.1in)

Height: 1.3m (51.4in)

Wheelbase: 257cm (101.1in)

Track: 154cm (60.6in) (front and rear)

Weight: 1630kg (3593lb)

Chevrolet **CAMARO Z28**

General Motors' answer to the Ford Mustang needed plenty of power to compete with the original pony car. The Z28 performance option on the Chevrolet Camaro was the answer. It dramatically improved handling and power.

'...factory built race car.'

'Designed to compete in Trans Am racing, the high-revving Z28 is a factory built race car. Underrated at 290bhp, the over-square 4949cc (302ci) V8 engine is peaky and nothing much happens until the engine revs past 4000rpm. Suddenly the tachometer needle is pointing to 7000rpm and the car really comes to life. It's upper end power like this where the Z28 gives you easy 193km/h (120mph) performance. Complementing the overabundance of high end power, the Z28 is garnished with a four-speed transmission, seven-inch rims and competition suspension.'

The interior of this race-modified Z28 uses bucket seat, roll cage and a fire extinguisher.

Milestones

1966 First Camaro appears

based on the Chevy II frame. The standard powertrain is only a 3769cc (230ci) six cylinder.

Only 602 Camaro Z28s were built in its first year, 1967.

1967 Regular production

option Z28 is introduced with a 4949cc (302ci) engine, just inside the 4999cc (305ci) limit set for Trans Am racing. Z28s finish third and fourth at the Sebring 12 Hours, winning the Trans Am category.

1968 Z28 dominates

Trans Am, easily winning the championship with the Roger Penske-prepared cars. Driver Mark Donohue wins 10 out of the 13 rounds.

The Camaro's styling was radically altered for 1970.

1969 Crossram induction

is made available, but is put in only 205 cars.

1970 Model restyled

to be longer and heavier with egg-crate type grill, but the Z28 option lives on and is still found on today's hottest Camaros.

UNDER THE SKIN

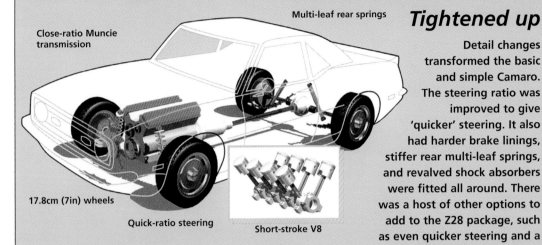

Close-ratio Muncie transmission

Multi-leaf rear springs

17.8cm (7in) wheels

Quick-ratio steering

Short-stroke V8

Tightened up

Detail changes transformed the basic and simple Camaro. The steering ratio was improved to give 'quicker' steering. It also had harder brake linings, stiffer rear multi-leaf springs, and revalved shock absorbers were fitted all around. There was a host of other options to add to the Z28 package, such as even quicker steering and a Muncie M-22 close-ratio four speed transmission.

THE POWER PACK

Hybrid V8

For the Z28, GM used the 327 cast iron block to give a 102mm (4in) bore and added a forged crankshaft (similar to the 283) with a 76mm (3in) stroke to make a rev-happy, over-square 4949cc (302ci) V8.

It operated a high (11.0:1) compression ratio, had 'Camelback' cylinder heads fitted with large 51mm (2.02in) intake and 41mm (1.60in) exhaust valves and had very radical valve timing. The engine is designed to give loads of top end performance, with its maximum power not coming in until 6000rpm.

2.02/1.60 valves

Holley carburetor

Shorter-stroke crankshaft

11.0:1 compression ratio

Longer, sleeker

The distinctive egg-crate grill is a definitive feature on the second-generation Camaro and was included on the Z28. It may not be the original, the rarest, or the most collectable Camaro variant, but it has a more obvious, overtly-sporting image. This shape remained in production, largely unchanged, until 1974.

The 1970 Camaros are more streamlined than first generation cars.

Chevrolet CAMARO Z28

To compete in the prestigious Trans Am championship, the rules required that Chevrolet had to build 1000 suitable cars ready for sale to the public to homologate the car for racing. The result was the Z28, a racing car for the road.

Performance V8
Chevrolet originally rated the Z28's short-stroke V8 at 290bhp. Some critics thought its potential was being deliberately underrated, and it could really produce something nearer to 350bhp at well over 6000rpm.

Coupe-only body style
You could not order the Z28 package with the convertible body because Chevrolet only needed to homologate the coupe for Trans Am racing.

Vented disc brakes
Z28s are heavy cars, so with the performance available they have to have vented front disc brakes. Even with the harder pads though, the Z28's braking isn't its strongest feature.

Close-ratio transmission
Standard Z28 transmission was an automatic but for $184 a Muncie four-speed manual was available that could also be ordered with close-ratio gears.

Harder brake linings
Although the Z28 carries rear drum brakes, just like stock Camaros, the linings are a harder compound to improve performance under sustained high-speed braking.

Rear spoiler
The rear spoiler is as much about adding just a touch of style to the rear of the Camaro as managing the airflow over the car to improve rear downforce.

Wide tyres

The Z28 used Goodyear WideTread tyres on relatively wide (for the time) 17.8cm (7in) rims.

Stiffer rear springs

The one major suspension change was the switch to multi-leaf instead of the stock single-leaf rear springs, which were 25 per cent stiffer than standard. Despite this change, the front spring rates did not need to be altered at all.

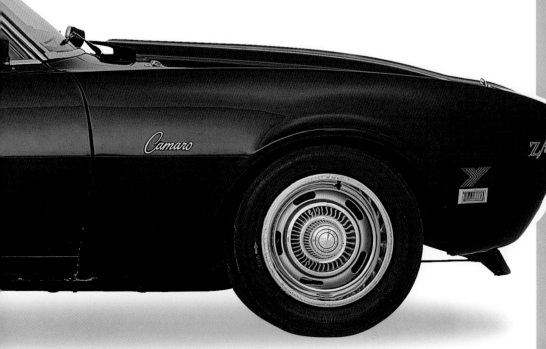

Specifications
1967 Chevrolet Camaro Z28

ENGINE

Type: V8

Construction: Cast-iron block and heads

Valve gear: Two valves per cylinder operated by single block-mounted camshaft via pushrods and hydraulic lifters

Bore and stroke: 102mm (4.0in) x 76mm (3.0in)

Displacement: 4949cc (302ci)

Compression ratio: 11.0:1

Induction system: Single four-barrel 800-cfm Holley carburettor

Maximum power: 290bhp at 5800rpm

Maximum torque: 290lb-ft at 4200rpm

Top speed: 259km/h (161mph)

0–96km/h (0–60mph): 5.2 sec

TRANSMISSION

Three-speed automatic or four-speed manual

BODY/CHASSIS

Unitary steel construction with two-door coupe body

SPECIAL FEATURES

This car has been fitted with a roll cage to comply with SCCA racing regulations.

RUNNING GEAR

Steering: Recirculating ball

Front suspension: Double wishbones with coil springs, telescopic shocks and anti-roll bar

Rear suspension: Live axle with multi-leaf semi-elliptic springs and telescopic shocks

Brakes: Front vented discs, 27.9cm (11in) dia., and rear drums, 22.8cm (9in) dia.**Wheels:** Steel disc, 17.8cm (7in) x 38.1cm (15in)

Tyres: Goodyear WideTread E70-15

DIMENSIONS

Length: 4.69m (184.7in)

Width: 1.84m (72.5in)

Height: 1.3m (51.4in)

Wheelbase: 274cm (108in)

Track: 151.3cm (59.6in) (front), 151.1cm (59.5in) (rear)

Weight: 1599kg (3525lb)

Chevrolet CAMARO ZL-1

GM supported the Automotive Manufacturers Association (AMA) ban in the 1960s by using its 6555cc (400ci) and larger engines only in full size cars and Corvettes. Through the Central Office Production Order system Vince Piggins, one of Chevrolet's officers, found a loop hole with the ban and created the ultimate Camaro – the ZL-1.

'...the apex of Chevy muscle.'

'This is the apex of Chevy's muscle cars. In the driver's seat, the car resembles a typical six-cylinder Camaro. When you start it up and listen to the aggressive engine, you soon realize you've slid behind the wheel of a true factory-built racer. With the addition of tubular headers, drag slicks and a super tune, one of these nasty Camaros could run the ¼ mile in 11.68 seconds at more than 193km/h (120mph). Few cars come close to offering the level of thrill that a ZL-1 can.'

Most ZL-1s had stripped cabins, but this one has a deluxe interior with woodgrain trim.

Milestones

1967 In response to the Mustang, Chevrolet launches the Camaro. The most powerful engine available is the 375bhp, 6489cc (396ci) V8. Because of the AMA ban, GM's intermediates weren't available with engines larger than 655cc (400ci). Meanwhile, some Chevy dealers were installing 427 V8s into these cars, especially Camaros.

In 1967 car dealers were installing 427 V8s into new Camaros.

1968 Don Yenko of Yenko Sports Cars becomes the largest dealer converting these Camaros. GM's Vince Piggins takes notice. Later that year, Piggins and Yenko get together to offer the conversion package from GM's COPO (Central Office Production Order) department for 1969.

Don Yenko's YSC Camaros got the ball rolling for the ZL-1.

1969 A few hundred COPO Camaros are built. While most come with cast iron 427s, 69 versions known as ZL-1s are built with aluminium big-block engines. Tuned ZL-1s made 500+bhp and could cover the ¼ mile in just under 12 seconds.

UNDER THE SKIN

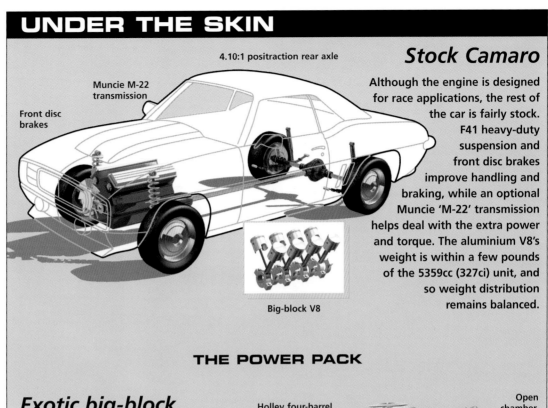

Muncie M-22 transmission

4.10:1 positraction rear axle

Front disc brakes

Big-block V8

Stock Camaro

Although the engine is designed for race applications, the rest of the car is fairly stock. F41 heavy-duty suspension and front disc brakes improve handling and braking, while an optional Muncie 'M-22' transmission helps deal with the extra power and torque. The aluminium V8's weight is within a few pounds of the 5359cc (327ci) unit, and so weight distribution remains balanced.

THE POWER PACK

Exotic big-block

The ZL-1 was unlike any other engine that GM made at that time. The engine is roughly equivalent to the L88 Corvette racing V8 but has an aluminium instead of cast-iron block. The reciprocating assembly consisted of a forged steel crankshaft, forged pistons that slide in steel cylinder liners and four-bolt main bearing caps. The aluminium cylinder heads have closed chambers and rectangle intake ports. A Holley 850-cfm four-barrel carburetor fed the massive engine the fuel it required.

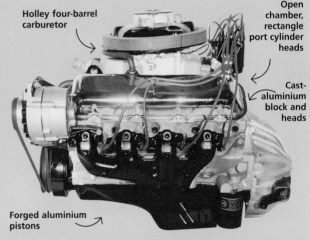

Holley four-barrel carburetor

Open chamber, rectangle port cylinder heads

Cast-aluminium block and heads

Forged aluminium pistons

Pure racer

ZL-1s are ranked with the Hemi Cuda convertible and Ram Air IV™ GTO® as one of the most desirable muscle cars ever produced. With only 69 built with the all-aluminium engine, they attract a premium price and often trade hands for $150,000 or more.

To this day, Chevrolet hasn't built a more powerful production car than the ZL-1.

Chevrolet **CAMARO ZL-1**

Most ZL-1s had plain bodies with skinny steel wheels – they didn't even have any badging to designate their model or engine size. This unique ZL-1 has the RS appearance package, vinyl top and 427 badging.

ZL2 cowl hood

All ZL-1s came with cowl induction hoods. It forced cool air into the engine from the high pressure area just below the windshield.

Expensive engine

You had to have a healthy bank account to be able to afford a ZL-1 Camaro. The engine's all-aluminium construction saved 73kg (160lb) over the cast-iron 427. Because it is virtually hand built, the engine alone cost $4160 – more than most cars of the period.

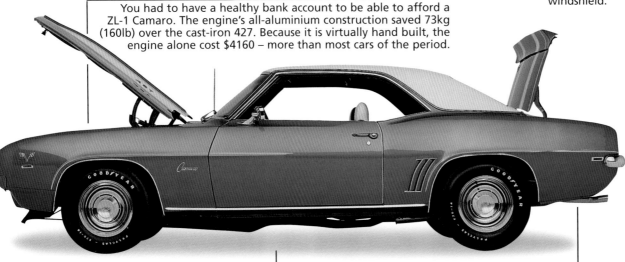

Better balance

Although it is a big-block unit, the ZL-1 engine weighs about 227kg (500lb), which is roughly the same as a 327, and so these special Camaros actually handle better than the stock SS 396™. However, these cars were designed for use in NHRA Super Stock drag racing events.

Standard exhaust system

ZL-1s left the factory with lots of mismatched parts because the owners were expected to do a lot of race development themselves. The stock exhaust manifolds restrict the flow of exhaust gases and were usually among the first items to be replaced.

The ZL-1 option package

All ZL-1s began life as SS 396s, but the engine and Super Sport™ option were deleted. Instead, the special cars received the ZL-1 option package, which included the aluminium engine, F41 suspension, front discs and a cowl induction hood.

Heavy duty suspension components

All ZL-1s were equipped with the heavy duty F41 suspension and front disc brakes. To better handle the 450lb-ft of torque from the powerful engines, ZL-1s were equipped with 12-bolt rear ends with 4.10 gears.

Performance transmission

Only two transmissions were strong enough to cope with the ZL-1 V8: the Muncie M-22 'Rock Crusher' four-speed or the equally stout TurboHydramatic 400 automatic.

Specifications

1969 Chevrolet Camaro ZL-1

ENGINE

Type: V8

Construction: Aluminium block and cylinder heads

Valve gear: Two valves per cylinder operated by a single camshaft

Bore and stroke: 108mm (4.25in) x 96mm (3.76in)

Displacement: 6997cc (427ci)

Compression ratio: 12.0:1

Induction system: Holley four-barrel carburettor

Maximum power: 430bhp at 5200rpm

Maximum torque: 450lb-ft at 4400rpm

Top speed: 201km/h (125mph)

0–96km/h (0–60mph): 5.5 sec

TRANSMISSION

Muncie M-22 four-speed manual

BODY/CHASSIS

Unitary steel chassis with two-door hardtop coupe body

SPECIAL FEATURES

Most ZL-1s have exposed headlights, but this car has the RS package.

RUNNING GEAR

Steering: Recirculating ball

Front suspension: Double wishbones with coil springs, telescopic shock absorbers and anti-roll bar

Rear suspension: Live axle with semi-elliptic leaf springs and telescopic shock absorbers

Brakes: Discs (front), drums (rear)

Wheels: Steel, 15.2cm (6in) x 38.1cm (15in)

Tyres: Goodyear Wide Tread GT, E70-15

DIMENSIONS

Length: 4.72m (186.0in)

Width: 1.88m (74.0in)

Height: 1.3m (51.0in)

Wheelbase: 274cm (108.0in)

Track: 151.4cm (59.6in) (front), 151.1cm (59.5in) (rear)

Weight: 1497kg (3300lb)

Chevrolet CHEVELLE SS 396

In 1966 the Chevelle Super Sport finally got serious with a larger engine and more muscular styling. Unfortunately, GM still retained on all of its mid-size high performers the 6555cc (400ci) cap that was instated in 1963. In response, the most powerful engine option was the ground-scorching 375bhp 6489cc (396ci) V8.

'...plenty of raw performance.'

"Not only is the 1966 SS tough-looking from the outside, it offers plenty of raw performance. Start the engine and savour the sound of the solid lifters. Straight-line acceleration is awesome and the force literally pushes you back into the seat. The engine is basically a detuned version of the largest engine option available in a 1965 Corvette®. With 375bhp only a touch of the throttle away, it was almost impossible not to get involved in a 0–96km/h (0–60mph) acceleration race.'

The interior features period pieces like a column-mounted tachometer and 4-speed shifter.

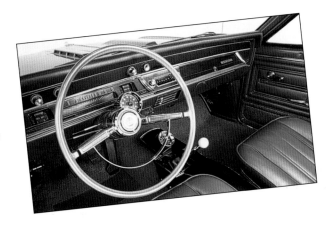

Milestones

1965 Chevrolet fits

the big-block 6489cc (396ci) Mark IV engine in the mid-size Chevelle Malibu SS. With 375bhp, the car is quick, but only 201 are built.

The 6489cc (396ci) V8 was first installed in the 1965 Corvette.

1966 Chevrolet introduces the SS 396 as a

Regular Production Order (RPO). Power is down, with the base engine rated at 325bhp and the L34 upgraded to 360bhp. A solid-lifter 375-bhp L78 unit is released in the spring and quickly establishes itself both on the street and at the strip. Of the 72,300 SS models built in 1966 only 3100 are equipped with the L78 engine.

The Camaro was also available with a Super Sport package.

1967 A mild facelift

greets the Chevelle, and front disc brakes and Rallye wheels join the options list. Sadly, the L78 engine is not listed this year, but returns for 1968.

UNDER THE SKIN

Body-on-the-frame construction

Rear-wheel drive

Independent front suspension

Front anti-roll bar

Big-block V8

Simple layout

Introduced in 1962, the Chevelle Malibu series employs body-on-the-frame construction. On SS versions the front anti-roll bar is thicker, the spring rates are increased by 30 per cent and stiffer shock absorbers are fitted. Prototypes had a rear anti-roll bar, but it wasn't used on production cars.

THE POWER PACK

Mark IV L78 Big-Block

In early 1965 Chevrolet brought out its new 6489cc (396ci) Mark IV big-block V8. The L78 version was the most powerful engine option available in the 1966 Chevelle. The 11.0:1 compression engine featured a steel crankshaft, a high-lift, long-duration camshaft with solid valve lifters and an aluminium high-rise intake manifold. It breathes better through its closed-chamber rectangle-port cast-iron cylinder heads. Topping off the 375bhp powerhouse is a Holley 800 cfm carb. If ultimate street performance was your goal, this was the engine to have.

Cast-iron block and cylinder heads

Two valves per cylinder

Aluminium intake manifold

Solid valve lifters

Rare beast

The 1967 is similar to the 1966 version, but has a few notable modifications, such as optional front disc brakes and a much more efficient three-speed automatic transmission. These cars, in fairly good condition, can cost about $10–25,000.

For 1967 the SS396 received only a new skin and some mechanical changes.

Chevrolet CHEVELLE SS 396

Launched in response to the Pontiac GTO and Oldsmobile 4-4-2, the Chevelle SS 396 soon gained many fans. Even in base 325bhp form, it was a force to be reckoned with and it proved to be the second best-selling muscle car, behind the GTO.

Standard drum brakes

In 1966 the SS 396 came with standard 24.1cm (9.5in) diameter drum brakes. Optional metallic brake linings provide better resistance to brake fade. Front discs became available in 1967.

Big-block engine

The 6489cc (396ci) V8 has canted valve cylinder heads, which allow better breathing. In 1966 a big-block Chevelle could be ordered with up to 375bhp.

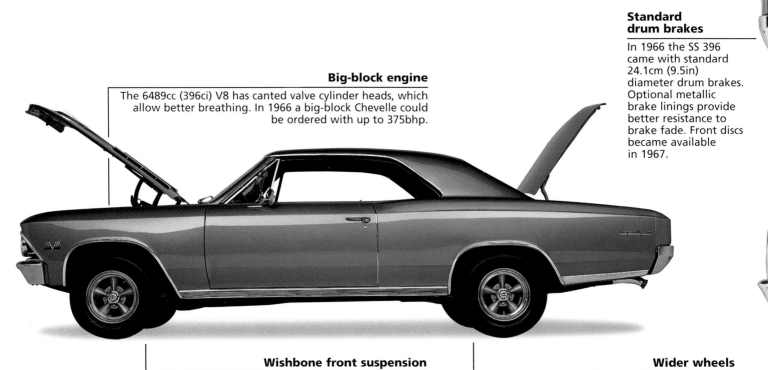

Wishbone front suspension

The standard Chevelle wishbone front suspension is beefed up with a larger diameter anti-roll bar, plus stiffer coil springs and shock absorbers.

Wider wheels

Chevelle SS models came with 35.6cm (14in) wheels as standard and small hub caps. Many owners in the 1960s fitted aftermarket wheels such as Cragars or these Torque Thrust-D items.

Rear axle brace

To deal with the strain of fierce acceleration and general high performance, a brace is fitted between each upper and lower control arm on the live axle and coil spring rear suspension. This helps to reinforce the frame.

Specifications

1966 Chevrolet Chevelle SS 396

ENGINE

Type: V8

Construction: Cast-iron block and heads

Valve gear: Two valves per cylinder operated by a single camshaft via pushrods, rockers and mechanical lifters

Bore and stroke: 104mm (4.09in) x 96mm (3.76in)

Displacement: 6489cc (396ci) (L78)

Compression ratio: 11.0:1

Induction system: Single Holley four-barrel carburetor

Maximum power: 375bhp at 5600rpm

Maximum torque: 415lb-ft at 3600rpm

Top speed: 209km/h (130mph)

0–96km/h (0–60mph): 6.0 sec

TRANSMISSION

Three- or four-speed manual or three-speed automatic

BODY/CHASSIS

Perimeter steel frame with two-door coupe body

SPECIAL FEATURES

This SS has been fitted with a rear stabilizer bar to improve handling.

These American Racing Torque Thrust-D magnesium wheels were a dealer-installed option on the 1966 Chevelle SS.

RUNNING GEAR

Steering: Recirculating ball

Front suspension: Double wishbones with coil springs, telescopic shock absorbers and anti-roll bar

Rear suspension: Live axle with upper and lower control arms, coil springs and telescopic shock absorbers

Brakes: Drums, 24.1cm (9.5in) dia. (front and rear)

Wheels: Steel disc, 15.2cm (6in) x 35.6cm (14in)

Tyres: US Royal Red Line 19.7cm (7.75in) x 35.6cm (14in)

DIMENSIONS

Length: 5m (197.0in)

Width: 1.9m (75.0in)

Height: 1.32m (51.9in)

Wheelbase: 292cm (115.0in)

Track: 147cm (58.0in) (front), 147cm (58.0in) (rear)

Weight: 1678kg (3700lb)

Power steering

Base-model Chevelles are heavy to drive and many owners ordered power steering. The steering wheel is huge and has a chromed centre section and horn ring.

Chevrolet CHEVELLE SS 454

In 1970, Chevrolet introduced the ultimate powerhouse for its midsize muscle car. It was also the year GM lifted its displacement ban on all of its midsize cars. For the Chevelle, it meant 450bhp from a stout LS-6 454 V8 for the Super Sport model. Today, it is regarded as one of the most fearsome muscle cars of all time.

'...all-out performance.'

'This is not a toy – it's an LS-6 Chevelle SS. It's one of those cars GM built just to show up Ford and Mopar. For years, the SS used semi-powerful 396 V8s, but when Chevy® released the LS-6 454, the competition shuddered. The all-out performance engine has a factory rating of 450bhp – no other muscle car production engine had a higher rating. The LS-6 Chevelle's only limitation was its tires. But even with the stock tread, the SS could be power shifted to 13.7 seconds in the ¼ mile.'

While most Chevelle Super Sports were ordered with custom buckets, this one has a bench seat.

Milestones

1969 SS is an option

package. Top-of-the-line engine is the L78 396 with 375bhp. But Vince Piggins, GM's performance products manager, had 323 COPO (Central Office Production Order) Chevelles built with L72 427 V8s. Producing 425bhp, they run the ¼ mile in 13.3 seconds at 175km/h (108 mph).

Earlier Chevelles had much boxier styling.

1970 General Motors

unleashes its wildest muscle cars yet, with revised styling. The LS-5 (360bhp) and LS-6 (454bhp) 454 V8s join the 396 in the Chevelle SS line up as a regular production order.

In 1970, the smaller-engined SS 396 was still available.

1971 The SS 454 returns,

though the LS-6 option is dropped. The less powerful LS-5 actually gains 5bhp, to 365. Only 9402 SS 454s are built. A new Chevelle arrives for 1973.

UNDER THE SKIN

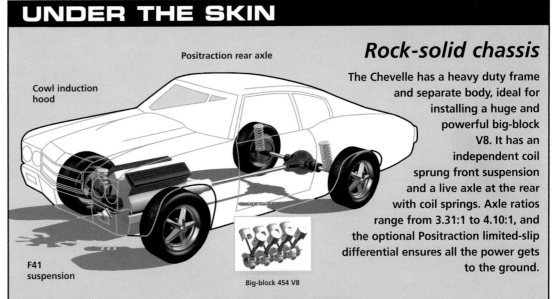

Cowl induction hood

Positraction rear axle

F41 suspension

Big-block 454 V8

Rock-solid chassis

The Chevelle has a heavy duty frame and separate body, ideal for installing a huge and powerful big-block V8. It has an independent coil sprung front suspension and a live axle at the rear with coil springs. Axle ratios range from 3.31:1 to 4.10:1, and the optional Positraction limited-slip differential ensures all the power gets to the ground.

THE POWER PACK

Hard-core power

The lightning and thunder raging under the bonnet of the highest performance Chevelle SS – the LS-6 – produces 450bhp and 500lb-ft of torque. The block shares the same 108mm (4.25in) bore as the 427 V8, but the stroke was increased to 102mm (4in). The longer stroke helps produce tons of low end power. The powerful LS-6 uses high (11.25:1) compression forged pistons, steel crankshaft, high-lift camshaft with mechanical lifters and closed-chamber, rectangle-port cylinder heads. It uses an aluminium intake manifold and a Holley 800 cfm carburetor. This engine means business.

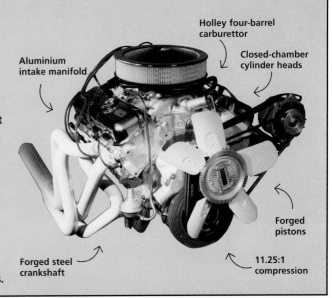

Aluminium intake manifold

Holley four-barrel carburettor

Closed-chamber cylinder heads

Forged pistons

Forged steel crankshaft

11.25:1 compression

Collector's cars

The 1970 Chevelle Super Sport was restyled from the 1969 model and again in 1971. A 1970 SS with the LS-6 is as rare as it is powerful. Only 4475 of these venomous vehicles were produced, making them popular and valuable among auto collectors.

Not many muscle cars come close to the tyre-shredding power of the LS-6 SS.

Chevrolet CHEVELLE SS 454

The LS-6 Chevelle was one of the most powerful muscle cars ever produced. It combined Chevrolet's largest engine with its sporty midsize car to give outrageous results.

Body stripes
By 1970 style was every bit as important as performance, and SS Chevelles were available with twin stripes running over the bonnet and rear decklid.

LS-6 454-cubic inch V8
The biggest performance option in 1970 was the LS-6 engine. It produces 450bhp at 5600rpm and 500lb-ft of torque at 3600rpm. It has high compression pistons, rectangle port cylinder heads and solid valve lifters. Few other muscle machines could rival the power of the LS-6.

M-22 'Rock crusher' transmission
With 500lb-ft of torque, only two transmissions were strong enough to cope with the LS-6 engine. This one has a Muncie M22 'Rock crusher' four-speed. This stout unit has a 2.20:1 straight-cut first gear.

Magnum 500 wheels
Magnum 500 steel wheels were used on all 1970 Chevelle Super Sports. The Polyglas F70x14 could barely handle the engine's torque.

Hardtop body
While all LS-6 engines were supposed to be installed in hardtops only, it's rumoured that a few found their way into convertibles.

Specifications
1970 Chevrolet Chevelle SS 454

ENGINE
Type: V8
Construction: Cast-iron block and heads
Valve gear: Two valves per cylinder operated by pushrods and rockers
Bore and stroke: 108mm (4.25in) x 102mm (4.00in)
Displacement: 7440cc (454ci)
Compression ratio: 11.25:1
Induction system: Holley four-barrel carburetor and aluminium intake manifold
Maximum power: 450bhp at 5600rpm
Maximum torque: 500lb-ft at 3600rpm
Top speed: 201km/h (125mph)
0–96km/h (0–60mph): 6.1 sec

TRANSMISSION
Manual four-speed, close-ratio M-22

BODY/CHASSIS
Steel body on separate steel chassis

SPECIAL FEATURES

These NASCAR-style tie-down bonnet pins were a popular item and helped keep the bonnet from lifting at high speed.

Upgraded suspension
The SS package included the F41 suspension, which has stiffer front springs to compensate for the weight of the big-block engine.

CNE 098

RUNNING GEAR
Steering: Recirculating ball
Front suspension: Independent with wishbones, anti-roll bar, coil springs and telescopic shock absorbers
Rear suspension: Live axle with coil springs and telescopic shock absorbers
Brakes: Disc, 27.9cm (11in) dia. (front), drum 22.8cm (9in) dia. (rear)
Wheels: Magnum 500, 14-in. dia.
Tyres: Polyglas F70x14

Cowl induction hood
A vacuum-controlled flap at the top of the hood draws air in from the high-pressure area at the base of the windshield to help the engine exploit its power. This is known as cowl induction.

Dual exhaust
A full-length 64mm (2.5in) dual exhaust system enables the LS-6 to optimize the engine's performance.

DIMENSIONS
Length: 4.8m (189in)
Width: 1.78m (70.2in)
Height: 1.34m (52.7in)
Wheelbase: 284cm (112in)
Track: 144cm (56.8in) (front), 145cm (56.9in) (rear)
Weight: 1814kg (4000lb)

Chevrolet CORVETTE STING RAY

When Chevrolet® introduced the Corvette Sting Ray in 1963, it was the quickest roadster Detroit had ever made. Its 5359cc (327ci) V8 gave the new Corvette serious muscle, and for the first time, an American sports car could out-gun its European rivals.

'America's favourite sports car.'

'Off the line, this Vette™ has the kind of low-end grunt that will leave most modern sports cars in a cloud of dust and burning rubber. First you hear the throaty rumble of the big-shouldered 427 V8, then the three two-barrel carbs snarl to life and you can feel the power throb through the chrome shifter. Both the steering and clutch are heavy, while the handling and brakes are crude by today's standards. But that snap-your-head-back lunge of power still makes the Sting Ray America's favourite sports car.'

The cockpit is spartan and functional with a classic hot rod feel often imitated but never quite equalled.

Milestones

1953 The first Motorama Corvette
show car enters production with a six-cylinder engine.

1955 Zora Arkus-Duntov,
father of the Sting Ray, becomes head of the Corvette programme, a position he held until retirement in 1982. Under him, manual transmission and the V8 engine are offered as options (1955) and fuel injection becomes available (1957).

1957 The Vette is the fastest
real production car in the world, showing what can be done when conventional engineering is applied well.

The 1963 convertible. Soft top is stored under a panel behind the seats.

1963 The first Sting Ray
production car is built, with all-independent suspension and the first coupe body. Its styling is based on a racing car design originally developed in 1958 by Bill Mitchell.

1965 Big-block
engine and disc brakes are available. The 6489cc (396ci) V8 with a solid cam is introduced with 425bhp.

1967 Pinnacle of performance
is the L88 6997cc (427ci) V8. This also marks the last year of this body style.

UNDER THE SKIN

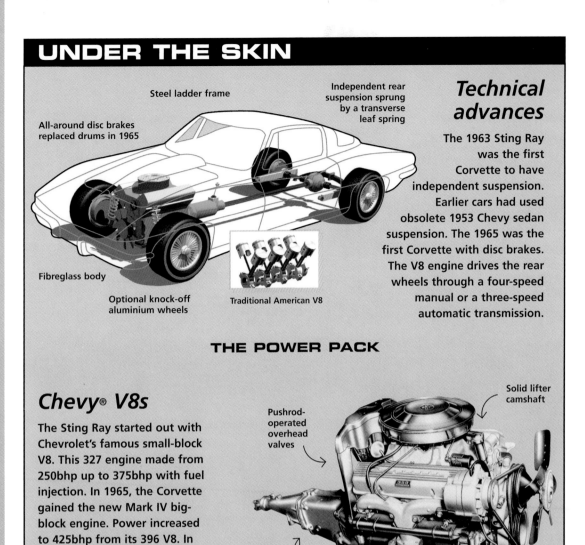

Steel ladder frame

Independent rear suspension sprung by a transverse leaf spring

All-around disc brakes replaced drums in 1965

Fibreglass body

Optional knock-off aluminium wheels

Traditional American V8

Technical advances

The 1963 Sting Ray was the first Corvette to have independent suspension. Earlier cars had used obsolete 1953 Chevy sedan suspension. The 1965 was the first Corvette with disc brakes. The V8 engine drives the rear wheels through a four-speed manual or a three-speed automatic transmission.

THE POWER PACK

Chevy® V8s

The Sting Ray started out with Chevrolet's famous small-block V8. This 327 engine made from 250bhp up to 375bhp with fuel injection. In 1965, the Corvette gained the new Mark IV big-block engine. Power increased to 425bhp from its 396 V8. In 1966, the engine was enlarged again to 6997cc (427ci) and made up to 425bhp. The 435bhp 427 L88 was offered the very next year.

Pushrod-operated overhead valves

Solid lifter camshaft

M-22 manual transmission

Cast-iron block

Split rear window

The most sought-after Sting Ray is the 1963 split rear window coupe model. The designer, Bill Mitchell, intended it to form a visual connection with the central raised sections on the hood. The feature was dropped because it spoiled rear vision. Some later cars have been retro-fitted with the centre pillar in an attempt to raise their values.

The split rear window coupe was available in 1963 only.

Chevrolet CORVETTE STING RAY

The Sting Ray was introduced in 1963, 10 years after the Corvette's first appearance. The engine is set well back in the frame, giving nearly 50/50 weight distribution and excellent handling for the day.

Fibreglass body

Like all Corvettes, the Sting Ray has a body made from a number of fibreglass panels mounted on a traditional separate frame.

Disc brakes all around

Vented discs with dual-pot calipers on each wheel were fitted from 1965. While old stocks lasted, buyers could opt for the discontinued drums to save money.

V8 engine

Apart from the very early models, all Corvettes are powered by V8 engines. There is a wide variety of displacements and states of tune. The 5359cc (327ci) engine in 350bhp tune is typical.

Optional side exhausts

The Sting Ray's enormous options list included the Side Mount Exhaust System. The side pipes are covered with a perforated shield to prevent the driver or passengers from burning themselves. Side exhausts were chosen mainly for visual effect.

No trunk lid

To preserve the contour of the car, there is no boot lid and access to the luggage compartment is from behind the seats.

Foldaway top

The Corvette's convertible top folds away completely when not in use and is stored beneath a flush-fitting fibreglass panel behind the driver. Optional hard top cost $231.75 in 1966.

Alloy gearbox and clutch housing

To save weight, the Sting Ray was given an alloy clutch housing and an alloy-cased gearbox. This also improved weight distribution.

Flip-up headlights

The headlights are rotated by two reversible vacuum operated motors – a postwar first for an American car.

Triple side vents

Side vent arrangement, like many minor details, changed over the years. The 1965 and '66 models like this one have three vents.

Independent rear suspension

Another Corvette first, the Sting Ray has a crude but effective system with a transverse leaf spring mounted behind the differential.

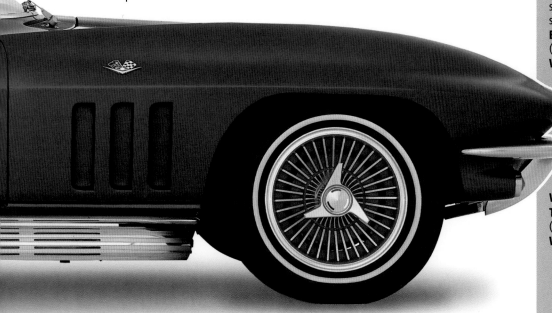

Specifications
1966 Chevrolet Corvette Sting Ray

ENGINE
Type: V8, 90°

Construction: Cast-iron block and heads; Single cam, pushrods

Bore and stroke: 102mm (4.0in) x 83mm (3.25in)

Displacement: 5359cc (327ci)

Compression ratio: 11:1

Induction system: Rochester fuel injection or one/two Carter four-barrel carbs

Maximum power: 375bhp at 6200rpm

Maximum torque: 350lb-ft at 4000rpm

Top speed: 217km/h (135mph)

0–96km/h (0–60 mph): 5.6 sec

TRANSMISSION
Three-speed automatic (optional four-speed manual)

BODY/CHASSIS
Steel ladder frame with two-door convertible or coupe fibreglass body

SPECIAL FEATURES

Soft top folds away neatly into compartment behind seats, with luggage space below.

RUNNING GEAR
Front suspension: Double wishbone, coil springs, anti-roll bar

Rear suspension: Semi-trailing arms, half-shafts and transverse links with transverse leaf spring

Brakes: Vented discs with four-pot calipers (optional cast-iron drums)

Wheels: Five-bolt steel (knock off aluminium optional) 15.2cm (6in) x 38.1cm (15in)

Tyres: 17cm (6.7in) x 38.1cm (15in) Firestone Super Sport 170

DIMENSIONS
Length: 4.45m (175.3in)

Width: 1.77m (69.6in)

Height: 1.26m (49.8in)

Wheelbase: 249cm (98in)

Track: 143cm (56.3in) (front), 145cm (57in) (rear)

Weight: 1429kg (3150lb)

Chevrolet CORVETTE

In 1968 Chevrolet introduced the third generation Corvette. Not everyone liked it, but with a 6997cc (427ci) engine under the bonnnet, it was one of the quickest production vehicles made in the late 1960s.

'...strong and torquey.'

'Compared to contemporary European sports cars, the 1969 Corvette is big and brash. The styling is controversial and the interior tight, but once you put your foot down all these criticisms are forgotten. The 6997cc (427ci) V8 is strong and torquey and will push the 'Vette to 96km/h (60mph) in under six seconds. Though most of the Corvette's weight is over the front wheels, it can hold a line or corner with most any other sports car.'

Early third generation Corvettes had easy-to-read gauges and comfortable bucket seats.

Milestones

1966 Mako Shark

show car, designed by GM stylist Larry Shinoda, is revealed.

Early third generation Corvettes use the optional 427 that first appeared in the 1967 model.

1968 The new Corvette, with both small-block and big-block V8s, debuts to mixed reviews. There are initial quality control problems, but testers comment on the excellent performance. The new model sets a production record, with 28,566 Corvettes built.

By 1977 the Corvette was more cruiser than bruiser.

1969 Chevrolet makes detail changes. The name Stingray is revived, but now as one word. The doors and rear taillights are slightly redesigned. The 350 replaces the 327 as the base small-block V8, and it also marks the final year the 427 V8 will be used. The following year will see the arrival of the 454 big block.

UNDER THE SKIN

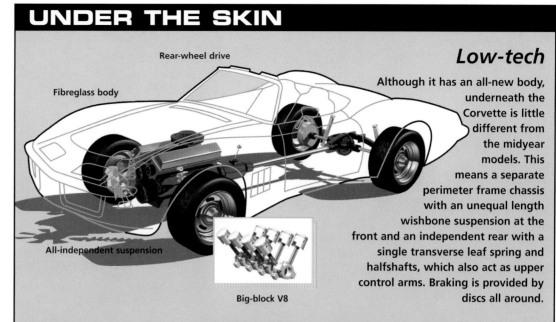

Rear-wheel drive

Fibreglass body

All-independent suspension

Big-block V8

Low-tech

Although it has an all-new body, underneath the Corvette is little different from the midyear models. This means a separate perimeter frame chassis with an unequal length wishbone suspension at the front and an independent rear with a single transverse leaf spring and halfshafts, which also act as upper control arms. Braking is provided by discs all around.

THE POWER PACK

Codes of power

In 1969 Chevrolet offered five 427 big-block V8 engines. The lowest powered 427 was the L36 which 'only' made 390bhp, while the L68 made 400bhp. Those who wanted more performance ordered the L71 (435bhp) which was available with optional aluminium heads. Both the L68 and L71 came with tri-power carbs. The over-the-edge engine was the L88, which was underrated from the factory at 430bhp (the actual figure was closer to 530bhp). There were also two all-alloy ZL-1 427s produced, which made over 500bhp.

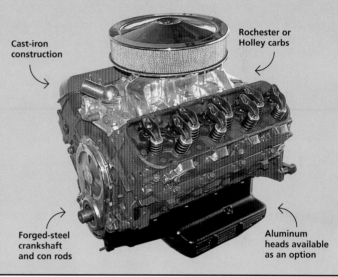

Cast-iron construction

Rochester or Holley carbs

Forged-steel crankshaft and con rods

Aluminum heads available as an option

Special order

Some of the rarest and most desirable of all the muscle-era Corvettes are those powered by the L88 engine. Factory rated at 435bhp, the true output is estimated at around 530bhp. Only 116 were built in 1969, and today are worth around $90,000.

The L88 Corvettes were available by special order only.

Chevrolet CORVETTE

Although overshadowed by the 1963–1967 Sting Ray, the later big-block Corvettes were equipped with some of Detroit's most powerful engines and are highly sought-after because of their performance.

Optional hard top

For an extra $252, owners who bought convertibles could order an optional hardtop that attaches to twin locating slots on the rear decklid and two on the top of the windshield frame. It can be installed when the soft top is down.

Big-block engine

Known as the Mark IV, the big-block 427 was only available in full-size Chevrolets and the Corvette as a regular production option in 1969. With this engine, Corvettes are capable of 13-second quarter-mile times at about 160km/h 100mph).

Limited-slip differential

A GM Positraction limited-slip differential was available for an extra $46.35 and most owners specified it. It helps to control wheel spin under hard acceleration.

Revised interior

The 1968 Corvette was criticized for its small interior, and so for 1969 it was modified with a smaller-diameter steering wheel and thinner door panels. A map pocket was also included in the glove compartment door.

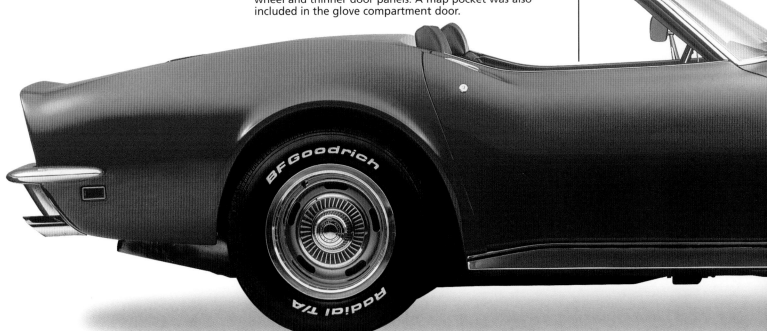

Windshield wiper panel

An unusual feature is a vacuum-operated panel that conceals the windshield wipers. When the wipers are turned on, it pops up and forward and can be left up to facilitate changing the wiper blades.

Specifications

1969 Chevrolet Corvette

ENGINE

Type: V8

Construction: Cast-iron block and heads

Valve gear: Two valves per cylinder operated by pushrods and rockers

Bore and stroke: 108mm (4.25in) x 96mm (3.76in)

Displacement: 6997cc (427ci)

Compression ratio: 11.0:1

Induction system: Single Rochester Quadrajet four-barrel carburettor

Maximum power: 435bhp at 5600rpm

Maximum torque: 460lb-ft at 4000rpm

Top speed: 217km/h (135mph)

0–96km/h (0–60mph): 5.5 sec

TRANSMISSION

Muncie M22, close ratio, four-speed

BODY/CHASSIS

Perimeter chassis with fibreglass body

SPECIAL FEATURES

1968–1969 Corvettes contain these gill-like fender air extractors.

RUNNING GEAR

Steering: Recirculating ball

Front suspension: Unequal length wishbones with coil springs and telescopic shock absorbers

Rear suspension: Independent with lower control arms, transverse leaf spring and telescopic shock absorbers

Brakes: Discs (front), drums (rear)

Wheels: Slotted Rally, 17.8cm (7in) x 38.1cm (15in)

Tyres: F60 15

DIMENSIONS

Length: 4.34m (171.0in)

Width: 1.72m (67.8in)

Height: 1.24m (48.9in)

Wheelbase: 2.48m (98.0in)

Track: 1.47m (57.9in) (front), 1.51m (59.6in) (rear)

Weight: 1427kg (3145lb)

Chevrolet CORVETTE ZR-1

**With its Lotus-designed quad-cam V8 engine, the ZR-1
has a more advanced powerplant and superior performance than the current
C5 Corvette. It is the ultimate Corvette – a genuine world-class supercar.**

'...the ultimate Corvette?'

*'Above 3500rpm, when all 16 injectors are pumping fuel as fast as
the engine can use it, the ZR-1's performance is astounding, even
for early models. With the later 405bhp engines, there were few
cars on the road to challenge the ZR-1's performance. The chassis
easily copes with the huge power output. The ride may be harsh
and the interior cramped, but this is a supercar with sensitive
steering, powerful brakes, and fine rear-wheel drive road manners.'*

**Lateral support in the ZR-1 is excellent, although the cockpit is difficult
to enter.**

Milestones

1984 A new Corvette
is finally introduced in 1983 as a 1984 model. The fourth-generation Corvette is the best in years, but, although it retains the front-engine rear-drive format, it severely needs more power.

By 1956 the Corvette finally matured, and turned into a serious sports car.

1986 The Corvette roadster
is revived, and goes on sale this year. It is selected as a pace car for the Indianapolis 500.

1990 After much hype,
the ZR-1 finally enters production. It has unique rear end styling to distinguish it from the standard Corvette.

An all-new, fifth-generation Corvette debuted in 1997.

1993 Power is boosted
to 405bhp and a special 40th anniversary trim package is available on all Corvettes. The ZR-1 returns for two more seasons with new five-spoke alloy wheels.

UNDER THE SKIN

American technology

Beneath the fibreglass body lies the heart of the ZR-1, the high-tech LT5 V8 engine. Backing it up is a standard six-speed ZF transmission (automatic was not available), which transmits power to a fully independent rear end. The rear body panels had to be widened to fit the huge 315/35 Goodyear tyres.

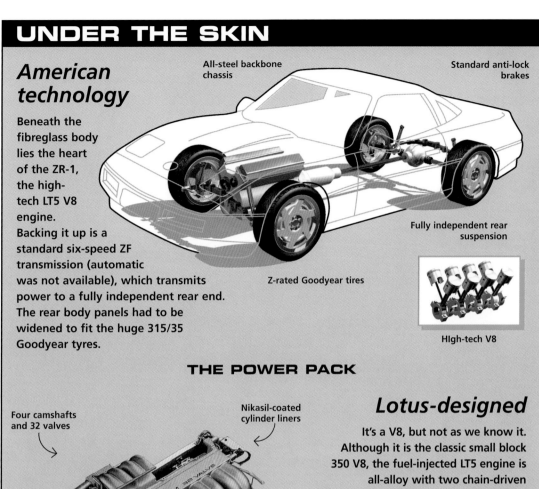

All-steel backbone chassis

Standard anti-lock brakes

Fully independent rear suspension

Z-rated Goodyear tires

HIgh-tech V8

THE POWER PACK

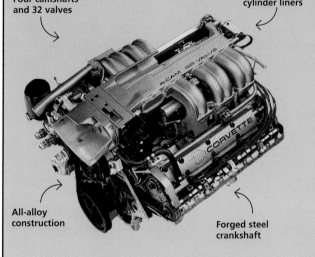

Four camshafts and 32 valves

Nikasil-coated cylinder liners

All-alloy construction

Forged steel crankshaft

Lotus-designed

It's a V8, but not as we know it. Although it is the classic small block 350 V8, the fuel-injected LT5 engine is all-alloy with two chain-driven camshafts per cylinder bank, which operate four valves per cylinder. The crankshaft is a very strong, cross-drilled, forged steel unit and the connecting rods are made from forged steel alloy. Chevrolet employed Lotus, in England, to design the engine and Mercury Marine, in the US, to build it. The sophisticated design meant that it could be tweaked to produce even more power.

Brute force

In 1993 Chevrolet began to make use of the powerful Lotus-designed LT5 V8, pushing up its output to 405bhp at 5800rpm and the torque to 385lb-ft. The early ZR-1s may have been fast, but the extra power of the later model really makes them move.

This post-1993 model has an increased power output of 405bhp.

Chevrolet CORVETTE ZR-1

With the ZR-1, Chevrolet proved that an exotic mid-mounted engine and $100,000 price tag are not required to offer true supercar performance.

Quad-cam V8

A technological masterpiece, the LT5 was originally intended for boats. Although all-alloy, it weighs more than a cast-iron Chevy small block.

Plastic springs

Like all Corvettes since the launch of the 1963 Coupe, the ZR-1 features transverse leaf springs. These are now made from plastic for reduced weight.

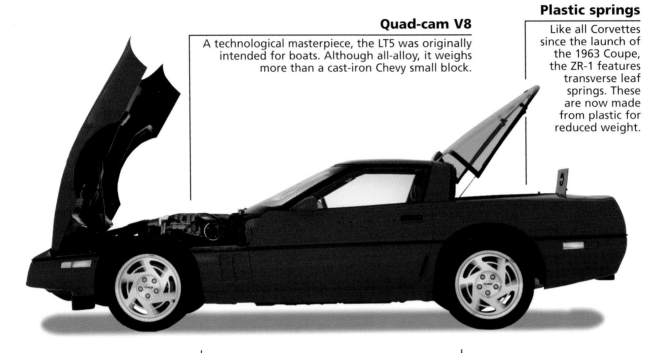

Traction control

Corvettes were often tricky to control on slippery roads. The introduction of ASR (Anti-Slip Regulation) considerably reduced the tendency for the car to slide on wet roads.

Tyre-pressure monitor

For 1989, all Corvettes received a tyre-pressure monitoring device that warns the driver, by means of a flashing light, if tyre pressures are low.

CAGS gear selection

Computer-Aided Gear Selection (CAGS) is a device which skips shifts in low gears at light throttle openings.

Valet key

To prevent certain individuals from experiencing the ZR-1's full performance, a special key can be used to restrict horsepower.

Fibreglass bodywork

The ZR-1, like all Corvettes, retains fibreglass bodywork. The back half of the car had to be widened to fit the ZR-1s large wheels.

Selective ride control

At the touch of a switch the ZR-1 driver can select three different suspension settings: Touring, Sport, or Performance. As speed increases, the shocks are stiffened by a computer that is able to make 10 adjustments per second.

Variable fuel injectio

During normal driving, the ZR-1's engine uses only eight primary ports and injectors. With the throttle floored and the engine turning above 3500rpm, the eight secondary injectors are brought into action, producing truly awesome performance.

Specifications
1991 Chevrolet Corvette ZR-1

ENGINE

Type: LT5 V8

Construction: Alloy block, heads and cylinder liners

Valve gear: Four valves per cylinder operated by four overhead camshafts

Bore and stroke: 99mm (3.90in) x 93mm (3.66in)

Displacement: 5735cc (350ci)

Compression ratio: 11:1

Induction system: Multi-port fuel injection

Maximum power: 375bhp at 5800rpm

Maximum torque: 371lb-ft at 4800rpm

Top speed: 290km/h (180mph)

0–96km/h (0–60mph): 5 sec

TRANSMISSION

ZF six-speed manual

BODY/CHASSIS

Separate steel chassis with fiberglass two-door coupe body

SPECIAL FEATURES

Prototype ZR-1s retained the original 1984 instrument panel layout.

RUNNING GEAR

Steering: Rack-and-pinion

Front suspension: Double wishbones, transverse plastic leaf springs, and telescopic adjustable shocks

Rear suspension: Upper and lower trailing links, transverse plastic leaf spring, telescopic adjustable shocks, and anti-roll bar

Brakes: Vented discs front and rear, 33cm (13in) dia. (front), 30.5cm (12in) dia. (rear)

Wheels: Alloy, 43.2cm (17in) x 24.1cm (9.5in) dia. (front), 43.2cm (17in) x 27.9cm (11in) dia. (rear)

Tyres: Goodyear Eagle ZR40, 275/40 ZR17 (front), 315/35 ZR17 (rear)

DIMENSIONS

Length: 4.5m (178.5in)

Width: 1.86m (73.2in)

Height: 1.19m (46.7in)

Wheelbase: 244cm (96.2in)

Track: 152cm (60in) (front), 157cm (62in) (rear)

Weight: 1596kg (3519lb)

Chevrolet CORVETTE GS

With the advent of the new C5 model on the horizon, Chevrolet wanted to send off the fourth generation version in typical Corvette style. So for its final year in production, Chevy® added a 330bhp LT4 small-block V8 and some interesting graphics that hark back to the original sports racer of the 1960s – and called it the Grand Sport.

'...a driving enthusiast's dream.'

'Because this is a limited edition Corvette, it needed more than radical graphics to give it collectible status. The engine reaches 330bhp thanks to redesigned cylinder heads and intake manifold. Its stable road manners and flat-out handling leave the driver with a strong feeling of confidence and enthusiasm. The firm suspension, responsive steering and potent brakes mated with the one-year-only engine option are a hard-core driving enthusiast's dream come true.'

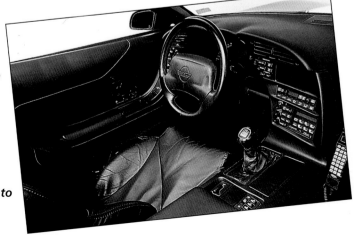

'Grand Sport' embroidery on each seat back is just one exclusive touch to this special Vette®.

Milestones

1954 The first V8
Corvette is built. It uses the 195bhp 'Turbo-Fire' 4343cc (265ci) V8.

1967 Most coveted
of all Corvettes is the L88 Sting Ray®. Only 20 are built.

1984 Late-model
technology in the form of a rigid chassis and race-car style suspension is the focus on the fourth-generation model.

The original Grand Sport cars were built for SCCA racing.

1990 'King of the Hill' is the name

given to the ZR-1®. It boasts a special Lotus-designed 32-valve all-alloy engine.

For the Corvette's 40th anniversary in 1993, a special appearance package was offered.

1996 The end of an era coincides with the

one-year-only LT4 small-block V8. Grand Sport production is limited to 1000 units.

UNDER THE SKIN

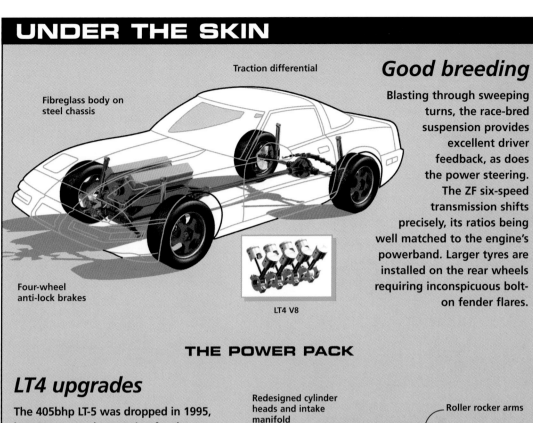

Traction differential

Fibreglass body on steel chassis

Four-wheel anti-lock brakes

LT4 V8

Good breeding

Blasting through sweeping turns, the race-bred suspension provides excellent driver feedback, as does the power steering. The ZF six-speed transmission shifts precisely, its ratios being well matched to the engine's powerband. Larger tyres are installed on the rear wheels requiring inconspicuous bolt-on fender flares.

THE POWER PACK

LT4 upgrades

The 405bhp LT-5 was dropped in 1995, but GM wanted an engine for the Corvette that would offer 10 per cent more power than the base LT1. The LT4 was the answer. The foundation is a 5735cc (350ci) engine with modified pistons, required to clear the 51/39mm (2.00/1.55in) hollow valves. This brings the compression ratio up to 10.8:1 from 10.5:1. Redesigned cylinder heads with modified ports are used with 45kg (100lb) valve springs, a hot cam and roller rocker arms. The LT4 makes 330bhp and also has a higher 6300rpm redline.

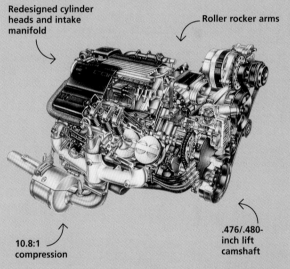

Redesigned cylinder heads and intake manifold

Roller rocker arms

10.8:1 compression

.476/.480-inch lift camshaft

Neat package

Models with the Z51 'Performance Handling Package' have a special attraction. The package increases the Grand Sport's cornering ability by means of thicker anti-roll bars, firmer shocks and stiffer springs. The ride is firm, but the trade-off is worth it.

In addition to its many dynamic qualities, the Grand Sport is very attractive.

Chevrolet **CORVETTE GS**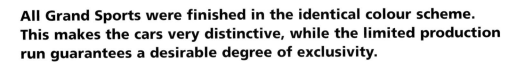

All Grand Sports were finished in the identical colour scheme. This makes the cars very distinctive, while the limited production run guarantees a desirable degree of exclusivity.

Small-block V8

To separate the 330bhp LT4 small-block from the base LT1, the ignition wires, intake manifold and 'Corvette' lettering on the plastic manifold covers are all painted red.

High-flow heads

The LT4's heads are a completely different casting than the LT1's. The exhaust ports are widened, the intake ports are raised by 3mm (0.1in) and the radius has been smoothed for better flow. They are assembled with larger 51mm (2.00in) hollow-stem intake valves, and 39mm (1.55in) sodium-filled exhaust valves and use stiffer valve springs.

Distinctive color

All Grand Sports are painted Admiral Blue Metallic with a white stripe down the centre of the body and red hash marks on the driver's side front fender.

Six-speed shifting

GM didn't think that an automatic unit would be strong enough to handle the engine's 10 per cent power gain. Because of this, all Grand Sports were available only with a strong ZF 6-speed manual transmission.

Performance wheels and tyres

High-performance Z-rated Goodyear GS-C tyres are fitted to black, powder-coated 43.2cm (17in) five-spoke wheels. Although they look like ZR-1 wheels, their offset is slightly different.

Special identification

To celebrate the Grand Sport's limited production run of only 1000 models, Chevrolet gave them a separate serial number sequence.

Aero shape

Although they have a large frontal area, fourth-generation Corvettes slice through the air quite effectively. Special fender flares in the rear have been added to house the wider 315/35 ZR17 tyres.

Specifications

1996 Corvette Grand Sport

ENGINE

Type: V8 (LT-4)

Construction: Cast-iron block and aluminium cylinder heads

Valve gear: Two valves per cylinder operated by a centrally mounted camshaft with pushrods and roller rocker arms

Bore and stroke: 102mm (4.00in) x 88m (3.48in)

Displacement: 5735cc (350ci)

Compression ratio: 10.8:1

Induction system: Sequential fuel injection

Maximum power: 330bhp at 5800rpm

Maximum torque: 340lb-ft at 4500rpm

Top speed: 270km/h (168mph)

0–96km/h (0–60mph): 4.7 sec

TRANSMISSION

Six-speed manual

BODY/CHASSIS

Fibreglass body on steel chassis

SPECIAL FEATURES

The five-spoke wheel design resembles that of the ZR-1, but is in fact unique.

Red 'Grand Sport' seat embroidery is just one of many identifying features.

RUNNING GEAR

Steering: Rack-and-pinion

Front suspension: Independent with aluminium upper and lower control arms, transverse leaf spring, gas shock absorbers and anti-roll bar

Rear suspension: Independent with five-link, transverse leaf spring and anti-roll bar

Brakes: Discs, 30.5cm (12in) dia. (front and rear)

Wheels: Aluminium, 24.1cm (9.5in) x 43.2cm (17in)

Tyres: Goodyear, 275/40 ZR17 (front), P315/35 ZR17 (rear)

DIMENSIONS

Length: 4.53m (178.5in)

Width: 1.80m (70.7in)

Height: 1.18m (46.3in)

Wheelbase: 244cm (96.2in)

Track: 147cm (57.7in) (front), 150cm (59.1in) (rear)

Weight: 1496kg (3298lb)

Chevrolet CORVETTE

Corvettes have been around for well over 40 years, but none has the sophistication of the latest model. It still has typical stunning performance, but without the compromise that made previous Corvettes hard to live with.

'...return to greatness.'

'The C5 signals Corvette's return to greatness: it is truly a perfect blend of performance and comfort. The alloy LS1 V8 engine revs instantly in response to its new electronic throttle control and sends the car soaring to 96km/h (60mph) in less than five seconds and past 241km/h (150mph) with ease. But thanks to a redesigned body that is four times stiffer than that of its predecessor, the car doesn't creak, groan or shudder over bumps, and the longer wheelbase and roomier cabin combine to make it much more comfortable.'

The completely redesigned cockpit makes the C5 Corvette more comfortable and user-friendly.

Milestones

1990 The ZR-1® has supercar status. Its quad-cam 32-valve V8 engine makes 375bhp and reaches 96km/h (60mph) in under five seconds.

The latest Corvette is the fifth generation car.

1995 ZR-1 production ends to make way for a more advanced Corvette, which will be launched the following year.

1997 A new generation of Corvette appears. It is slightly wider and taller, but the biggest difference is in the wheelbase, which is significantly longer and adds to the car's stability. The quad-cam V8 is not used because the all-alloy LS1 small block can produce 345bhp without the complexity of multiple overhead valves and cams.

The coupe was launched eight months before the convertible.

1997 The convertible appears eight months later. It is heavier than the coupe and has the same specification, but the convertible's inferior aerodynamics reduces the top speed – but only by 4.8km/h (3mph).

UNDER THE SKIN

Super stiff

Because the Corvette has a fibreglass body, it has to have a separate steel frame. A new composite floor has been added, with a balsa wood layer sandwiched between two steel sheets, to stiffen the whole structure. The suspension features cast-alloy arms, a multi-link rear end for maximum control, and monofilament leaf springs made of composite material, which are lighter and more space efficient.

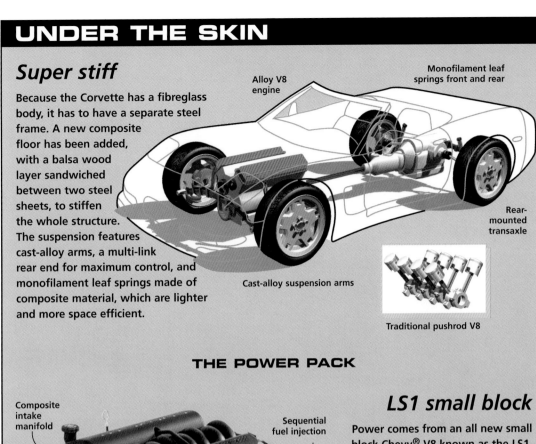

Alloy V8 engine

Monofilament leaf springs front and rear

Rear-mounted transaxle

Cast-alloy suspension arms

Traditional pushrod V8

THE POWER PACK

Composite intake manifold

Sequential fuel injection

Alloy oil pan

Alloy block and heads

LS1 small block

Power comes from an all new small block Chevy® V8 known as the LS1. The engine block is made of cast aluminium and fortified with 6-bolt main bearing caps and an alloy oil pan. It is still a traditional overhead-valve pushrod design with roller rocker arms, but thanks to redesigned cylinder heads, composite induction system, advanced engine management and electronic fuel injection, the LS1 revs flawlessly through its power band. Maximum power is reached at 5400rpm, while peak torque comes on strong at 4200rpm.

Newcomer

The Convertible features a body-colour tonneau cover that extends between the front seats, echoing the original Corvettes. But as in more modern cars, the easy-folding convertible top has a lightweight magnesium alloy frame.

The Corvette Convertible looks good with its top up or down.

Chevrolet CORVETTE

It looks softer and less aggressive than the ZR-1, but don't be deceived. With its latest Corvette, Chevrolet has produced one of the best sports cars in the world.

Fibreglass body

A fibreglass body is as much a Corvette tradition as the front-mounted V8 engine, and both are retained on the new Corvette.

Alloy V8

The 5686cc (347ci) engine is new to the Chevy V8 family. Some of its features include 6-bolt main bearing caps, composite intake manifold and an electronic throttle.

Alloy suspension arms

The Corvette's suspension deserves to be exposed rather than hidden away, as the various control arms are made from forged alloy instead of heavier pressed steel.

Balsa wood floor

One of the many innovative features on the Corvette is the use of a balsa wood and steel sheet sandwich material for the floor. This is light, but extremely rigid, and makes the car feel more like a conventional steel monocoque design, despite the separate steel chassis.

Six-speed transmission

For the first time, the Corvette benefits from a rear transaxle. Standard equipment is a four-speed automatic, but buyers can order a six-speed manual with a very high overdrive ratio of 0.50:1.

Tyre-pressure monitor

Like the previous Vette®, the C5 has a tyre-pressure monitor which alerts the driver when the tyre pressure is low. As a backup (and because there is no room for a spare, the tyres can run flat for 322km (200 miles).

Magnesium roof frame

The suspension is not the only area where Chevrolet has opted for alloy rather than steel. The convertible roof frame is made from light, yet very strong, magnesium.

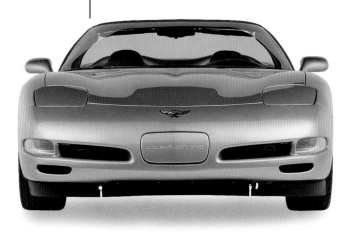

Traction control

Working in tandem with the ABS, the Corvette has traction control. When wheelspin is detected, the system automatically reduces the power until traction is restored.

Rear transaxle

For even better packaging and weight distribution, the transmission is now mounted at the rear. This means that a slim torque tube is used, which makes the interior roomier.

Specifications
1998 Chevrolet Corvette

ENGINE

Type: V8

Construction: Alloy block and heads

Valve gear: Two valves per cylinder operated by a single block-mounted camshaft

Bore and stroke: 99m (3.9in) x 92mm (3.62in)

Displacement: 5686cc (347ci)

Compression ratio: 10.1:1

Induction system: Electronic sequential fuel injection

Maximum power: 345bhp at 5400rpm

Maximum torque: 350lb-ft at 4200rpm

Top speed: 281km/h (175mph)

0–96km/h (0–60mph): 4.7 sec

TRANSMISSION

Four-speed automatic or optional six-speed manual, rear-mounted transaxle

BODY/CHASSIS

Separate steel chassis with fibreglass and composite two-door convertible body

SPECIAL FEATURES

The roof folds neatly under this stylish, body-coloured cover.

RUNNING GEAR

Steering: Rack-and-pinion

Front suspension: Double unequal length wishbones, transverse leaf spring, telescopic shocks and anti-roll bar

Rear suspension: Five-link system with transverse leaf spring, telescopic shocks and anti-roll bar

Brakes: Vented discs with ABS, 32.5cm (12.8in) dia. (front), 30.5cm (12in) dia. (rear)

Wheels: Magnesium, 43.2cm (17in) x 21.6cm (8.5in) (front), 45.7cm (18in) x 24.1cm (9.5in) (rear)

Tyres: Goodyear F1 EMT 245/45 ZR17 (front), 275/40ZR17 (rear)

DIMENSIONS

Length: 4.56m (179.7in)

Width: 1.87m (73.6in)

Height: 1.21m (47.7in)

Wheelbase: 265cm (104.5in)

Track: 157cm (62in) (front), 158cm (62.1in) (rear)

Weight: 1544kg (3427lb)

Chevrolet **IMPALA SS 427**

When Chevrolet put the engine used in the Corvette® in very nearly the same tune into the big Impala SS™, the car's sheer size meant the result wasn't quite as dramatic. It did, however, produce a high-speed cruiser with plenty of power to spare.

'...full-size muscle monster.'

'For some, bigger is better, and this is certainly true of the SS 427. The front bucket seats are huge. The monster 6997cc (427ci) V8 has enough torque to move mountains and motivates the tremendous bulk of the Impala down the road at maximum velocity. It would be natural to think that the SS 427 would plough through corners, but a wide track and well-located rear end ensure this is one of the better behaved full-size muscle monsters of the late 1960s.'

The Impala SS has full instrumentation and tremendous interior space.

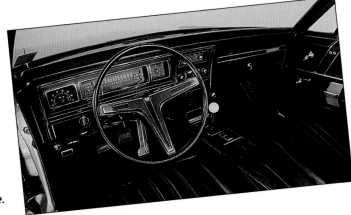

Milestones

1965 Impalas are redesigned

with smoother, more modern contours and a new perimeter chassis, plus revised suspension. The Impala SS returns with available bucket seats and a new optional Mark IV 6489cc (396ci) V8 engine. The 409 will be dropped at the end of the year.

The last year for the boxy, square Impala SS was 1964.

1966 Externally, few changes mark

this year's full-size Chevys®. The big news is under the bonnet. The 396 engine is joined by a 6997cc (427ci) unit available in 390bhp and 425bhp versions.

1965 Impala SS models came standard with an in-line six.

1967 A new fastback

roof is grafted to the Impala Sport Coupe.

1969 Having reverted

to an option package in 1968, the Impala SS is retired this year.

UNDER THE SKIN

Body-on-frame construction

Power front disc brakes

Live rear axle

Big-block V8

Strong frame

For the 1965 model year, Chevrolet introduced a new perimeter chassis frame for the Impala, and revised the suspension with a wider front and rear track that made the car more stable during high-speed cornering. The frame had to be strong so that the pillarless two-door coupe bodies of the SS versions could be fitted without flexing. The faster SS versions had superior rear axle location with four, rather than three, links.

THE POWER PACK

The fat rat

In 1966, Chevrolet launched its 427, an enlarged version of the 6489cc (396ci) V8, which was more common to find in a Corvette than a full-size car. The following year, it was available in full-size cars. The standard 427 engine returned for 1968 with a power output of 385bhp and a four-barrel carburetor in full-size cars (GM outlawed multi-carb setups in 1967 on all models but the Corvette). The engine continued until 1969, by which time it thumped out 390bhp.

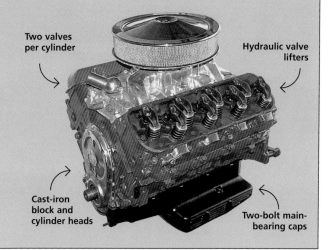

Two valves per cylinder

Hydraulic valve lifters

Cast-iron block and cylinder heads

Two-bolt main-bearing caps

Milestone SS

1967 was a milestone for the SS Impala. The Impala was reskinned with larger, swoopier sheet metal. It was also the first and last year that the SS 427 was a model in its own right. Today, these cars make an interesting alternative to Chevelles and Camaros.

The 1967 Impala SS with fastback styling and the 427 is the one to go for.

93

Chevrolet **IMPALA SS 427**

'For the man who'd buy a sports car if it had this much room' was how Chevrolet marketed the Impala SS 427. It was a fine machine, with a huge torquey V8, seating for five and a well-engineered suspension.

Four transmissions

The big V8s could be matched to a variety of transmissions: a three- or four-speed heavy-duty manual; Powerglide; or strong TurboHydramatic 400 three-speed automatic.

V8 engine

The fastest of all the Impalas, the SS 427 is powered by the same short-stroke cast-iron 6997cc (427ci) engine found in the Corvette. Despite its size, it is happy to rev and produces its maximum power at 5200rpm with maximum torque coming in at 3400rpm. In its highest state of tune, Chevrolet claimed 385bhp for the Impala engine.

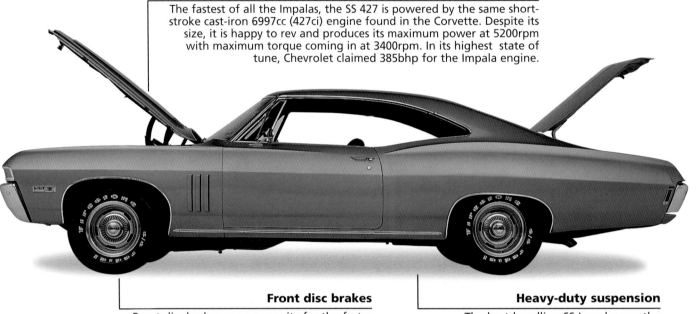

Front disc brakes

Front disc brakes are a necessity for the faster SS models with their high performance and weight. For the SS, Chevrolet made front discs an option, which came with different wheels for $121.15.

Heavy-duty suspension

The best-handling SS Impalas use the optional heavy-duty F41 suspension with its stiffer springs and shocks. At just $31.60, it was a very small price to pay for the extra handling security.

Fastback style

The fastback style was very fashionable in the 1960s and helped give a sporty look to very large cars. The size of cars like the Impala and the Ford Galaxie meant they could have a long sloping rear roof line and still have room for rear passengers.

Front parking lights

The ends of the front fenders contain what look like turn signals. In fact, they are just parking lights, with the turn signals located in the lower grill assembly.

Pillarless construction

Chevrolet gave the Impala its sleek look by the use of two styling features. As well as the long, sloping rear fastback, the car has pillarless construction. This accentuates the side window glass area and makes it appear bigger than it really is.

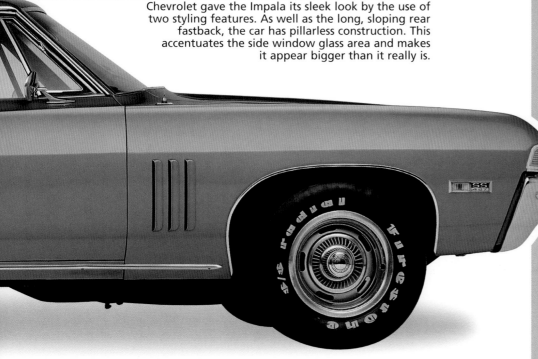

Specifications

1968 Chevrolet Impala SS 427

ENGINE

Type: V8

Construction: Cast-iron block and heads

Valve gear: Two valves per cylinder operated by a single camshaft with pushrods and rockers

Bore and stroke: 108mm (4.25in) x 96mm (3.76in)

Displacement: 6997cc (427ci)

Compression ratio: 10.3:1

Induction system: Single four-barrel carburettor

Maximum power: 385bhp at 5200rpm

Maximum torque: 460lb-ft at 3400rpm

Top speed: 201km/h (125mph)

0–96km/h (0–60mph): 8.5 sec

TRANSMISSION

M21 four-speed manual

BODY/CHASSIS

Box-section perimeter chassis with two-door fastback hardtop body

SPECIAL FEATURES

For 1968, all cars sold in the US had to have side marker lights. In addition to the lights, the SS also had proper engine identification.

RUNNING GEAR

Steering: Recirculating ball

Front suspension: Double wishbones with coil springs, telescopic shock absorbers and anti-roll bar

Rear suspension: Live axle with four links, Panhard rod, coil springs and telescopic shock absorbers

Brakes: Discs, 27.9cm (11in) dia. (front), drums, 27.9cm (11in) dia. (rear)

Wheels: Steel discs, 15.24cm (6in) x 38.1cm (15in)

Tyres: 20.9cm (8.25in) x 38.1cm (15in)

DIMENSIONS

Length: 5.42m (213.2in)

Width: 2.03m (79.9in)

Height: 1.4m (55.4in)

Wheelbase: 302cm (119.0in)

Track: 159cm (62.5in) (front), 158cm (62.4in) (rear)

Weight: 1741kg (3835lb)

Chevrolet **MONTE CARLO SS 454**

Super Sport™ is the meaning behind the SS designation, and the big-block Monte Carlo lives up to that name proudly. Grand-touring comfort is backed by a 360-horsepower, 7440cc (454ci) V8, making this one of the first executive-class luxury performance cars of all time.

'...unbelievable authority.'

'Only a light touch of the throttle is needed to get a sneak preview to what lies ahead. When the big Quadrajet is running at wide open throttle, the stout 7440cc (454ci) big-block makes unbelievable mid-range power. As soon as the tyres bite, the engine's 500lb-ft. of torque will pin you deeply into the back of the seat with unbelievable authority. Yet the ride remains comfortably smooth and the big Monte will cruise happily at 160km/h (100mph) all day long.'

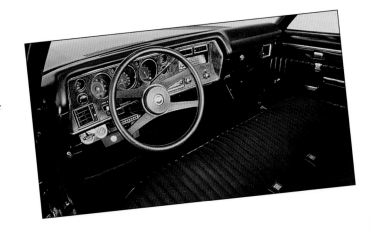

Plenty of room and plenty of comfort. The Monte SS is the ultimate highway cruiser.

Milestones

1970 Chevrolet
enters the personal luxury field with the Monte Carlo – a two-door coupe based on the Chevelle chassis. It boasts the longest bonnet ever fitted to a Chevrolet. In SS form it is available with the monster 454 V8. The moderate LS-5 makes 360bhp and the bone-crushing LS-6 puts out 450bhp.

The big 454 V8 in SS tune was also offered in the Chevelle.

1971 Having proved
to be a great success, the Monte Carlo returns for another season with a revised grill. The muscular SS 454 also returns, but with rising insurance premiums and lower octane fuel it is not popular, with just 1919 built.

A 'new' Monte Carlo SS arrived for 1983. This is a 1986 model.

1972 The Monte
Carlo enters its last season with the original body. The SS 454 is no longer available, but Monte Carlo sales remain strong with 180,819 built.

UNDER THE SKIN

Body-on-frame construction

Coil-sprung live rear axle

Power front disc brakes

Big-block V8

Chevelle based

The Monte Carlo was built on the Chevelle platform, but using the 295cm (116in) wheelbase of the four door. Suspension is also Chevelle, with unequal length wishbones at the front and a live rear axle. Due to its more luxurious nature, the Monte has more sound deadening, plus additional rubber mountings between body and chassis to reduce vibration from the road.

THE POWER PACK

Biggest stock Rat

Arriving in 1970, the big-block 454 was part of the Mk IV V8 series which were first introduced in Chevrolet passenger cars in 1965. It has a cast-iron block and cylinder heads, plus a forged-steel crankshaft and connecting rods. The LS-5 has a 10.25:1 compression ratio, hydraulic lifters and a single Rochester Quadrajet four-barrel carburettor. It thumps out an impressive 360bhp at a low 4400rpm and a hefty 500lb-ft of torque. If fitted with the infamous LS-6 it makes 450bhp in 1970 and 425bhp in 1971.

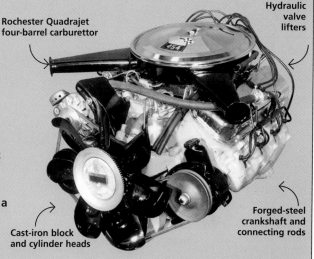

Rochester Quadrajet four-barrel carburettor

Hydraulic valve lifters

Cast-iron block and cylinder heads

Forged-steel crankshaft and connecting rods

Good buy

SS 454 Montes were only built for two years and production totalled just 5742. Although rare, they are often overlooked. Excellent examples can be picked up for as little as $8000, making the Monte Carlo 454 one of the best big-block muscle buys.

Few muscle cars could match the performance and luxury of the SS 45.

Chevrolet MONTE CARLO SS 454

To order an SS 454, you had to check RPO Z20 on the options list. Considering the added performance, this option was a bargain at $420.25. Surprisingly, less than 4000 buyers chose the option in 1970.

Rally wheels

To go with its high-performance image, all SS 454s had G70-15 wide oval white stripe tyres fitted on 17.8cm (7in) x 38.1cm (15in) Rally wheels.

Big-block muscle

The long 102mm (4in) stroke in Chevrolet's famous cast-iron LS-5 big-block V8 is the reason this 7440cc (454ci) Rat motor produces 500lb-ft. of torque at a very usable 3200rpm. Its forged crankshaft is nitride and cross-drilled, making the bottom end virtually bullet proof. Big-valve cast-iron cylinder heads and a Rochester Quadrajet carburetor complete the package.

Front-end style

The bold front end sports a pair of single headlights surrounded by wide chrome bezels. The handsome grill has chrome trim and features a special badge in the centre.

Vinyl top

To increase appeal for the luxury car buyer, a special vinyl top was made available as an option. For only $126.40, there was a choice of five distinct colours: black, blue, dark gold, green or white.

Distinctive styling

Built only as a two-door hardtop, the Monte Carlo's exterior styling is very European-looking with its long bonnet and short deck design. The pronounced fender profile that runs front to back is vaguely reminiscent of the old Jaguar XK models.

Special suspension

In addition to GM's normal practice of using unequal length A-arms up front and a solid, live axle at the rear, all SS 454s contained a unique Automatic Level Control system with built-in air compressor.

Optional interior

An optional console could be fitted between a pair of comfortable bucket seats upholstered in soft vinyl. Simulated burred-elm wood inlays were applied to the instrument panel.

Specifications

1970 Chevrolet Monte Carlo SS 454

ENGINE

Type: V8

Construction: Cast-iron block and heads

Valve gear: Two valves per cylinder operated by a single camshaft, pushrods and rocker arms

Bore and stroke: 108mm (4.25in) x 102mm (4.00in)

Displacement: 7440cc (454ci)

Compression ratio: 10.25:1

Induction system: Rochester Quadrajet four-barrel carburettor

Maximum power: 360bhp at 4400rpm

Maximum torque: 500lb-ft at 3200rpm

Top speed: 208km/h (129mph)

0–96km/h (0–60mph): 6.5 sec

TRANSMISSION

GM TurboHydramatic 400 automatic

BODY/CHASSIS

Separate steel body and frame

SPECIAL FEATURES

Discreet badges on the rocker panel are the only giveaway of the 454.

RUNNING GEAR

Steering: Recirculating ball

Front suspension: Unequal length A-arms, telescopic shock absorbers, coil springs and anti-roll bar

Rear suspension: Live solid axle with telescopic shock absorbers and coil springs

Brakes: Discs (front), drums (rear)

Wheels: Rally, 17.8cm (7in) x 38.1cm (15in)

Tyres: Goodyear Polyglas, G70-15

DIMENSIONS

Length: 5.23m (206.0in)

Width: 1.93m (76.0in)

Height: 1.32m (52.0in)

Wheelbase: 295cm (116.0in)

Track: 157cm (61.9in) (front), 155cm (61.1in) (rear)

Weight: 1751kg (3860lb)

Chevrolet **NOVA SS396**

Redesigned and larger for 1968, Chevy's compact now had room for big-block engines. The 6489cc (396ci) rat motor was officially offered in 350-bhp tune, but those who lived by the phrase 'excess is best' selected the L78 engine option and got the 375-bhp 396 turning the plain-looking Nova into a street terror.

'...Dr. Jekyll and Mr. Hyde aura.'

'Traditionally, the Nova has been stereotyped as a timid base-model with zero performance potential. This 396 V8 version proves this to be a blatant misconception. True, inside and out, it is plain and unadorned, but upon start up, you soon realize that this so-called "grocery-getter" has a real Dr. Jekyll and Mr. Hyde aura. Grab the four-speed shifter, hit the pedal and listen to the tyres spin effortlessly. Its quick-ratio steering and stiff suspension give a fun-to-drive feel that is missing from other muscle cars.'

Nova SSs are ideal racers because they're kept light with a minimum of interior embellishments.

Milestones

1968 The Chevy II™ is redesigned

and now rides on a 282cm (111in) wheelbase. Hardtop coupes are dropped, leaving just two-door, pillared coupes and four-door sedans. The SS option returns, and for the first time a 6489cc (396c), big-block V8 is available.

The Nova Super Sport finally got a 5359cc (327ci) V8 in 1965.

1969 Thanks to a strong

advertising campaign, sales are high. Of the 106,200 Novas built, only 7209 are ordered as SS™ models.

The most powerful engine available in 1971 was a four-barrel 270bhp, 5735cc (350ci) V8.

1970 Nova is now the official name,

ousting the original Chevy II title. Despite an auto workers' strike early in the year, production is up. The number of SS models that are sold are doubled from the previous year. This is the final season for the 6489cc (396ci) V8 in Novas.

UNDER THE SKIN

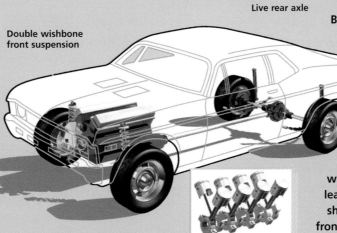

Double wishbone front suspension

Live rear axle

Unitary construction

Big-block V8

Sharing parts

Built on a bigger X-body platform from 1968, the Nova has unitary construction. Front end components, notably the subframe, suspension pieces, engine mounts and radiator, are shared with the Camaro®. All Novas from this period have front coil springs with a live rear axle suspended on leaf springs. SS models have stiffer shocks and springs and a standard front anti-roll bar. Quick-ratio power steering and front disc brakes were available as options.

THE POWER PACK

Mark IV monster

Introduced in 1965 as a replacement for the 409, the 396 was the smallest of the Mark IV series of big-block Chevrolet V8s. First made available in big Chevrolets and the Corvette®, the 396 became a Nova option partway through 1968. In L78 trim, it has a cast-iron block but features an aluminium dual-plane intake manifold and heads borrowed from the 427 with larger valves. Other high performance features include solid lifters and an 800-cfm Holley four-barrel carburetor. Horsepower is rated at 375bhp at 5600rpm, while torque is a substantial 415lb-ft. With this engine, the 1542kg (3400lb) Nova could run the ¼-mile in 14.5 seconds bone stock.

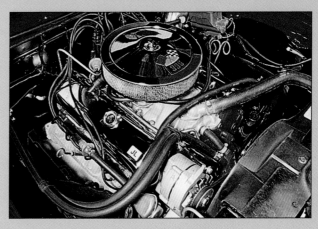

Speed king

With a very favourable weight distribution, the Nova SS396 was one of the most surprising and quickest muscle cars of the late 1960s. Those equipped with the 375bhp, solid-lifter, L78 engine are especially sought after by collectors today.

Those who wanted lots of power in a light car were drawn to the Nova SS396.

Chevrolet NOVA SS396

Serious racers saw the Nova as the perfect street brawler. For just $280 they could transform their bare-bones coupe into a machine that could nearly outrun just about every GTO, Mustang and Road Runner in town.

Rat motor

The key to the Nova's surprising performance is the 6489cc (396ci), big-block V8. Although not highlighted in factory brochures, the L78 version of this engine with its solid cam could be ordered by those who wanted a serious performance machine.

Pillared coupe styling

When the Chevy II was enlarged in 1968, the hardtop bodystyle was dropped, leaving the pillared coupe and sedan as the only choices. Even with SS badging, the 1969 Chevy II Nova is still demure in appearance.

Four-speed transmission

Back in the late 1960s, most racers still wanted a manual transmission. The Muncie M21, close-ratio four-speed was ideal for the torquey 6489cc (396ci) engine.

Side marker lights

From 1969, all cars sold in the U.S. required side marker lights (amber) front and (red) rear.

Rally wheels

When new, the SS396 came from the factory with 35.6cm (14in) steel wheels and poverty hubcaps. Chevy Rally wheels were available as an option and were without a doubt more attractive. Unusually, not many Novas were ordered with them.

Short gearing

With its greater size and weight, plus multileaf springs at the rear, the SS396 launches off the line better than its predecessor. To further lower 0–96km/h (0–60mph) acceleration, this Nova is equipped with a set of 3.55:1 rear gears and a Positraction limited-slip differential.

Specifications

1969 Chevrolet Nova SS396

ENGINE

Type: V8

Construction: Cast-iron block and heads

Valve gear: Two valves per cylinder operated by a single centrally mounted camshaft with pushrods and rockers

Bore and stroke: 104mm (4.09in) x 96mm (3.76in)

Displacement: 6489cc (396ci)

Compression ratio: 10.0:1

Induction system: Holley 800-cfm four-barrel downdraft carburettor

Maximum power: 375bhp at 5600rpm

Maximum torque: 415lb-ft at 3600rpm

Top speed: 193km/h (20mph)

0–96 km/h (0–60mph): 5.9 sec

TRANSMISSION

Muncie M21 four-speed manual

BODY/CHASSIS

Unitary steel chassis with two-door coupe body

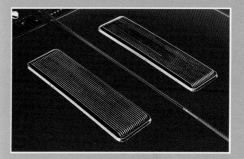

SPECIAL FEATURES

These non-functional bonnet vents are part of the SS package.

RUNNING GEAR

Steering: Recirculating ball

Front suspension: Unequal length A-arms with coil springs, telescopic shock absorbers and anti-roll bar

Rear suspension: Live axle with semi-elliptic leaf springs and telescopic shock absorbers

Brakes: Discs (front), drums (rear)

Wheels: Rally, 17.8cm (7in) x 35.6cm (14in)

Tyres: E70 14

DIMENSIONS

Length: 4.81m (189.4in)

Width: 1.79m (70.4in)

Height: 1.33m (52.4in)

Wheelbase: 282cm (111.0in)

Track: 149.9cm (59.0in) (front), 149.6cm (58.9in) (rear)

Weight: 1542kg (3400lb)

Chevrolet YENKO CHEVELLE

Best known for his hopped-up Camaros®, Don Yenko also offered a small number of hot Chevelles during 1969 – made possible due to a GM corporate loophole – powered by 6997cc (427ci) engines. Properly tuned, these cars could run the ¼ mile in about 12 seconds.

'...highly tuned street car.'

'If the bold stripes don't tell you that this Chevelle is a highly tuned street car, then upon start up the loud engine note will. Replacing the nasty 375bhp 6489cc (396ci) is an even more belligerent Corvette-spec 427 that cranks out a whopping 450bhp. During part throttle acceleration, the Yenko Chevelle is notchy and disobedient. But if it's all-out racing excitement you crave, step on the accelerator all the way and listen to the throaty 427 bellow its true intention.'

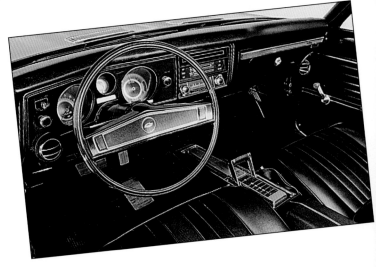

The interior looks stock with the exception of the column-mounted Stewart Warner tach.

Milestones

1967 After building a small number of hot Corvairs, Cannonsburg speed shop owner Don Yenko strikes a deal with Vince Piggins at Chevrolet to build 6997cc (427ci) Camaros. Stock SS 396 models are sent to the Yenko dealership where their engines are swapped out for 427s. A total of 118 are built up to 1968.

The factory Chevelle for 1969 was the SS 396 – mainstream muscle.

1969 Using a loophole known as the Central Office Production Order, Yenko convinces Chevrolet to build 427 powered Camaros on the production line. These are then sent to Cannonsburg for installation of decals and trim.

Filling the Yenko's shoes in 1970 was the mighty Chevelle SS 454.

1969 Following on from the Camaros are a small number of 427 Chevelles. Yenko orders 99 with SS hoods, 4.10 gears and front disc brakes.

UNDER THE SKIN

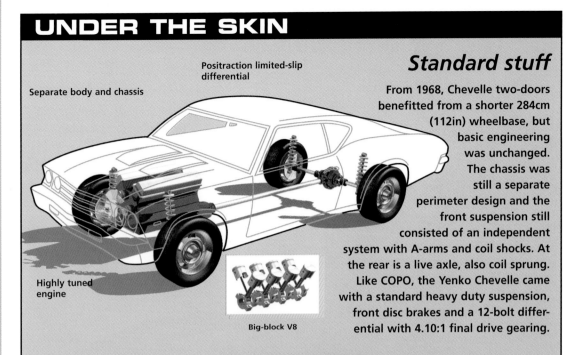

Separate body and chassis

Positraction limited-slip differential

Highly tuned engine

Big-block V8

Standard stuff

From 1968, Chevelle two-doors benefitted from a shorter 284cm (112in) wheelbase, but basic engineering was unchanged. The chassis was still a separate perimeter design and the front suspension still consisted of an independent system with A-arms and coil shocks. At the rear is a live axle, also coil sprung. Like COPO, the Yenko Chevelle came with a standard heavy duty suspension, front disc brakes and a 12-bolt differential with 4.10:1 final drive gearing.

THE POWER PACK

Tyrannical L-72

Due to a corporate edict, the largest engine officially available in the Chevelle in 1969 was a 396. By ordering his cars as COPO specials, tuning specialist Don Yenko was able to have 427s factory installed in Chevelles. All these cars have L-72 engines which feature a cast-iron block with four-bolt main bearing caps, rectangular exhaust ports with closed combustion chambers, low restriction exhaust manifolds, an aluminium intake, a solid lifter camshaft and a 800cfm Holley four-barrel carburettor. GM quoted output at a conservative 425bhp, but Yenko and the National Hot Rod Association rated them as a more truthful 450bhp.

Super Car

Only 99 1969 Yenko Chevelles were built. All models had L-72 engines and Positraction 12-bolt rear ends. As some of the quickest GM intermedi-ates of the 1960s, these cars command high prices today, and perfectly restored examples sell for $80,000 or more.

Rarest of all Yenko Chevelles are the automatic cars – only 28 were built.

Chevrolet YENKO CHEVELLE

Going a step beyond what the factory had to offer, the Yenko Chevelles, adorned with Yenko SC (Super Car) logos, were part of a select band of street warriors and among the finest Detroit muscle cars ever built.

Heavy-duty transmission

The only transmissions deemed strong enough to cope with the raucous 427 were a Muncie M21 and M22 'Rock-crusher' four-speed manual or, as in this car, a strengthened TH400 three-speed automatic.

Big-block engine

All Chevelles built as part of the COPO order received L-72 6997cc (427ci) V8s with four-barrel carburettors and solid lifters. For an additional charge, Yenko could fit a pair of Mickey Thompson Super Scavenger headers, making the Chevelle a genuine 12-second street car.

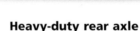

Heavy-duty rear axle

Intended as straight-line screamers, the 427 COPO Chevelles and Yenkos were fortified with strengthened GM 12-bolt rear ends with 4.10:1 gearing for maximum acceleration. A Posi-traction limited-slip differential was standard.

Gaudy graphics

Yenko liked to dress up his cars, so the Chevelles got side and hood stripes with SC (Super Car) emblems. Like the factory 396SS Chevelles, Yenkos came with a blacked-out Super Sport grill and rear valance along with the intimidating SS hood.

Base interior

As all the 427 Chevelles were part of a COPO order, they received base Malibu interiors, but many had front bench seats and a centre console. Some of the Yenko cars also came with three-spoke, wood-rimmed steering wheels and Hurst shifters.

Power front disc brakes

Because it could scream to 96km/h (60mph) in less than six seconds, the Chevelle needed considerable power to bring it to a halt. Front disc brakes were thus mandatory.

Specifications

1969 Chevrolet Yenko Chevelle

ENGINE

Type: V8

Construction: Cast-iron block and heads

Valve gear: Two valves per cylinder operated by a single camshaft with pushrods and rockers

Bore and stroke: 108mm (4.25in) x 96mm (3.76in)

Displacement: 6997cc (427ci)

Compression ratio: 11.0:1

Induction system: Holley cfm 800 four-barrel carburetor

Maximum power: 450bhp at 5000rpm

Maximum torque: 460lb-ft at 4000rpm

Top speed: 177km/h (110mph)

0–96km/h (0–60mph): 5.7 sec

TRANSMISSION

TH400 three-speed automatic

BODY/CHASSIS

Separate steel chassis with two-door coupe body

SPECIAL FEATURES

All 6997cc (427ci) V8s were built at GM's Tonawanda plant in NY.

RUNNING GEAR

Steering: Recirculating ball

Front suspension: Unequal length A-arms, coil springs, telescopic shock absorbers and anti-roll bar

Rear suspension: Live axle, coil springs, lower links and telescopic shock absorbers

Brakes: Discs (front), drums (rear)

Wheels: Steel Rally 17.8cm (7in) x 38.1cm (15in)

Tyres: Goodyear Polyglas GT F70-15

DIMENSIONS

Length: 4.73m (186.4in)

Width: 1.96m (77.2in)

Height: 1.41m (55.6in)

Wheelbase: 284cm (112.0in)

Track: 157cm (61.9in) (front), 155cm (61.0in) (rear)

Weight: 1724kg (3800lb)

Dodge **CHALLENGER R/T**

As the muscle car movement reached its peak in 1970, Dodge finally got a ponycar of its own. Aptly named Challenger, it offered a huge range of engines and options. Enthusiasts were drawn to the R/T model. In 440 Six Pack form, it could run with the best of them.

'...muscle at its finest.'

'There is something really magical about E-body Mopars. The seats may offer little support and the light steering can make the Challenger feel a little unwieldy at times, but take the car for a blast and you cannot help but fall in love with it. The 440 Six Pack engine, coupled to a Pistol Grip four-speed enables the R/T to accelerate like a speeding bullet, accompanied by tremendous tyre squealing and a thundering exhaust roar; it is muscle at its finest.'

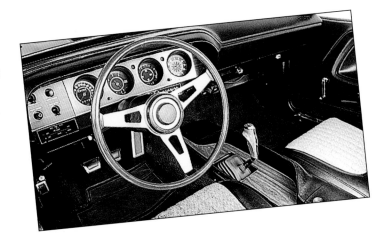

R/Ts got the Rallye Pack instrument cluster. This car has the rare Pistol-Grip shifter.

Milestones

1970 Dodge enters the ponycar war

with its new Challenger. It is offered as a coupe or convertible with one of the longest option lists available, including nine engines. An R/T model caters to the performance crowd and was available with a 383, 440 or 426 Hemi engine.

The Challenger shares its firewall and front inner structure with B-bodies like this Charger.

1971 Due to rising insurance

rates, safety issues and emissions regulations, the performance market enters its twilight years. The Challenger returns with just minor styling tweaks, but its sales figures drop by 60 percent – just 4630 R/Ts are built this year.

The Cuda was Plymouth's version of the R/T. This is a 1971 model.

1972 High-horse-power engines,

convertibles and the R/T package depart, leaving a Rallye 340 as the top performer.

UNDER THE SKIN

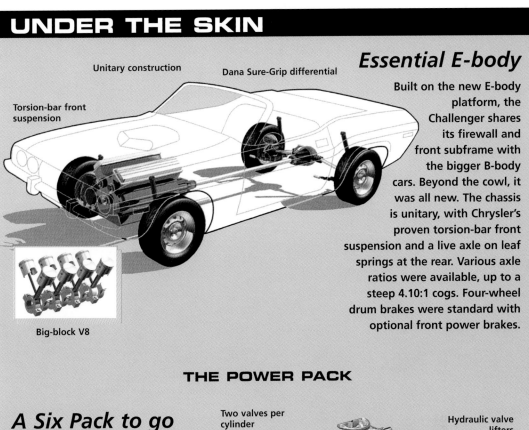

Unitary construction

Dana Sure-Grip differential

Torsion-bar front suspension

Big-block V8

Essential E-body

Built on the new E-body platform, the Challenger shares its firewall and front subframe with the bigger B-body cars. Beyond the cowl, it was all new. The chassis is unitary, with Chrysler's proven torsion-bar front suspension and a live axle on leaf springs at the rear. Various axle ratios were available, up to a steep 4.10:1 cogs. Four-wheel drum brakes were standard with optional front power brakes.

THE POWER PACK

A Six Pack to go

Base Challengers came with the bulletproof but hardly exciting 3687cc (225ci) Slant-Six, but eight V8s were optional. R/T models got a standard 335bhp, 6276cc (383ci) mill, though the mighty Hemi and 440 were available. The 440 is an immensely robust and torquey engine, which cranks out a whopping 480lb-ft at 3200rpm. In Six Pack form, with a trio of Holley two-barrel carburetors, the 440 gets an additional 10lb-ft of torque.

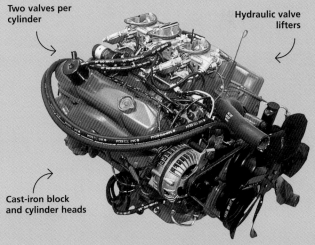

Two valves per cylinder

Hydraulic valve lifters

Cast-iron block and cylinder heads

SE Comfort

As with most Chrysler products, owners were free to order virtually any option on their Challenger R/T. If ordered in the sporty SE guise, these hot Dodges came with soft leather seats, a sporty vinyl top and smaller rear window.

1970 R/T-SEs are very rare: only 3979 were built.

109

Dodge CHALLENGER R/T SE

Smoothly styled and an able performer in R/T guise, the Challenger was well received when new, and remains today as one of the most sought-after early muscle cars.

Special Edition

An SE, or Special Edition, package was basically a luxury trim package on the Challenger. It added a vinyl roof with a smaller rear window, upgraded interior appointments and exterior trim. It could be ordered on both base and R/T models.

Mopar Power

Although the 383 was standard fare, the big 440 Magnum was an ideal choice for those into serious racing. Adding the Six-Pack option with three two-barrel carburetors resulted in 390bhp and 490lb-ft of torque. A good running Six Pack was a threat to just about anything with wheels.

Manual transmission

Although the standard Challenger transmission was a three-speed manual, R/Ts ordered with the 440 or Hemi got the robust TorqueFlite automatic transmission. A handful were, however, fitted with four-speed manuals, complete with Hurst shifters with a wood-grain Pistol-Grip shift handle.

Standard R/T hood

Most Challenger R/Ts left the factory with a performance hood, which included dual scoops and a raised center section. For $97.30, however, buyers could order a Shaker bonnet scoop that attached directly to the air cleaner.

Dana Sure-Grip differential

A good way to reduce quarter-mile ETs was to order the Performance Axle Package with a 3.55:1 ring and pinion with a Sure-Grip limited-slip differential. Steeper 4.10:1 cogs could be specified as part of the Super Track Pak.

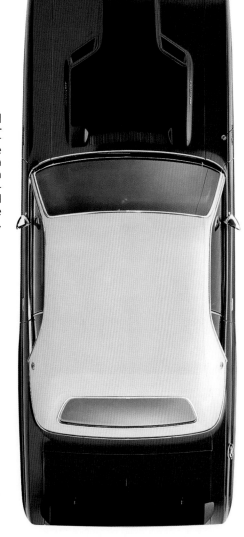

Heavy-duty suspension

As the R/T was the standard performance model, it has a heavy-duty suspension with thicker front torsion bars and stiffer rear leaf springs, plus a beefy front anti-roll bar.

Wide wheels

For the early 1970s, 15.2cm (6in) wide wheels were considered large. The Rallye rims fitted to the R/T are only 35.6cm (14in) in diameter, shod in F-70 14 Goodyear Polyglas tyres. Bigger G-60 15 tyres and 38.1cm (15in) Rallyes could be ordered, resulting in slightly improved grip.

Specifications

1970 Dodge Challenger R/T-SE 440

ENGINE

Type: V8

Valve gear: Two valves per cylinder operated by a single V-mounted camshaft via pushrods, rockers and hydraulic lifters

Bore and stroke: 110mm (4.32in) x 95mm (3.75in)

Displacement: 7210cc (440ci)

Compression ratio: 10.1:1

Induction system: Three Holley two-barrel carburetors

Maximum power: 390bhp at 4700rpm

Maximum torque: 490lb-ft at 3200rpm

Top speed: 200km/h (124mph)

0–96km/h (0–60mph): 6 sec

TRANSMISSION

Four-speed manual

BODY/CHASSIS

Unitary steel chassis with steel body panels

SPECIAL FEATURES

All Challengers came with a racing-style fuel filler cap, which is also found on the bigger intermediate Charger.

As it was the performance model, the R/T got a full set of gauges.

RUNNING GEAR

Steering: Recirculating ball

Front suspension: A arms with longitudinal torsion bars, telescopic shock absorbers and anti-roll bar

Rear suspension: Live axle with semi-elliptic leaf springs, telescopic shock absorbers and anti-roll bar

Brakes: Drums, 27.9cm (11.0in) dia. (front and rear)

Wheels: Stamped steel, 35.6cm (14in) x 15.2cm (6in)

Tyres: Fibreglass belted, F-70 14

DIMENSIONS

Length: 4.88m (192in)

Width: 1.93m (76.1in)

Height: 1.29m (50.9in)

Wheelbase: 279cm (110.0in)

Track: 152cm (59.7in) (front), 154cm (60.7in) (rear)

Weight: 1559kg (3437lb)

Dodge CHALLENGER T/A

With the SCCA's Trans Am wars in full swing, Dodge jumped in to the foray with its aptly named Challenger T/A. Built for only one year and powered by a 5572cc (340ci) V8, it was conceived as a road racer but became a factory street rod.

'...mindwarping acceleration.'

'Unlike its big-block counterparts, the T/A is a better-balanced package with less weight over the front wheels. It therefore offers more nimble handling. The rev-happy 5557cc (340ci) V8 engine, with its triple carburettors and the bulletproof TorqueFlite transmission give mind-warping acceleration. For its time, the power-assisted steering is smooth and the brakes firm, but the sound of the V8 blowing through the side pipes is enough to stir anyone's soul.'

Full instrumentation and black upholstery give the interior a real sporty feel.

Milestones

1970 Dodge finally

launches its own ponycar – the Challenger. An R/T performance model is offered with standard big-block power. With the popularity of Trans Am racing Dodge develops a homologation special: the Challenger T/A. Street versions are fitted with a 5572cc (340ci) V8, a fibreglass lift-off bonnet, side pipes and large rear tyres. Only 2142 are built this year.

In 1969, the top performing Dodge small block muscle car was the Dart GTS 383.

1971 With factory

support in Trans Am racing on the decline, the T/A does not return, although the big-block R/T makes it second and last appearance. Only 4630 R/Ts are built and Challenger sales in general are less than half those of 1970.

The 1971 Demon is also powered by a 5572cc (340ci) V8.

1972 Big-block engines

are no longer available and the performance model is a new Challenger 360 Rallye. The Challenger itself lasts until 1974.

UNDER THE SKIN

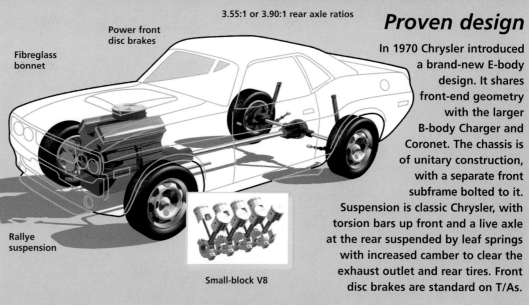

3.55:1 or 3.90:1 rear axle ratios

Power front disc brakes

Fibreglass bonnet

Rallye suspension

Small-block V8

Proven design

In 1970 Chrysler introduced a brand-new E-body design. It shares front-end geometry with the larger B-body Charger and Coronet. The chassis is of unitary construction, with a separate front subframe bolted to it. Suspension is classic Chrysler, with torsion bars up front and a live axle at the rear suspended by leaf springs with increased camber to clear the exhaust outlet and rear tires. Front disc brakes are standard on T/As.

THE POWER PACK

Rev-happy magnum

The T/A proved that the hemi or the 440 Magnum are not necessary to produce real power. The 5572cc (340ci) unit used in the Dart Swinger is fitted with a special Edelbrock intake manifold, on which sits three two-barrel Holley carburetors. The advertized output was 290bhp at 5000rpm, although this was purely for insurance reasons. With this engine the Challenger T/A and its AAR 'Cuda twin are a serious threat on the street and hydraulic lifters ensured that they were always ready for action.

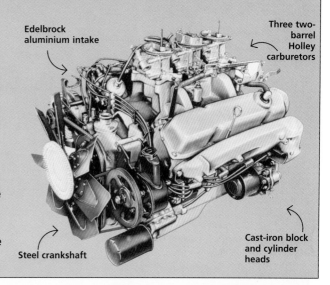

Edelbrock aluminium intake

Three two-barrel Holley carburetors

Steel crankshaft

Cast-iron block and cylinder heads

Loud T/A

In 1970 Dodge finally got serious about SCCA racing and launched its T/A. On the race circuit, all cars ran a 4998cc (305ci) V8 which was nothing more than a destroked 340. To make the street versions more fun, an Edelbrock intake and trio of Holley carbs were added.

The Challenger T/A has handling to match its massive power output.

Dodge CHALLENGER T/A

With its matte black bonnet and wide stripes, the Challenger T/A might just be one of the most stylish cars Dodge built during the heyday of muscle cars. It was equally at home taking high speed turns or accelerating in a straight line.

V8 engine

When all six barrels of the carburetors are wide open, the 5572cc (340ci) has rocket-like acceleration. Though it's a smaller engine than what most Mopar enthusiasts consider to be powerful, it really holds its own against larger-engined cars.

Panther Pink paint

Believe it or not, this colour was offered by Dodge. It's called Panther Pink and it's one of the optional High Impact colours.

Limited-slip differential

Despite the larger rear tyres, many T/A buyers specified a Positraction limited-slip differential to reduce wheel spin and increase bite.

'Six-pack' carburettors

In order to extract maximum performance out of the 5572cc (340ci) small-block, Dodge installed three Holley two-barrel carburettors atop the engine. During normal driving, only the centre carburettor is used, but punching the throttle opens the outboard units and produces astonishing acceleration.

Hardtop body

The Challenger was available in coupe and convertible forms, but all T/A models were hardtop coupes. However, a vinyl roof was available.

Torsion bar suspension

Unlike its rivals, Chrysler used torsion bar front suspension on its cars in the early 1970s. These are more robust than coil springs and result in a smoother ride over rough surfaces.

Big rear wheels

The Challenger T/A was one of the first Detroit production cars to feature different size front and rear tyres. At the back are massive G60 x 15 Goodyear Polyglas GTs, which give the T/A excellent straight-line traction.

Four-speed transmission

The standard transmission on the T/A is a Hurst-shifted four-speed with a direct-drive top ratio. The only option was a TorqueFlite three-speed automatic.

Specifications
1970 Dodge Challenger T/A

ENGINE
Type: V8

Construction: Cast-iron block and heads

Valve gear: Two valves per cylinder operated by pushrods and rockers

Bore and stroke: 102mm (4.03in) x 84mm (3.31in)

Displacement: 5571cc (340ci)

Compression ratio: 10.5:1

Induction system: Three Holley two-barrel carburetors

Maximum power: 290bhp at 5000rpm

Maximum torque: 345lb-ft at 3200rpm

Top speed: 201km/h (125mph)

0–96km/h (0–60mph): 5.8 sec

TRANSMISSION
TorqueFlite three-speed automatic

BODY/CHASSIS
Unitary steel construction with two-door four-seater coupe body

SPECIAL FEATURES

All Challengers are fitted with this racing-style chromed fuel filler cap.

At the rear, Challengers have a single, large back up light behind the Dodge lettering.

RUNNING GEAR
Steering: Recirculating ball

Front suspension: Double wishbones with longitudinal torsion bars, telescopic shock absorbers and anti-roll bar

Rear suspension: Live axle with semi-elliptic leaf springs, telescopic shock absorbers and anti-roll bar

Brakes: Discs (front), drums (rear)

Wheels: Steel discs, 17.8cm (7in) x 38.1cm (15in)

Tyres: E60 x 38.1cm (15in) (front), G60 x 38.1cm (15in) (rear)

DIMENSIONS
Length: 4.86m (191.3in)

Width: 1.93m (76.1in)

Height: 1.31m (51.7in)

Wheelbase: 279cm (110.0in)

Track: 154cm (60.7in) (front), 155cm (61.2in) (rear)

Weight: 1656kg (3650lb)

Dodge CHARGER

In 1966, responding to market tastes for sporty coupes, Dodge launched the Charger, a swoopy fastback coupe derived from the Coronet. Outfitted with the 426 Hemi, it was a truly formidable street fighter.

'...Hemi-equipped fastback.'

'Looking to boost its image as a manufacturer that can make cars look as good as they perform, Dodge introduced its fastback Charger in 1966. While its main rival, the GTO, was powerful with its Tri-Powered, 6375cc (389ci) V8, it was no match for one of Dodge's Hemi-equipped fastbacks – especially ones packing a 4-speed and a Sure Grip-fortified rear differential. While base versions came with four-wheel drums, Hemi cars benefitted from the extra stopping performance of front disc brakes.'

A fully functional and well stocked interior keep the driver well informed.

Milestones

1966 Entering mid-year as part
of the 'Dodge Rebellion' is the Charger. Built on the 297cm (117in) wheelbase Coronet chassis, it boasts hidden headlights and V8 power. Rallye suspension and Hemi V8 are available, but the latter is only installed in 468 Chargers this year.

The R/T package, new on Chargers for 1967, continued with the new 1968 model.

1967 An R/T performance
package becomes available and the full-length centre console is made optional. Charger production drops this year.

Third generation Chargers entered production in 1971 on a 297cm (117in) wheelbase.

1968 A new second-generation
Charger, with swoopy 'coke bottle' contours, arrives. The R/T package continues, but with a standard Magnum 7210cc (440ci) V8.

UNDER THE SKIN

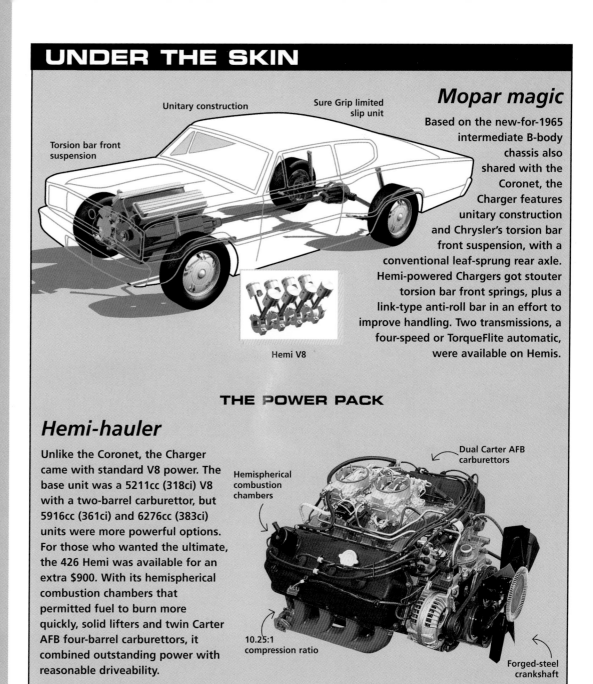

Torsion bar front suspension

Unitary construction

Sure Grip limited slip unit

Hemi V8

Mopar magic

Based on the new-for-1965 intermediate B-body chassis also shared with the Coronet, the Charger features unitary construction and Chrysler's torsion bar front suspension, with a conventional leaf-sprung rear axle. Hemi-powered Chargers got stouter torsion bar front springs, plus a link-type anti-roll bar in an effort to improve handling. Two transmissions, a four-speed or TorqueFlite automatic, were available on Hemis.

THE POWER PACK

Hemi-hauler

Unlike the Coronet, the Charger came with standard V8 power. The base unit was a 5211cc (318ci) V8 with a two-barrel carburettor, but 5916cc (361ci) and 6276cc (383ci) units were more powerful options. For those who wanted the ultimate, the 426 Hemi was available for an extra $900. With its hemispherical combustion chambers that permitted fuel to burn more quickly, solid lifters and twin Carter AFB four-barrel carburettors, it combined outstanding power with reasonable driveability.

Hemispherical combustion chambers

Dual Carter AFB carburettors

10.25:1 compression ratio

Forged-steel crankshaft

Rare rocket

Hemi-engined Mopars are among the most sought-after of all muscle cars and the 1966 6981cc (426ci) Charger is right up there with them. Perhaps the most desirable is a 1967 Hemi (just 118 built) with the Rallye package and four-speed transmission.

1967 was the second and last year for the original Charger.

Dodge CHARGER

Although previous Dodge muscle machines were outstanding performers, they lacked a racy image. The slick Charger changed all that and thrust hot Mopars into the spotlight during the mid-1960s.

Drum brakes

Like most muscle cars of the time, the Charger came from the factory with four-wheel drum brakes. All Hemi-equipped cars came with front discs as standard.

The hemispherical edge

Launched in 1964 and offered in street trim from 1966, the Hemi was the engine to beat. With solid valve lifters, dual quad carburetion and massive hemispherical combustion chambers, it was more powerful and efficient than rival big-blocks.

Heavy-duty suspension

The Hemi required a heavy-duty suspension. The front torsion bars were increased to 23mm (0.92in) in diameter and a front anti-roll bar was fitted to reduce body roll. Even so, the nose-heavy car can become a handful around corners with an inexperienced driver at the wheel.

Slippery styling

Although its shape is visually appealing, the Charger's slippery lines were important for high speed aerodynamics in NASCAR races. It proved to be so successful this year that David Pearson took the NASCAR championship in 1966 driving a Hemi Charger.

Hidden headlights

A standard feature of early Chargers are the hidden headlights. The doors concealing them are activated by vacuum canisters.

Futuristic cabin

One of the Charger's main selling points was the interior. Strictly a four-seater, due to the long centre console, the cabin also features deeply set gauges with brushed metal housings. The rear seats can be folded flat to free up rear luggage space.

Specifications

1966 Dodge Charger

ENGINE

Type: V8

Construction: Cast-iron block and heads

Valve gear: Two valves per cylinder operated by a single camshaft with pushrods and rockers

Bore and stroke: 108mm (4.25in) x 95mm (3.75in)

Displacement: 6981cc (426ci)

Compression ratio: 10.25:1

Induction system: Twin Carter AFB four-barrel carburettors

Maximum power: 425bhp at 5000rpm

Maximum torque: 490lb-ft at 4000rpm

Top speed: 216km/h (134mph)

0–96km/h (0–60mph): 5.3 sec

TRANSMISSION

Four-speed manual

BODY/CHASSIS

Steel unitary chassis with two-door fastback body

SPECIAL FEATURES

Magnum steel wheels were a popular option among Charger buyers.

RUNNING GEAR

Steering: Recirculating ball

Front suspension: Unequal-length wishbones with longitudinal torsion bars, telescopic shock absorbers

Rear suspension: Live axle with semi-elliptic leaf springs and telescopic shock absorbers

Brakes: Discs (front), Drums (rear)

Wheels: Magnum 500 steel, 35.6cm (14in) dia.

Tyres: Blue Streak, 20/9cm (8.25in) x 35.6cm (14in)

DIMENSIONS

Length: 5.17m (203.6in)

Width: 1.91m (75.2in)

Height: 1.37m (53.8in)

Wheelbase: 297cm (117.0in)

Track: 151cm (59.3in) (front), 149cm (58.5in) (rear)

Weight: 1810kg (3990lb)

Dodge **CHARGER 440**

One of the biggest two-door coupes built, the awesome Charger had the extrovert style and extreme performance to go with its massive size, making it the ideal street machine.

'...obeys every command.'

'Don't be fooled by the Charger's size. It has enough power under the bonnet to tame the wildest performance cars in its class. While the 400bhp 7210cc (440ci) V8 engine and TorqueFlite automatic transmission is the common driveline, a 425-bhp, 426 Hemi V8 with dual four-barrel carburettors and heavy duty four-speed transmission unleashes the Charger's potential. Hemi-powered Chargers, if equipped with a Traction Loc differential and 4.10:1 gears, will run the standing 1/4 mile in 13.7 seconds. With power like this, it's no wonder the Dodge Charger obeys every command.'

Black plastic fascia dominates the Charger's interior. The tachometer carries a clock in its centre.

Milestones

1966 The first Chargers are genuine high performers, especially with the 425bhp Hemi-engined version.

More than 400 Chargers were destroyed during the filming of the TV series 'The Dukes of Hazzard'.

1968 Second-generation Chargers get a restyle. Seven different power outputs are available from a range of V8 engines. The 1969 model year Charger 500 is a limited edition NASCAR special.

The 1970 Charger is more refined than the 1968 model.

1969 Dodge dominates NASCAR with the Charger Daytona, a racing car with aerodynamic nose, tall rear wing and a top speed beyond 322km/h (200mph).

1970 Last year of the classic Charger, in which styling is changed from the previous year. Its dimensions are almost the same but the car loses its appeal as the 1970s unfold.

UNDER THE SKIN

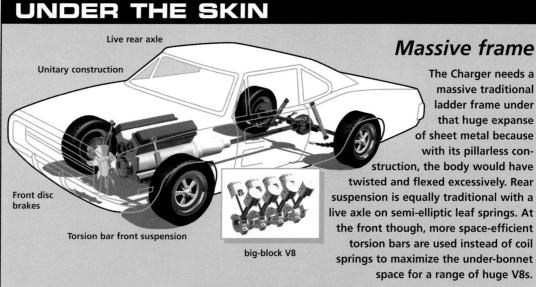

Live rear axle

Unitary construction

Front disc brakes

Torsion bar front suspension

big-block V8

Massive frame

The Charger needs a massive traditional ladder frame under that huge expanse of sheet metal because with its pillarless construction, the body would have twisted and flexed excessively. Rear suspension is equally traditional with a live axle on semi-elliptic leaf springs. At the front though, more space-efficient torsion bars are used instead of coil springs to maximize the under-bonnet space for a range of huge V8s.

THE POWER PACK

Classic V8

There were seven different power outputs available from a range of V8s in this style of Charger from 1968 to 1970, culminating in the mighty Hemi with 6981cc (426ci) and 425bhp. The name 'Hemi' derives from the engine's hemispherical combustion chamber design. This design has the same efficient combustion chamber as overhead-cam engines while using pushrods and a single cam. This enables the engine to produce more power at higher rpm. Since they were made to run in the upper rpm range, street Hemis came equipped with dual carburetors. The larger 440 V8 would give 375bhp as standard, which nearly equalled the Hemi.

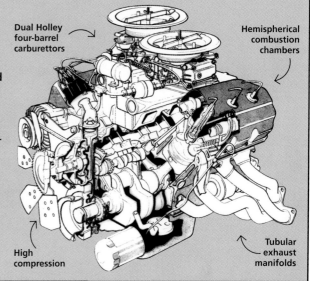

Dual Holley four-barrel carburettors

Hemispherical combustion chambers

High compression

Tubular exhaust manifolds

Charger Daytona

Pride of the 1969 Charger fleet was the Daytona, built for long-distance NASCAR races like the Daytona 500. It was distinguished from the rest of the range by an aerodynamic nose with chin spoiler and concealed headlamps, a flush-window fastback roof and a huge rear adjustable wing. Dodge built only 503 examples in order to homologate the car for competition.

The Charger Daytona was conceived for long-distance NASCAR races.

121

Dodge CHARGER 440

With style and performance to burn why modify a good thing? When the changes are subtle, unseen and increase performance and handling, why not make a good thing even better?

Concealed headlamps

One of the Charger's consistent features is its concealed headlamps, seen on all the models from 1966 to 1970. When the four lights were not needed, all you could see was the full-width grill.

Tuned V8

The 7210cc (440ci) Chrysler V8 relies on neat design and its sheer size to give 375bhp standard output without stressing the engine at all. This modified car has been fitted with two large four-barrel carburettors and a free-flowing exhaust to liberate further power without sacrificing reliability.

Torsion bar front suspension

It would have been hard to place the right sized front coil springs between the Charger's double wishbones, so the bottom wishbone is connected to a long torsion bar on each side.

TorqueFlite transmission

A manual four-speed was a no-cost option on the Charger, but most buyers opted for the superb Chrysler TorqueFlite three-speed auto without really losing anything in performance.

Radial tyres

In the late-1960s, R/T Chargers rode on F70 x 35.6cm (14in) tyres like most of the powerful opposition. Tyre technology has moved on and this modified Charger has more grip and control thanks to its modern radials.

Optional disc brakes

Even on the most powerful of the 1968 to 1970 generation Charger front discs were listed as an option, costing $41.75 extra.

Leaf spring rear suspension

Although the Charger has only a leaf spring rear suspension, the faster versions were given stiffer springs thanks to six rather than four leafs.

Standard bodywork

Given the rising value of the 1968–1970 Charger as a classic car, it pays to make modifications reversible so as not to affect the car's value. This car has immaculate standard bodywork.

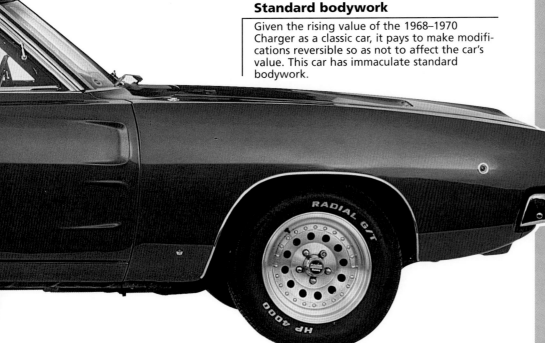

Specifications
1968 Modified Dodge Charger 440

ENGINE

Type: V8

Construction: Cast-iron block and heads

Valve gear: Two valves per cylinder operated by single block-mounted camshaft via pushrods, rockers and hydraulic lifters

Bore and stroke: 110mm (4.32in) x 95mm (3.75in)

Displacement: 7210cc (440ci)

Compression ratio: 10.0:1

Induction system: Two four-barrel carburetors

Maximum power: 400bhp at 4800rpm

Maximum torque: 410 ft-lb at 3600rpm

Top speed: 225km/h (140mph)

0–96km/h (0–60mph): 7.5 sec

TRANSMISSION

Three-speed TorqueFlite automatic

BODY/CHASSIS

Unitary construction with additional ladder frame and two-door pillarless coupe body

SPECIAL FEATURES

R/T stands for Road/Track and denotes the installation of Dodge's popular performance package.

RUNNING GEAR

Steering: Recirculating ball

Front suspension: Double wishbones with longitudinal torsion bars and telescopic shocks

Rear suspension: Live axle with semi-elliptic leaf springs and telescopic shocks

Brakes: Drums, 27.9cm (11in) dia. (front), drums 25.4cm (10in) dia. (rear)

Wheels: Alloy, 35.6cm (14in) x 13.9m (5.5in)

Tyres: F70 x 35.6cm (14in)

DIMENSIONS

Length: 5.28m (208in)

Width: 1.95m (76.6in)

Height: 1.35m (53.2in)

Wheelbase: 297cm (117in)

Track: 151cm (59.5in) (front), 150cm (59.2in) (rear)

Weight: 1622kg (3574lb)

Dodge CHARGER 500

'Win on Sunday, sell on Monday' was a Detroit mantra in the late 1960s. With Chrysler being trounced by Ford on the super speedways, it needed a worthy contender. The result was the high-performance, limited-production Dodge Charger 500.

'...breathtaking acceleration.'

'Turn the key and hear the distinctive starter crank the mighty Hemi. Although it requires premium fuel, the 6981cc (426ci) V8 powers the Charger around town without stumbling in low revs like some engines, although fast street racing is its call. Planting your foot to the floor brings a howl of delight from under the bonnet and, combined with the four-speed transmission, the acceleration is breathtaking – the Hemi pulls all the way up to the redline.'

Charger 500s came with a stock R/T (Road and Track) interior, and woodgrain trim.

Milestones

1967 A second-generation
Charger, with coke bottle fender line, is released for 1968. The R/T model comes with either a 375bhp, 7210cc (440ci) or 425bhp 6981cc (426ci) Hemi V8.

The Charger debuted for 1966 with fastback styling.

1968 With Chrysler losing
the battle in NASCAR to Ford, Mopar produce the Charger 500. It has a plugged grill with exposed headlights and a flush back window. It is sold as a 1969 model.

Regular Charger R/Ts got a split hidden headlight grill for 1969.

1969 The slippery Charger 500s
manage to capture 18 NASCAR victories this year. Unfortunately, Ford's more aerodynamic Talladegas won 30.

1969 A more streamlined
Daytona replaces the 500 later this year. It has a pointed nose cone and tall rear wing.

UNDER THE SKIN

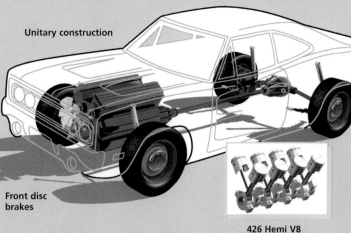

Heavy-duty R/T suspension

Unitary construction

Front disc brakes

426 Hemi V8

Heavy duty

As a member of Chrysler's B-body intermediate line up, the Charger 500 has a unitary body/chassis with a separate front subframe bolted to it. At the rear is a Dana live axle with a Sure-Grip differential, while the front has upper and lower A-arms but with longitudinal torsion bar springs in place of more conventional coils. Front disc brakes were standard, though 27.9cm (11in) drums are retained at the rear.

THE POWER PACK

Ultimate Hemi

Like the standard Charger R/T, the 500 was offered with just two engines – the 375bhp, 7210cc (440ci) Magnum or 6981cc (426ci) Hemi V8. The Hemi, installed in a mere 32 Charger 500s, was perhaps the ultimate muscle car engine. With 425bhp, 490lb-ft of torque and an aluminium intake manifold with twin Carter AFB four-barrel carburettors, it is a fearsome powerplant. Equipped with this engine and 4.10:1 rear gearing, a Charger 500 can zip through the ¼-mile in just 13.7 seconds.

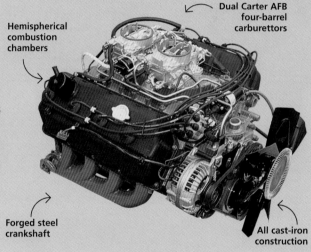

Hemispherical combustion chambers

Dual Carter AFB four-barrel carburettors

Forged steel crankshaft

All cast-iron construction

Rare Hemis

Built as a homologation exercise, the Charger 500 is exceedingly rare. The Hemi V8-engined cars are even more exclusive, with just 32 built. As with all muscle Mopars, these machines are highly sought-after today and mint examples can cost $50,000.

Exposed headlights, flush-fit grill and smooth rear window distinguish the 500.

Dodge CHARGER 500

Although marginally faster than the standard Charger on the speedways, the 500 really came into its own on the street. One magazine even went as far as to call it a showroom racer – surprisingly docile on the street circuit.

Hemi V8

Only two engines were available in the limited edition 500. The first was the big 7210cc (440ci) Magnum, installed in the majority (340) of the cars. The second was the mighty Hemi, which produced an incredible 425bhp and 490lb-ft of torque.

Body modifications

To combat problems of turbulence on the second-generation Charger, the 500 was fitted with a flush-mounted grill and smooth rear window. The latter necessitated a shorter boot lid and an extended rear backlight shelf.

Heavy-duty suspension

All Charger 500s were fitted with the same suspension. This included heavy-duty shocks, stiffer front torsion bars and an extra leaf in the right rear spring, plus a thicker and tighter front anti-roll bar.

Out-of-house conversion

The Charger 500 started life as a 1968 Charger but, besides the nose and window alterations, it got 1969 style taillights and was marketed as a 1969 model. The conversion was undertaken by Creative Industries – an aftermarket car crafter based in Michigan.

Front disc brakes

Base model Chargers came with four-wheel drum brakes, although R/T models have 27.9cm (11in) units front and rear. Charger 500s, however, have front discs as standard equipment.

Dual exhaust

Like the vast majority of muscle cars, the Charger 500 needed a large exhaust system. It is fitted with twin full-length 57mm (2¼in) diameter pipes.

Specifications

1969 Dodge Charger 500

ENGINE

Type: V8

Construction: Cast-iron block and heads

Valve gear: Two valves per cylinder operated by a single camshaft with pushrods and rockers

Bore and stroke: 108mm (4.25in) x 95mm (3.75in)

Displacement: 6981cc (426ci)

Compression ratio: 10.25:1

Induction system: Twin Carter AFB four-barrel carburettors

Maximum power: 425bhp at 5000rpm

Maximum torque: 490lb-ft at 4000rpm

Top speed: 225km/h (140mph)

0–96 km/h (0–60mph): 6.5 sec

TRANSMISSION

Four-speed manual

BODY/CHASSIS

Steel unitary chassis with two-door fastback body

SPECIAL FEATURES

All Chargers from 1968 to 1970 have this racing style fuel filler cap on the left rear quarter panel.

RUNNING GEAR

Steering: Recirculating ball

Front suspension: Unequal length A-arms with longitudinally mounted torsion bars, telescopic shock absorbers and anti-roll bar

Rear suspension: Live axle with semi-elliptic leaf springs and telescopic shock absorbers

Brakes: Discs, 27.9cm (11in) dia. (front), drums, 27.9cm (11in) dia. (rear)

Wheels: Steel discs, 12.7cm (5in) x 35.6cm (14in)

Tyres: F70-14

DIMENSIONS

Length: 208.0in)

Width: 76.5in)

Height: 53.1in)

Wheelbase: 116.0in)

Track: 59.5in) (front), 29.2in) (rear)

Weight: 1860kg (4100lb)

Dodge CHARGER DAYTONA

There was a street version of the Charger Daytona because Dodge had to build a certain number to qualify for NASCAR racing. With its Hemi-engined 322km/h (200mph) missile, Dodge went on to win 22 races in 1969.

'...shattering performance.'

'You do not notice the aerodynamic aids until you are well past 193km/h (120mph), but they really came into play on superspeedways, helping to keep the cars stable as they passed each other at around 322km/h (200mph). It is unlikely you will reach that speed in a street-spec Hemi V8 since it only has 425bhp; but that is still enough for earth shattering performance and acceleration. Low gearing and light steering do not give an immediate sense of confidence, but it is fairly accurate.'

The interior of the street Charger is much more civilized than that of its NASCAR sibling.

Milestones

1969 Race goers at Alabama's

Talledega track get first sight of the racing Charger Daytona. Charlie Glotzbach laps the track at just under 322km/h (200mph). Charger driver Richard Brickhouse wins the race, and the Charger Daytona takes another 22 chequers this season.

Plymouth's version of the Charger was the Superbird.

1970 Plymouth builds

a sister to the Charger Daytona in the shape of the almost-identical Superbird.

Chargers and Superbirds often went head to head on the track.

1971 Both the Charger

Daytona and the Plymouth Superbird are effectively outlawed from racing when NASCAR insists on a reduction in engine size by 25 per cent. To prove a point, Dodge organizes a run at Bonneville on the Salt Flats, where Daytona 500 winner Bobby Isaacs reaches over 349km/h (217mph).

UNDER THE SKIN

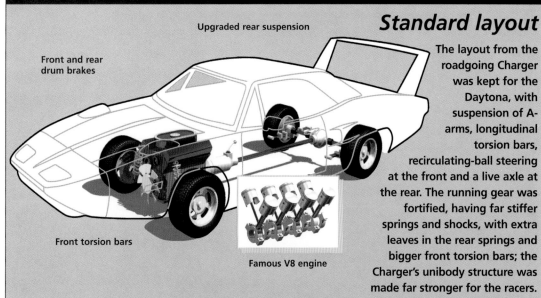

Upgraded rear suspension

Front and rear drum brakes

Front torsion bars

Famous V8 engine

Standard layout

The layout from the roadgoing Charger was kept for the Daytona, with suspension of A-arms, longitudinal torsion bars, recirculating-ball steering at the front and a live axle at the rear. The running gear was fortified, having far stiffer springs and shocks, with extra leaves in the rear springs and bigger front torsion bars; the Charger's unibody structure was made far stronger for the racers.

THE POWER PACK

MOPAR Muscle

The immortal Hemi engine first appeared in 1964, when Chrysler seriously decided to take on Ford in NASCAR. It is an all-cast-iron unit with a single camshaft in the V operating canted valves in highly efficient hemispherical combustion chambers through a combination of pushrods, solid lifters and rockers. It is oversquare with a large bore to allow room for the large valves. With its shorter stroke, it is designed to rev high, up to 7200rpm. The 6981cc (426ci) alloy-headed, high-compression race engines gave over 650bhp when fitted into the front of the Charger Daytona.

Special

The distinctive looks of the Charger Daytona have ensured its status as a cult classic. All cars are supremely powerful, but Keith Black (builder of MOPAR performance engines) prepared a promotional version with hair-raising performance.

The Daytona has one of the most outrageous wings ever seen on a stock car.

Dodge **CHARGER DAYTONA**

The Charger Daytona's outrageous look was no styling gimmick; the sharp extended nose and huge rear wing really did make the car far more aerodynamic and quicker around the track.

6981cc (426ci) Hemi

The street version of the Hemi gave less power than the higher tuned race engines, with their outputs of 575–700bhp. Also, they ran with iron heads, lower compression ratios, and later hydraulic rather than solid tappets that kept the potential engine speeds lower.

Four-speed transmission

Street versions of the Charger Daytona came with a standard three-speed manual, but the racers were equipped with a close-ratio, four-speed with a Hurst shifter. Customers could specify a four-speed as a no-cost option or opt for the TorqueFlite three-speed auto.

Two four-barrel carburettors

For the street Hemi engine there were two Carter four-barrel carburettors, arranged to open progressively. Just two barrels of the rear carb open at low throttle.

Extended nose

The new nose was made of fibreglass and was some 43.2cm (17in) long. It made the car more aerodynamically efficient. The poor fit, which is a feature of all Charger Daytonas and Plymouth Superbirds, clearly had no effect on the aerodynamics of this 322km/h (200mph) car.

Unitary construction

Although it looks like a classic example of a traditional body-on-frame piece of American design, the Charger Daytona is a unitary vehicle, with the bodywork acting as the chassis.

Pop-up lights

With the addition of the sharp extended nose, the standard headlights were covered and had to be replaced by a new arrangement of pop-up light pods, with each having two headlights.

Rear wing

That distinctive rear wing is mounted more than 60cm (24in) above the boot lid, so there is room for the boot to open. But its real benefit is to allow it to operate in clean air.

Specifications

1969 Dodge Charger Daytona

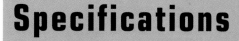

ENGINE

Type: V8

Construction: Cast-iron block and heads

Valve gear: Two valves per cylinder operating in hemispherical combustion chambers opened by a single V-mounted camshaft with pushrods, rockers and solid lifters

Bore and stroke: 108mm (4.25in) x 95mm (3.75in)

Displacement: 6981cc (426ci)

Compression ratio: 10.25:1

Induction system: Two Carter AFB 3084S carburettors

Maximum power: 425bhp at 5600rpm

Maximum torque: 490lb-ft at 4000rpm

Top speed: 217km/h (135mph)

0–96km/h (0–60mph): 5 sec

TRANSMISSION

Four-speed manual

BODY/CHASSIS

Unitary monocoque construction with steel body panels and fibreglass nose section

SPECIAL FEATURES

The black rear wing distinguishes the Charger from the Plymouth Superbird.

RUNNING GEAR

Steering: Recirculating-ball

Front suspension: A-arms with longitudinal torsion bars, telescopic shock absorbers and anti-roll bar

Rear suspension: Live axle with asymmetrical leaf springs and telescopic shock absorbers

Brakes: Drums, 27.9cm (11.0in) dia. (front), 27.9cm (11.0in) dia. (rear)

Wheels: Stamped steel, 35.6cm (14in) x 15.2cm (6in)

Tyres: F70 x 35.6cm (14in)

DIMENSIONS

Length: 5.3m (208.5in)

Width: 1.95m (76.6in)

Height: 1.35m (53.0in)

Wheelbase: 297cm (117.0in)

Track: 152cm (59.7in) (front), 150cm (59.2in) (rear)

Weight: 1665kg (3671lb)

Dodge **CORONET R/T**

The Coronet R/T was the first mid-size Dodge muscle machine to feature all the performance and luxury features in a single package. With a powerful 7210cc (440ci) V8, it didn't disappoint.

'...it just keeps on going.'

'Unlike previous mid-size Chrysler muscle cars, the Coronet R/T has a more sporty feel. With a distinctive start-up sound, the giant Magnum V8 roars into life. Smooth and refined, the big V8 has plenty of torque. Dropping the pedal launches the car forward and it just keeps on going, daring you to go faster. Watch out for the corners though; the nose-heavy R/T doesn't handle very well and its 480lb-ft of torque will surely result in oversteer.'

The Coronet R/T has standard bucket seats, a centre console and full instrumentation.

Milestones

1967 Dodge introduces its Coronet R/T (Road and Track). It is a complete high-performance package and is fitted with a standard 7210cc (440ci) V8, although the Hemi engine is also available. This year sales figures total 10,181.

The Coronet R/T debuted in both hardtop and convertible forms.

1968 The R/T returns with handsome new sheet-metal on an unchanged wheelbase.

1969 After a major facelift in 1968, changes this year are minor, with a new grill and rear tail panel. Engine choices remain the same.

The race-ready Super Bee was the Coronet's high performance stablemate.

1970 Greater competition in a heavily crowded market takes its toll on the Coronet R/T and sales fall to just 2,615. Only 13 of these cars are fitted with the Hemi V8.

UNDER THE SKIN

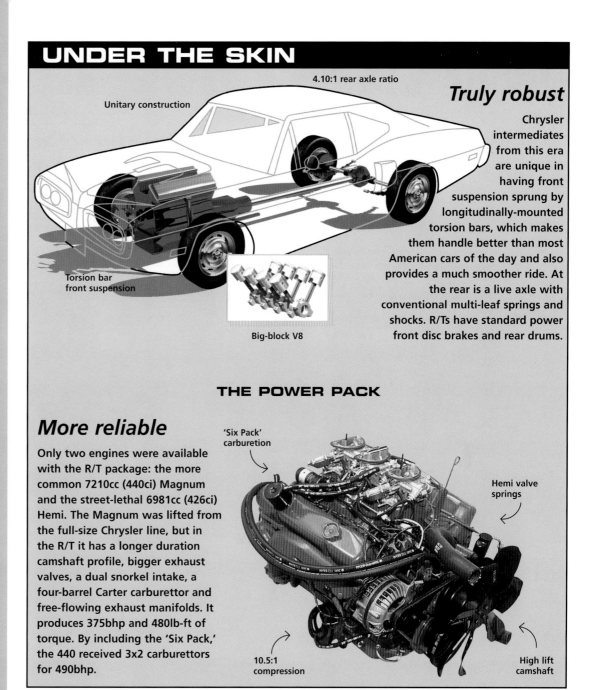

4.10:1 rear axle ratio

Unitary construction

Torsion bar front suspension

Big-block V8

Truly robust

Chrysler intermediates from this era are unique in having front suspension sprung by longitudinally-mounted torsion bars, which makes them handle better than most American cars of the day and also provides a much smoother ride. At the rear is a live axle with conventional multi-leaf springs and shocks. R/Ts have standard power front disc brakes and rear drums.

THE POWER PACK

More reliable

Only two engines were available with the R/T package: the more common 7210cc (440ci) Magnum and the street-lethal 6981cc (426ci) Hemi. The Magnum was lifted from the full-size Chrysler line, but in the R/T it has a longer duration camshaft profile, bigger exhaust valves, a dual snorkel intake, a four-barrel Carter carburettor and free-flowing exhaust manifolds. It produces 375bhp and 480lb-ft of torque. By including the 'Six Pack,' the 440 received 3x2 carburettors for 490bhp.

'Six Pack' carburetion

Hemi valve springs

10.5:1 compression

High lift camshaft

Short life

When the Coronet was launched in 1967, its styling was boxy and upright. A new, smoother body was introduced the following year, which was carried over to 1969 with few changes. 1970 models feature an aggressive twin 'horse collar'-type grill.

1970 was the last year for the convertible Coronet.

Dodge CORONET R/T

This peppermint green 1970 Coronet 440 is one of just 2615 R/Ts built that year. With so much competition in the muscle car arena, sales plummeted in 1970, making this a desirable muscle car today.

Torsion bar suspension

Chrysler was unique in employing torsion bars for the front suspension. Mounted lengthways, they are extremely simple and robust.

Street racer's powerplant

Easier to maintain, more flexible and less temperamental than the Hemi, the 440 delivers plenty of torque and is perfect for drag racing. It is nicknamed the 'Wedge' because of the shape of its combustion chambers.

Bulletproof TorqueFlite

The V8 in this R/T is backed up by the optional 727 TorqueFlite three-speed automatic. This transmission is extremely reliable and has been used in countless Mopars over the years.

Bigger wheels

For 1970 handsome 38.1cm (15in) Rallye wheels became available on the Coronet R/T. They feature chrome beauty rings and centre caps.

Bumble bee stripe

A tail end stripe, usually in black, white or red, was available at no extra cost.

Aggressive front

Twin 'horse collar'-type grills are unique to 1970 Coronets and give the car an aggressive appearance. The bonnet scoops are an R/T-only feature and are nonfunctional.

Specifications
1970 Dodge Coronet R/T

ENGINE

Type: V8

Construction: Cast-iron block and heads

Valve gear: Two valves per cylinder operated by pushrods and rockers

Bore and stroke: 110mm (4.32in) x 95mm (3.75in)

Displacement: 7210cc (440ci)

Compression ratio: 10.5:1

Induction system: Single Carter AFB downdraft four-barrel carburettor

Maximum power: 375bhp at 4600rpm

Maximum torque: 480lb-ft at 3200rpm

Top speed: 198km/h (123mph)

0–96km/h (0–60mph): 6.6 sec

TRANSMISSION

TorqueFlite 727 three-speed automatic

BODY/CHASSIS

Steel monocoque with two-door body

SPECIAL FEATURES

Side-mounted scoops are only fitted to 1970 Coronet R/Ts and are purely decorative features.

Though the engine in this Coronet R/T makes 375bhp, it is the base engine. Also available was a 390bhp version with three two-barrel carbs, and a 426 Hemi that made 425 bhp.

RUNNING GEAR

Steering: Recirculating ball

Front suspension: Longitudinally mounted torsion bars with wishbones and telescopic shocks

Rear suspension: Live rear axle with semi-elliptic leaf springs and telescopic shocks

Brakes: Discs (front), drums (rear)

Wheels: Steel disc, 38.1cm (15in) dia.

Tyres: Goodyear Polyglas GT F60 15

DIMENSIONS

Length: 7.82m (207.7in)

Width: 205m (80.6in)

Height: 1.33m (52.5in)

Wheelbase: 297cm (117in)

Track: 150cm (8.9in) (front and rear)

Weight: 1608kg (3546lb)

Dodge DART GTS

In 1968, the humble Dart finally entered the muscle car fraternity when it was fitted with the 383 V8. An even larger 440 V8 was fitted in 1969. This turned the Dart into a very accomplished performer and a serious threat on the streets.

'...pulls hard to 193km/h (120mph).'

'A horizontal sweep speedometer and a plain interior give away the budget origins of the GTS, but its 383 V8 performance puts the car in a different league. At idle, the 330bhp engine vigorously and uncontrollably shakes the car. With the sure-shifting TorqueFlite at the command of your right hand, the Dart will rocket off the line with the slightest touch of the throttle, but its real strength lies when the throttle is nailed from about 32km/h (20 mph); then it pulls hard to 193km/h (120mph).'

The narrow steering wheel and pedestrian-looking dash show the Dart's humble character.

Milestones

1967 Chrysler offers new A-body

compacts with unitary construction. Both the Dodge Dart and Plymouth Valiant get more important and curvier styling. At Dodge, performance is endowed in the Dart GT, which can get a 230bhp, 4425cc (270ci) V8.

The Dart GTS was only offered for 1968 and 1969.

1968 A hotter GTS version

is launched with a standard 5572cc (340ci) small-block engine. With an excellent power-to-weight ratio, it can run 14-second ¼-mile times. A larger 6276cc (383ci) unit is optional.

Based on the Dart, the Dodge Demon 340 debuted for 1971.

1969 In an attempt to improve

performance, the 383 engine undergoes some tweaks, resulting in 330bhp. This is the final year for the GTS. The Swinger is the sole performance Dart for 1970.

UNDER THE SKIN

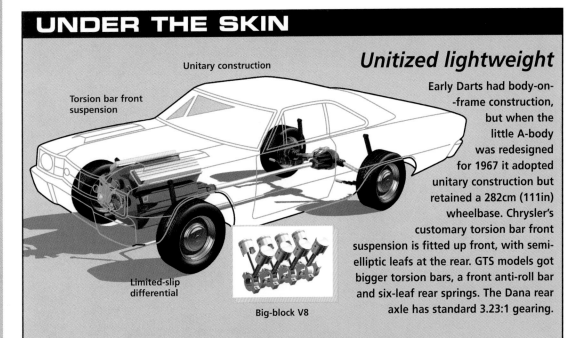

Unitary construction

Torsion bar front suspension

Limited-slip differential

Big-block V8

Unitized lightweight

Early Darts had body-on-frame construction, but when the little A-body was redesigned for 1967 it adopted unitary construction but retained a 282cm (111in) wheelbase. Chrysler's customary torsion bar front suspension is fitted up front, with semi-elliptic leafs at the rear. GTS models got bigger torsion bars, a front anti-roll bar and six-leaf rear springs. The Dana rear axle has standard 3.23:1 gearing.

THE POWER PACK

Magnum force

The GTS was powered by a standard 5572cc (340ci) engine, but in 1968 Dodge finally gave the Dart some serious muscle under the bonnet when the little compact was fitted with a big block. The 6276cc (383ci) V8, the staple of run-of-the-mill big Dodge sedans, underwent some modifications for 1969 using experience from the 1968 Super Bee. These included free-breathing cylinder heads, a stronger crankshaft, stiffer valve springs, a higher lift camshaft and low-restriction exhaust manifolds. Fuel is fed through a single Carter AFB four-barrel carburettor. With 330bhp and 410lb-ft of torque, 14.4-second ¼-miles are a regular occurrence.

GT Sport

One of the most unassuming performers of the late 1960s, the Dart is still underrated when compared with its larger stablemates. Good 383-equipped cars can sell in the $20,000 range and have equal if not better acceleration than B-bodies.

GTS Darts could be bought with 5572cc (340ci) and 6276cc (383ci) engines.

Dodge DART GTS

Although adding the 383 engine upset the Dart's balance somewhat, the problem was addressed in 1969 by modifying the front suspension. The resulting car runs excellent ETs, provided care is taken with the throttle.

TorqueFlite transmission

In 1969, either a four-speed manual or a TorqueFlite automatic transmission could be ordered. Typically, the smooth, quick-shifting TorqueFlite was tough to beat.

Small- or big-block V8

The standard engine in the GTS is the free-revving, small-block 5572cc (340ci) which offers outstanding performance. The big 6276cc (383ci), despite its extra 55bhp, offers only marginally better acceleration but in the right hands it makes for a lethal junior muscle car. Power for the Darts didn't stop there. Some GTSs received 375bhp 7210cc (440ci) V8s.

Torsion-bar front suspension

Because the 6276cc (383ci) engine puts more weight over the front wheels than the 7210cc (340ci), the front torsion bars were increased and a thicker front anti-roll bar fitted. This gives a stiffer ride and better handling than the base model Darts.

Bias-ply tyres

The E70 x 35.6cm (14in) tyres are not really capable of harnessing 410lb-ft of torque and careless acceleration can result in uncontrollable wheelspin. Deflating the tyres a few psi greatly improves its traction under hard acceleration.

Rugged rear end

A Dana 9¾ rear axle with a Sure-Grip limited-slip differential and standard 3.23:1 gears transfer the power to the pavement. Shorter 3.55:1 or 3.90:1 ratios were available for those who craved quicker acceleration.

Specifications

1969 Dodge Dart GTS 383

ENGINE

Type: V8

Construction: Cast-iron block and heads

Valve gear: Two valves per cylinder operated by a single centrally mounted camshaft with pushrods and rockers

Bore and stroke: 108mm (.25in) x 86mm (3.38in)

Displacement: 6276cc (383ci)

Compression ratio: 10.0:1

Induction system: Carter AFB four-barrel downdraft carburettor

Maximum power: 330bhp at 5200rpm

Maximum torque: 410lb-ft at 3600rpm

Top speed: 193km/h (120mph)

0–96km/h (0–60mph): 6.0 sec

TRANSMISSION

TorqueFlite 727 three-speed automatic

BODY/CHASSIS

Steel unitary chassis with two-door hardtop coupe body

SPECIAL FEATURES

With a horizontal speedometer, the tach had to be mounted on the centre console. The transmission is a TorqueFlite three-speed automatic.

Steel wheels with centre caps and trim rings give this GTS its 'sleeper' appearance.

RUNNING GEAR

Steering: Recirculating ball

Front suspension: Unequal length A-arms with longitudinal torsion bars, coil springs, telescopic shock absorbers and anti-roll bar

Rear suspension: Live axle with semi-elliptic leaf springs and telescopic shock absorbers

Brakes: Discs (front), drums (rear)

Wheels: Pressed steel, 35.6cm (14in) dia.

Tyres: Redline, E70 x 35.6cm (14in)

DIMENSIONS

Length: 4.98m (196.0in)

Width: 1.78m (70.0in)

Height: 1/37m (53.9in)

Wheelbase: 279cm (111.0in)

Track: 146cm (57.4in) (front), 141cm (55.6in) (rear)

Weight: 1588kg (3500lb)

Unitary chassis

From 1967, Darts adopted unitary construction, which gives a stiffer structure. The front suspension is attached to a subframe.

Plain interior

Most Darts have spartan interiors – the GTS included – but optional front bucket seats, a centre console and deluxe steering wheel add a little luxury.

Dodge **SUPER BEE**

In the late 1960s, Chrysler went all out to better the competition when it came to muscle cars. One of the fastest of all was the Super Bee, created by stuffing the monster 440 into the lightest intermediate bodyshell.

'...throws you back in the seat.'

'Take a good, long look at the Super Bee before you slide behind the wheel. The matte-black, fibreglass bonnet with its massive scoop and bare-bone steel wheels tell you that this Dodge means business. A full set of instruments greets you inside, but otherwise the interior is fairly plain. Punch the pedal and this car turns into a real animal. It throws you back in the bucket seat, and there is little you can do but stare at the rising speedometer and listen to the screaming engine.'

Super Bees came with full instrumentation, but a centre console was optional.

Milestones

1966 The Chrysler Corporation issues a paper about a new high-performance engine designed for regular street driving.

1968 Dodge releases the no-frills Super Bee in response to the Plymouth Road Runner. It is offered as a two-door coupe with a 6276cc (383ci) or a 6981cc (426ci) Hemi V8.

The classic 1969 Charger R/T came with standard 440 power.

1969 Realizing that there is still a market for outlandishly fast, yet low-buck, street racers, Dodge unveils the Super Bee 440 Six Pack. It comes with a fibreglass lift-off bonnet. 1907 are built this year.

Super Bees are the performance variant of base Coronets.

1970 The Coronet is facelifted with a twin horsecollar front grill. The Super Bee 440 Six Pack returns for its second and final season.

UNDER THE SKIN

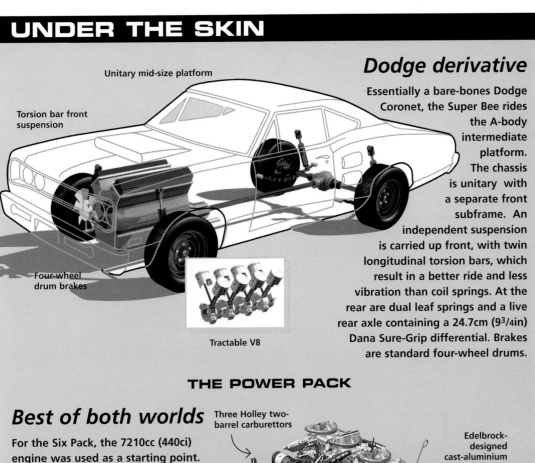

Unitary mid-size platform

Torsion bar front suspension

Four-wheel drum brakes

Tractable V8

Dodge derivative

Essentially a bare-bones Dodge Coronet, the Super Bee rides the A-body intermediate platform. The chassis is unitary with a separate front subframe. An independent suspension is carried up front, with twin longitudinal torsion bars, which result in a better ride and less vibration than coil springs. At the rear are dual leaf springs and a live rear axle containing a 24.7cm (9³/₄in) Dana Sure-Grip differential. Brakes are standard four-wheel drums.

THE POWER PACK

Best of both worlds

For the Six Pack, the 7210cc (440ci) engine was used as a starting point. Items such as the forged steel crankshaft, connecting rods and aluminium pistons were retained. To boost performance, a higher lift camshaft, stronger valve springs and free-flowing heads were specified. Sitting atop the engine is a special Edelbrock aluminium manifold and three Holley two-barrel carburettors. Although it has less power than the 426 Hemi, the 440 is more tractable and easier to keep in tune.

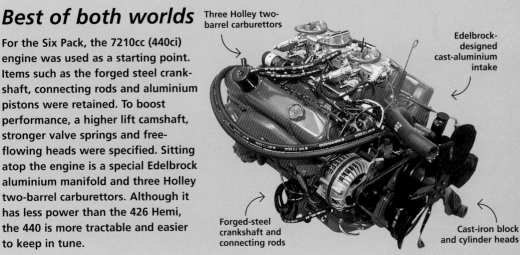

Three Holley two-barrel carburettors

Edelbrock-designed cast-aluminium intake

Forged-steel crankshaft and connecting rods

Cast-iron block and cylinder heads

First year

Six Pack Super Bees were built for only two years and only in small numbers. Collectors tend to prefer the 1969 models with their cleaner styling, plus the fibreglass scoop which is unique to this year and the aluminium intake. Good Six Packs can cost $35,000.

Super Bee 'Six Packs' left the factory with 35.6cm (14in) steel wheels.

Dodge SUPER BEE

With its enormous cop-baiting bonnet and loud paint, the Super Bee Six Pack is certainly no street sleeper. It is, however, a true high performance machine, able to take on any challenger on the street or at the strip.

Fibreglass bonnet

The feature that probably brings more attention than any other element of the car is the bonnet. It is a one-piece fibreglass affair with a massive functional scoop.

Six Pack 440 engine

In normal driving, the engine requires only the fuel from the centre carburettor. However, when the accelerator pedal meets the floorboard, the front and rear carburetors feed the engine more fuel. With this engine, the Super Bee can run the ¼-mile in a shade under 14 seconds.

Heavy-duty suspension

Super Bee Six Packs are fitted with the same heavy-duty torsion bar suspension used on Hemi-powered Chryslers. This gives them surprisingly good roadholding for what is, after all, primarily a straight line rocket.

Hardtop styling

Introduced in 1968, the second-generation Coronet is one of the best-looking intermediates of the period. When launched early in 1968, the Super Bee was available only as a pillared coupe, though a hardtop version arrived later in the year.

Rugged rear end

Back in the 1960s, ultra-low rear axle ratios were available from the factory on many muscle cars. In 1969, Super Bee Six Packs came with 4.10:1 gearing in an almost bulletproof Dana rear end – this enables the driver to really exploit the power and torque of the six-barrel engine.

Dual exhaust

One of the signature factory performance enhancers in the 1960s was dual exhaust. It released the engine's back pressure, enabling the engine to make more power.

Specifications

1969 Dodge Super Bee 440

ENGINE

Type: V8

Construction: Cast-iron block and heads

Valve gear: Two valves per cylinder operated by a single camshaft via pushrods and rockers

Bore and stroke: 110mm (4.32in) x 95mm (3.75in)

Displacement: 7210cc (440ci)

Compression ratio: 10.5:1

Induction system: Three Holley two-barrel carburetors (Six Pack)

Maximum power: 390bhp at 4700rpm

Maximum torque: 490lb-ft at 3200rpm

Top speed: 209km/h (130mph)

0–96km/h (0–60mph): 6.0 sec

TRANSMISSION

Four-speed manual

BODY/CHASSIS

Steel unitary chassis with two-door hardtop coupe body

SPECIAL FEATURES

Because of its bare-bone image, the only wheels that the Super Bees came with were these low-budget black steel wheels with chrome lug nuts.

The one-piece, lift-off fibreglass bonnet is held in place by four tie-down pins and made routine oil checks a two-person job.

RUNNING GEAR

Steering: Recirculating ball

Front suspension: Unequal length wishbones with longitudinally mounted torsion bars, telescopic shock absorbers and anti-roll bar

Rear suspension: Dana 60 rear axle with semi-elliptic leaf springs and telescopic shock absorbers

Brakes: Drums (front and rear)

Wheels: Steel discs, 17.8cm (7in) x 35.6cm (14in)

Tyres: F70-14

DIMENSIONS

Length: 5.25m (206.6in)

Width: 1.95m (76.7in)

Height: 1.39m (54.8in)

Wheelbase: 297cm (117.0in)

Track: 151cm (59.5in) (front), 149cm (58.5in) (rear)

Weight: 1860kg (4100lb)

Dodge VIPER

The Viper was designed as a modern incarnation of the legendary Shelby Cobra of the 1960s – no nonsense, no frills, just big bags of brute power. The massive V10 is the biggest engine currently shoehorned into a production car.

'...a street brawler.'

'Some owners describe it as "a great motor looking for a car". Cruising at 121km/h (75mph), the wind batters you, the exhaust drones, engine and exhaust heat cook your feet. But when you put your foot down, all of the faults disappear. The engine has so much torque it's possible to drive away in 3rd, then shift to 6th at 56km/h (35mph). With its 8l (488ci), the V10 pulls at 500rpm. This is a no-holds-barred street brawler that will rattle your fillings and your neighbours' windows.'

Functional cockpit with stark white instruments. A very high 6th gear (85km/h, 53mph per 1000rpm) is required to pass California emission laws.

Milestone

1989 The Viper was originally a 'concept car' – a car taken to the motor shows to gauge public reaction. It is shown at the Detroit International Auto Show in January 1989. Public reaction is overwhelming.

Early racers had a huge rear spoiler.

1991 Carroll Shelby drives a prototype Viper as the pace car in the Indianapolis 500.

1992 The car goes on sale and proves a massive success. Chrysler has taken a huge risk building a car that costs nearly $60,000 and doesn't even have windows or air conditioning. It is a long-odds gamble that soon proves to be a winner for Chrysler.

1996 The GTS Coupe, first seen as a 'concept car' in 1993, finally goes on sale in Europe. Its chassis is stiffer and the engine and car are lighter, while the V10's power is increased to 450bhp. The superior aerodynamics of the fixed hard top also help make it faster.

Sleek and fast: Viper GTS Coupe.

UNDER THE SKIN

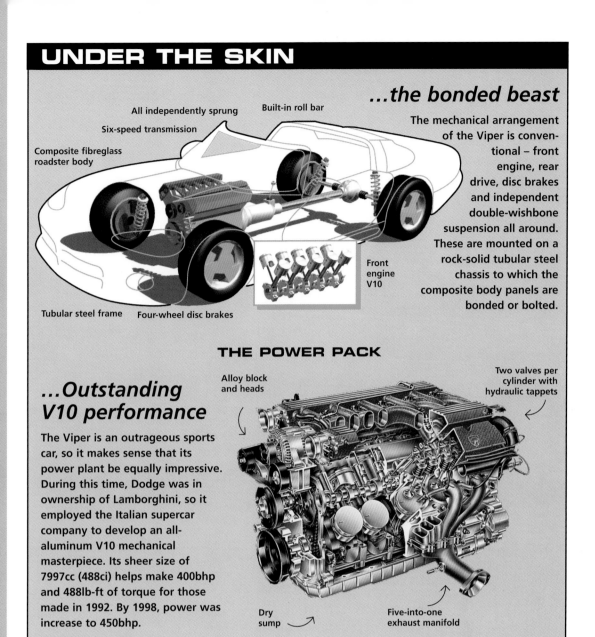

...the bonded beast

The mechanical arrangement of the Viper is conventional – front engine, rear drive, disc brakes and independent double-wishbone suspension all around. These are mounted on a rock-solid tubular steel chassis to which the composite body panels are bonded or bolted.

Labels: All independently sprung; Built-in roll bar; Six-speed transmission; Composite fibreglass roadster body; Tubular steel frame; Four-wheel disc brakes; Front engine V10

THE POWER PACK

...Outstanding V10 performance

The Viper is an outrageous sports car, so it makes sense that its power plant be equally impressive. During this time, Dodge was in ownership of Lamborghini, so it employed the Italian supercar company to develop an all-aluminum V10 mechanical masterpiece. Its sheer size of 7997cc (488ci) helps make 400bhp and 488lb-ft of torque for those made in 1992. By 1998, power was increase to 450bhp.

Labels: Alloy block and heads; Two valves per cylinder with hydraulic tappets; Dry sump; Five-into-one exhaust manifold

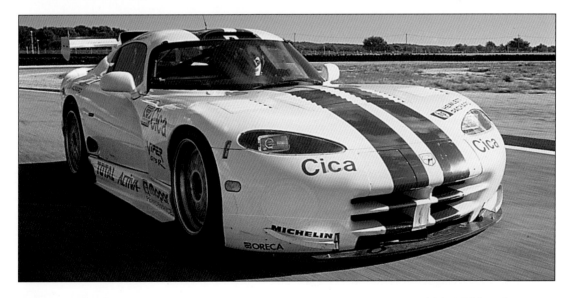

Viper Venom

As if the normal car wasn't powerful enough, John Hennessey produced the Venom version with a staggering 550bhp – 150bhp more than the original. It's enough to send a brave Viper driver to 160km/h (100mph) in under 10 seconds and on to a top speed of 280km/h (174 mph).

With 150bhp of extra bite, the Viper Venom is a car for the brave.

Dodge VIPER

The Viper's dramatic look of controlled aggression expresses the elemental power of its awesome V10 8l (488ci) engine. It was styled by an in-house Chrysler design team led by Tom Gale.

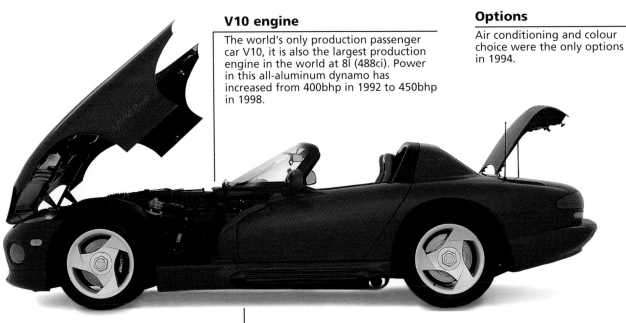

V10 engine

The world's only production passenger car V10, it is also the largest production engine in the world at 8l (488ci). Power in this all-aluminum dynamo has increased from 400bhp in 1992 to 450bhp in 1998.

Options

Air conditioning and colour choice were the only options in 1994.

Six-speed transmission

Borg-Warner six-speed transmission has an electronic shift lockout that automatically changes from 1st to 4th at light throttle.

Functional roll bar

Built-in roll bar stiffens body structure as well as adding protection. Removable rear window snaps into rollbar.

Limited slip differential

Limited slip differential helps to put the Viper's huge power down onto the road by reducing wheel spin.

Ellipsoidal headlights

Dodge describes the headlights on the Viper as Aero-Polyellipsoid. Behind those teardrop-shaped lenses are powerful halogen bulbs.

Tubular steel chassis

Steel tube chassis with steel cowl and sill structures; some composite body panels are bolted or bonded to the frame.

Unequal-sized tyres

Different size tyres and wheels front and rear help balance handling.

Exhaust air vents

The exaggerated cutaway sections in front of the doors form functional vents through which the hot engine compartment air is exhausted.

Plastic composite body

With a separate chassis, you would expect a fibreglass body, but the Viper uses more advanced plastic composite material with far greater damage resistance properties.

Specifications
1992 Dodge Viper RT/10

ENGINE

Type: V10, 90°

Construction: Aluminium heads and block with cast iron sleeves

Valve gear: Two valves per cylinders pushrods, roller hydraulic lifters

Bore and stroke: 102mm (4.0in) x 99mm (3.9in)

Displacement: 7998cc (488ci)

Compression ratio: 9:1

Induction system: Multi-port electronic injection with ram tuning

Maximum power: 400bhp at 4600rpm

Maximum torque: 488lb-ft at 3600rpm

Top speed: 261km/h (162mph)

0–96km/h (0–60mph): 5.4 sec

TRANSMISSION

Borg-Warner T-56 six-speed manual with electronic shift lock out

BODY/CHASSIS

Tubular steel chassis with two-seat fibreglass reinforced plastic convertible body

SPECIAL FEATURES

The Viper is the only production car with a V10 engine.

RUNNING GEAR

Steering: Power-assisted rack-and-pinion

Front suspension: Unequal A-arms, anti-roll bar, coil springs, adjustable gas shocks

Rear suspension: Unequal A-arms, anti-roll bar, coil springs, toe-control links, adjustable gas shocks

Brakes: Brembo 33cm (13in) vented disc with four-piston caliper (front); Brembo (33cm (13in) vented disc with sliding caliper (rear)

Wheels: Alloy 25.4cm (10in) x 43.2cm (17in) (front), 33cm (13in) x 43.2cm (17in) (rear)

Tyres: 275/40 ZR17 (front), 335/35 ZR17 (rear)

DIMENSIONS

Length: 4.45m (175in)

Width: 1.92m (75.6in)

Height: 1.1m (44in)

Wheelbase: 244cm (96.2in)

Track: 151cm (59.5in) (front), 154cm (60.6in) (rear)

Weight: 1577kg (3477lb)

Dodge VIPER GTS

It has a quicker ¼ mile time than a Ferrari F355, has better lateral acceleration than a Porsche 911 Carrera and can out-slalom a C5 Corvette. The Dodge Viper GTS might just be the best all-round performance car built that doesn't cost more than $100,000.

'...fantastic all around.'

'After just a few minutes at the wheel, you have no doubt that the Viper GTS is a fantastic all-round sports car. It takes effort to depress the clutch pedal, the gear shift is notchy and the brakes require a big stamp to get the most out of them. However, the sheer torque of the V10 engine allows a ¼ mile time of 12.6 seconds at 188km/h (117mph), its handling is tuned to give a lateral acceleration of .98 g and it can reach over 96km/h (60mph) in a 213m (700ft) slalom. Enough said.'

The GTS features power windows, a CD player and even has adjustable pedals.

Milestones

1989 The Viper
legend is born when a revitalized Chrysler Corporation displays it as a concept car at the Detroit Motor Show.

Race-prepared Vipers have been successful in GT endurance racing since they were introduced.

1991 A Viper RT/10
paces the prestigious Indianapolis 500 race with Carrol Shelby behind the wheel.

1992 The
production Viper RT/10 roadster finally goes on sale and buyers line up.

By popular demand the Viper RT/10 roadster was put into production in 1991.

1993 A GTS coupe
version is put on display as a future production proposition.

1996 The GTS finally goes
on sale after tremendous media acclaim. Current Viper roadster owners are allowed to put their orders in first for the new car.

UNDER THE SKIN

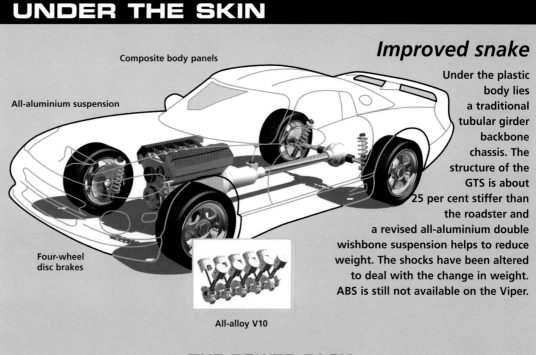

Composite body panels

All-aluminium suspension

Four-wheel disc brakes

All-alloy V10

Improved snake

Under the plastic body lies a traditional tubular girder backbone chassis. The structure of the GTS is about 25 per cent stiffer than the roadster and a revised all-aluminium double wishbone suspension helps to reduce weight. The shocks have been altered to deal with the change in weight. ABS is still not available on the Viper.

THE POWER PACK

King of the cubes

The Viper's visceral heart is its amazing engine. There is no substitute for cubic centimetres, and the Viper has 7997cc (488ci) of them. The Lamborghini-designed V10 engine features two valves per cylinder, pushrods and hydraulic valve lifters. The block is all-aluminium and uses cross-bolted main bearing caps. It is the same engine found in the Viper R/T. In the GTS coupe version power has been bumped up to 450bhp, although torque still stands at an incredible 490lb-ft.

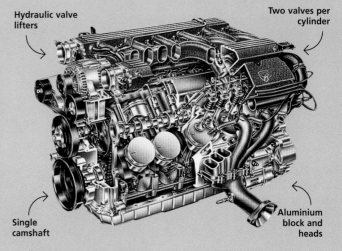

Hydraulic valve lifters

Two valves per cylinder

Single camshaft

Aluminium block and heads

Hard nut

By adding a solid roof, Dodge took the Viper to a new level with the GTS model. Thanks to its 490 lb-ft of torque, the GTS gets up to a maximum speed of 288km/h (179mph) in no time. With this much torque, it's no wonder it's designed to have mild understeer.

The GTS takes the original Viper concept a stage further.

Dodge VIPER GTS

In a world where the premiere performance cars are thought to come from Maranello, Italy and Stuttgart, Germany, its great to know that, with the Viper GTS, the U.S. has a supercar that can crush both Ferrari and Porsche.

V10 engine
The V10 puts out 450bhp and an incredible 490lb-ft of torque. The Viper is the only current production car powered by a V10 engine.

Large boot
The GTS satisfies that seemingly overridingly important criterion, namely that the boot should be able to accommodate more luggage than you would expect.

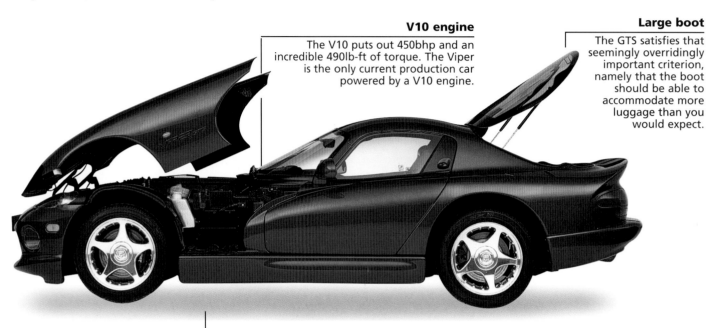

Six-speed transmission
The Viper was one of the first road cars to use a six-speed transmission. However, in reality, the six-speed unit was specified to obtain an improved fuel economy rating to satisfy tough fuel consumption standards. Both fifth and sixth are overdrive gears.

Huge brakes
Vented disc brakes at all four corners are among the largest used on any production car. They measure 33cm (13in) across and can stop the GTS from very high speeds.

Sleeker shape
Compared to the RT/10 roadster, the GTS has smoother, more aerodynamic lines and a drag figure of 0.39. Body panels are not interchangeable with the roadster.

Polished alloy wheels
The alloy wheels have a beautifully polished finish and are huge – 43.2cm (17in) diameter and 25.4cm (10in) wide at the front and 33cm (13in) at the rear.

Plastic bodywork
The body of the GTS is made almost entirely of composite materials, with some steel strengthening in the doors. This suits the low-volume production of the Viper. The GTS weighs 19.1kg (42.2lb) less than the RT/10 roadster.

Specifications
1998 Dodge Viper GTS

ENGINE
Type: V10

Construction: Aluminium cylinder block and heads

Valve gear: Two valves per cylinder operated by a single chain-driven camshaft

Bore and stroke: 102mm (4in) x 99mm (3.88in)

Displacement: 7997cc (488ci)

Compression ratio: 9.6:1

Induction system: Sequential fuel injection

Maximum power: 450bhp at 5200rpm

Maximum torque: 490lb-ft at 3700rpm

Top speed: 288km/h (179mph)

0–96km/h (0–60mph): 4.7 sec

TRANSMISSION
Six-speed manual

BODY/CHASSIS
Monocoque tubular backbone chassis with composite two-door coupe body

SPECIAL FEATURES

Huge 43.2cm (17in) five-spoke wheels were fitted on Viper roadsters in 1995.

RUNNING GEAR
Steering: Rack-and-pinion

Front suspension: Unequal length wishbones with coil springs, shocks and anti-roll bar

Rear suspension: Unequal length wishbones with coil springs, shocks and anti-roll bar

Brakes: Vented discs, 33cm (13in) dia. (front and rear)

Wheels: Alloy, 43.2cm (17in) dia.

Tyres: 275/40 ZR17 (front), 335/35 ZR17 (rear)

DIMENSIONS
Length: 4.45m (175.1in)

Width: 1.92m (75.7in)

Height: 1.12m (44in)

Wheelbase: 244cm (96.2in)

Track: 151cm (59.6in) (front), 154cm (60.6in) (rear)

Weight: 1535kg (3384lb)

Ford **FAIRLANE 427**

To fight its opposition on the street, Ford built the Fairlane 427, which had widened shock towers and larger front coil springs to fit a detuned 427 V8. Unfortunately, the Fairlane 427 was costly to build, so only 70 units were made in 1966 and 200 in 1967. Most went to pro racers for NHRA Super Stock competition.

'...uses a detuned race engine.'

'Only a Borg-Warner 'Top-Loader' four-speed transmission was able to handle the 480lb-ft of torque that the massive engine was capable of making. It uses a detuned version of its race engine, the brutal 427, and if equipped with dual four-barrel carbs, it "only" makes 425bhp. On the street, the Fairlane 427 was very competitive. Only a handful were made and at $5100 were very pricey, thus giving a slight edge to the competition.'

The only indication of power from the vinyl-clad interior was a 9000rpm tachometer.

Milestones

1964 After minimal success on the drag strips with the larger Galaxies, Ford creates the Thunderbolt – a specially prepared 427-powered lightweight Fairlane sedan. These factory-built race cars helped Ford secure the NHRA manufacturers' championship.

The first Fairlanes to be equipped with the 427 were the competition-only Thunderbolts.

1966 A new, bigger Fairlane is released, which has plenty of room for 427 FE V8 engines. Only 70 white hardtops and coupes are built to qualify for Super Stock drag racing.

The 1966 Fairlane has similar styling to the 1966–67 Galaxie.

1967 The 427 returns as a regular production option for its second and final season. Only 200 Fairlanes are equipped with the side-oiler 427 and are available in a variety of colours and optional trim packages.

UNDER THE SKIN

Special handling package

Front-disc brakes

Larger rear leaf springs

427 FE V8

Muscle bound

The 1966 Fairlane is larger and wider than its predecessor. It has a unitary body chassis, with a leaf-sprung live axle at the rear and coil-sprung wishbones at the front. A special handling package, front disc brakes, longer leaf springs and 38.1cm (15in) wheels and tyres were included. Only a 'Top Loader' transmission was available with the 427.

THE POWER PACK

The side-oiler

Oiling was a problem on the 406 and 427 FE engines, and so in 1965 Ford introduced a new block design known as the 'side-oiler'. It is this version of the 6997cc (427ci) engine that powers the Fairlane. Instead of routing the main oil gallery down the centre of the block, like other FE engines, the side-oiler has the main oil gallery positioned low on the left side near the pump outlet. It is rated at 410bhp with a single four-barrel carburettor and 425bhp with a dual carburettor set up.

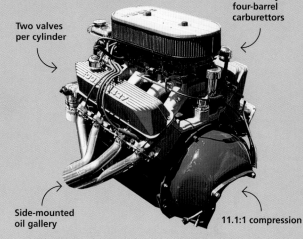

Two valves per cylinder

Two Holley four-barrel carburettors

Side-mounted oil gallery

11.1:1 compression

Rare beast

Although the 1966 models are very rare, this no-frills homologation special isn't very refined. For 1967, Ford offered the Fairlane 427 in a variety of colours and exterior trim. The cars still had the potent 427 V8 and also carried the equally potent price tag.

The 1967 Fairlane 427s were a serious threat on the streets and at the track.

Ford **FAIRLANE 427**

Although it was one of the quickest muscle cars around in 1966, the rarity of the Fairlane 427 prevented it from having the same impact among street racers as a Chevelle SS396 or a tri-power GTO.

Heavy-duty suspension

To cope with the weight and power of the 427 engine, the standard Fairlane suspension was reworked with stiffer spring rates and larger front coil springs. This unit also took up considerable space, which necessitated relocating the front shock towers.

Race-derived engine

The 6997cc (427ci) engine was available with the base model trim only and was never used in the plusher GT/GTA model. After all, it was a thinly disguised race car and potential purchasers were carefully screened by dealers.

Four-speed transmission

Unlike the Fairlane GT/GTA, the 427 was available with only one transmission: a Borg-Warner 'Top Loader' T-10 four-speed.

Handling package

A special handling package, consisting of manual front disc brakes, longer rear leaf springs and larger blackwall tyres, was available. This particular car is one of the very few to be fitted with these items.

Smooth styling

For 1966, the Fairlane hardtop received similar styling to the Pontiac GTO, with stacked headlights and smooth-flowing contours.

Specifications
1967 Ford
Fairlane 427

ENGINE
Type: V8
Construction: Cast-iron block and heads
Valve gear: Two valves per cylinder actuated by a single camshaft via pushrods, rockers and solid lifters
Bore and stroke: 107mm (4.23in) x 96mm (3.78in)
Displacement: 6997cc (427ci)
Compression ratio: 11.1:1
Induction system: Two Holley four-barrel downdraft carburettors with aluminium intake manifold
Maximum power: 425bhp at 6000rpm
Maximum torque: 480lb-ft at 3700rpm
Top speed: 195km/h (121mph)
0–96km/h (0–60mph): 6.0 sec

TRANSMISSION
Borg-Warner 'Top Loader' T-10 four-speed

BODY/CHASSIS
Steel unitary chassis with two-door body

SPECIAL FEATURES

Stacked headlights are a feature of 1966–1967 Fairlanes. The lower units are the high beams.

RUNNING GEAR
Steering: Recirculating ball
Front suspension: Double wishbones with heavy duty coil springs, telescopic shock absorbers, anti-sway bar
Rear suspension: Live axle with long semi-elliptic leaf springs and telescopic shock absorbers
Brakes: Discs front, drums rear
Wheels: 35.6cm (14in) x 14cm (5.5in)
Tyres: 19.6cm (7.75in) x 35.6cm (14in)

DIMENSIONS
Length: 5.0m)197.0in)
Width: 1.9m (74.7in)
Height: 1.38m (54.3in)
Wheelbase: 295cm (116.0in)
Track: 147cm (58.0in)
Weight: 1860kg (4100lb)

Fibreglass bonnet

In 1966 all 427 Fairlanes were built with a fibreglass lift-off bonnet with four tie-down pins. For 1967 a steel bonnet was available alongside the fibreglass unit.

Ford FALCON

In the early 1960s, Ford embarked on its 'Total Performance' sales campaign. It also brought a number of Ford Falcons to Europe for use in racing and rallying, where they performed incredibly well.

'...means business.'

'With its full roll cage and gutted interior, you can tell that this Falcon means business. Turn the key and the 4736cc (289ci) V8 rumbles to life. Thanks to its side mounted exhaust, the sound is impressive. Being fairly compact and light, the Falcon makes the most of its power and pulls hard in all gears. With stiffer springs than stock, a front anti-roll bar, and large tyres it tackles sharp corners with enthusiasm, understeering mildly.'

Only the bare essentials are retained, with just a single bucket seat for the driver.

Milestones

1960 Ford introduces its new
compact car, the Falcon. It proves a tremendous success with 410,876 examples built.

1961 Midway through the year a sporty
Falcon Sprint model is revealed with bucket seats and V8 power.

1964 Falcons gained boxier styling than the 1963 car.

1962 Ford begins its total performance
campaign and sends race-prepared Falcons to Europe for use in rallying events.

1963 Driving a Falcon, Bo Ljungfeldt
achieves a class win in the Monte Carlo Rally.

The Falcon Sprint was also available as a convertible.

1964 Restyled Falcons continue to do
battle, but are soon replaced in rallying by the sportier Mustang. The survivors continue in use as road racers through the 1960s.

UNDER THE SKIN

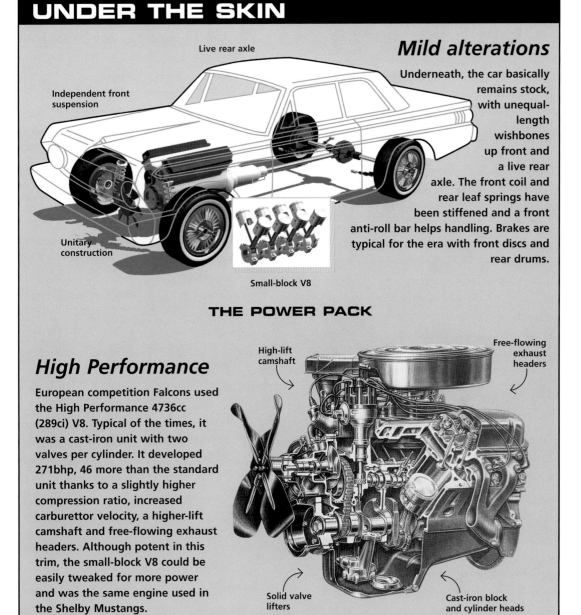

Live rear axle

Independent front suspension

Unitary construction

Small-block V8

Mild alterations

Underneath, the car basically remains stock, with unequal-length wishbones up front and a live rear axle. The front coil and rear leaf springs have been stiffened and a front anti-roll bar helps handling. Brakes are typical for the era with front discs and rear drums.

THE POWER PACK

High Performance

European competition Falcons used the High Performance 4736cc (289ci) V8. Typical of the times, it was a cast-iron unit with two valves per cylinder. It developed 271bhp, 46 more than the standard unit thanks to a slightly higher compression ratio, increased carburettor velocity, a higher-lift camshaft and free-flowing exhaust headers. Although potent in this trim, the small-block V8 could be easily tweaked for more power and was the same engine used in the Shelby Mustangs.

High-lift camshaft

Free-flowing exhaust headers

Solid valve lifters

Cast-iron block and cylinder heads

Falcon Futura

For rallying, Ford campaigned Futura Sprint two-door hardtops with fibreglass body panels and standard 289 V8s. After their rallying career was over, a handful were raced in the British Saloon Car Championship until the early 1970s.

After rallying, a few Falcons raced in the British Saloon Car Championship.

FORD **FALCON**

While high performance Falcons were generally used for drag racing in the U.S., the European-spec cars had a more powerful engine and were successfully campaigned as road racers in the 1960s.

Crisper styling

Falcons were restyled for 1964, with squarer, neater lines and a concave grille. This restyle carried over into 1965 with few changes. V8 engines transformed the Falcon's performance image.

V8 engine

This Falcon has considerable go thanks to the 4736cc (289ci) V8 engine. This was the powerplant that made the cars highly competitive in rallying and circuit racing during the 1960s, and which continues to do so in historic events today.

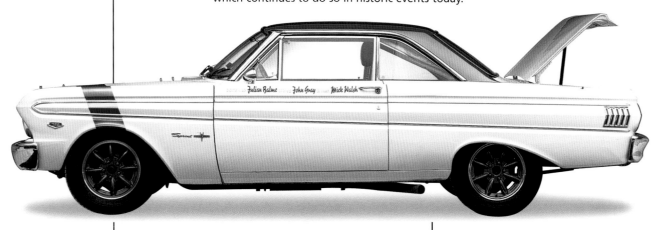

Stiffened suspension

For more responsive handling, the springs have been stiffened. Today, Falcons demonstrate excellent poise in FIA historic racing events across Europe.

Original-style brakes

Under FIA rules, even the original braking set up of front discs and rear drums must be retained. Braking ability contrasts sharply with modern machinery.

Fibreglass body panels

In order to reduce weight and increase performance, the front fenders, bonnet and boot are made from fibreglass.

Specifications
1964 Ford Falcon

ENGINE

Type: V8

Construction: Cast-iron block and heads

Valve gear: Two valves per cylinder operated by pushrods and rockers

Bore/stroke: 102mm (4in) x 73mm (2.87in)

Displacement: 4736cc (289ci)

Compression ratio: 10.5:1

Induction system: Twin four-barrel Holley cfm 600 carburettors

Maximum power: 271bhp at 6000rpm

Maximum torque: 312lb-ft at 3400rpm

Top speed: 217km/h (135mph)

0–96km/h (0–60mph): 6.4 sec

TRANSMISSION

Borg Warner T-10 four-speed

BODY/CHASSIS

Steel monocoque with two-door body

SPECIAL FEATURES

Circular taillights are a trademark of early 1960s Fords.

The elastic retaining strap on the bonnet looks crude but was actually homologated by Ford for racing.

RUNNING GEAR

Steering: Recirculating ball

Front suspension: Unequal length wishbones, coil springs, telescopic shocks and 2.5cm (1in) dia. anti-roll bar

Rear suspension: Live rear axle with semi-elliptic leaf springs and telescopic shocks

Brakes: Discs to front, drums to rear

Wheels: 17.8cm (7in) x 38.1cm (15in) Minilite spoked alloy wheels

Tyres: 205 60R 15

DIMENSIONS

Length: 4.58m (180.2in)

Width: 1.95m (76.6in)

Height: 1.33m (52.4in)

Wheelbase: 278cm (109.5in)

Track: 121cm (47.5in) (front), 109cm (43.1in) (rear)

Weight: 1275kg (2811lb)

Four-speed transmission

Manual transmissions are essential for track racing so this Falcon features an original equipment Borg Warner T-10 four-speed transmission.

Ford MUSTANG

Following its 1964 launch, the Mustang was a massive hit. Creating a place in the pony car market, its sales continued to increase. A modification of a 1966 car was the next step for this almost perfect package.

'...no ordinary Mustang.'

'Do not be fooled by its looks; this is no ordinary Mustang. Underneath there have been a multitude of changes. The supercharged engine delivers considerable power, and the modified chassis gives more stability and poise than the original. Great attention has been paid to the interior, which blends well with the orange exterior. You would be hard-pressed to find a better example of a 1966 Mustang.'

The carpet of this car is taken from Mercedes and it certainly looks elegant.

Milestones

1961 Inspirational Ford
President Lee Iacocca decides that the company should produce a sporty-looking car. Prototypes are built using a German four-cylinder engine.

1966 Mustangs came as convertibles as well as hardtops.

1964 Six months ahead
of the 1965 calendar year, Ford releases the Mustang. It is an instant hit, sparking a host of imitators from other manufacturers as the pony car war heats up.

The Mustang's first major design changes were introduced on the 1967 model, a bigger car.

1974 After a series of styling
changes, the original Mustang is replaced by the Mustang II. Initially a strong seller, it falls victim to the impending oil crisis and becomes a bloated, underpowered version of its previous self. Sales suffer as a result.

UNDER THE SKIN

Omni steering rack

Four wheel disc brakes

DOHC 4.6L modular engine shock absorbers

All-alloy V8

Uprated chassis

The original 1966 Mustang has a simple chassis layout that was adequate for the times, but feels its age now. Many changes have been made in the suspension. Up front, Mustang II parts have been incorporated and a chrome Ford 22.8cm (9in) axle is in the rear. Disc brakes have been installed all around. Transmission is a Ford AOD-E automatic with a Lokar shifter. The rack-and-pinion steering is taken from a Dodge Omni.

THE POWER PACK

4.6l (281ci) "modular" V8

In 1966, the Mustang was available with a 3277cc (200ci) inline six or a 4736cc (289ci) V8, in either 200bhp or 225/271bhp state of tune. The venerable cast-iron motor was considered too heavy for this Mustang and has been replaced by a 32-valve, 4.6l (281ci) modular Ford V8 unit with all-alloy construction. From its relatively small displacement, it produces 392bhp with the aid of a Kenne Bell twin-screw whipplecharger running at 2.7kg (6lb) of boost. This is in combination with a multipoint electronic fuel-injection system and a modern engine layout of four valves per cylinder operated by four chain-driven overhead camshafts.

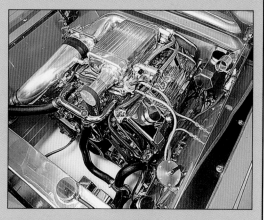

Dynamite

For some people, the pre-1967 Mustangs are the best of the breed. The lines are uncluttered and classic. When mated with a stiff chassis and powerful engine, excellence is created – exactly what this 1966 example is.

Tasteful modifications have not betrayed the Mustang's good looks.

Ford MUSTANG 1966

If you like the looks but not the performance, what can you do? Build your ideal car, of course. With nearly 400bhp and a chassis that can handle the power, this Mustang would be your dream car.

Supercharged engine

To get phenomenal performance from the Mustang, a 32-valve, all-alloy 4.6l (281ci) 'modular' Ford V8 engine, from a late-model Mustang Cobra, has been fitted. The power has been upped to 392bhp by the addition of a Kenne Bell supercharger running at 2.7kg (6lb) of boost.

Tangerine dream

Completing the modified look is the tangerine pearl custom paint scheme. The side scallops are finished in a blend of gold pearl and candy root beer.

Billet grill

A lot of attention has been paid to the look of this car. This is illustrated by the six-bar chrome front grill and the five-bar rear fascia, which incorporates 900 LEDs.

Four-wheel disc brakes

To balance the enhanced performance, disc brakes have been installed. At the front these are 27.9cm (11in) in diameter with 22.8cm (9in) ones at the rear.

Custom interior

As much work has gone into customizing the interior as modifying the mechanicals of this car. There are two shades of leather upholstery, cream and biscuit. There is also a wool carpet from a Mercedes, as well as modified 1965 T-Bird front seats.

Upgraded suspension

As with many modified first-generation Mustangs, this car uses the coil-sprung front suspension from the Mustang II. A chrome 22.8cm (9in) rear axle combines with a Global West stage III suspension system out back.

Specifications
1966 Ford Mustang

ENGINE
Type: V8

Construction: Alloy block and heads

Valve gear: Four valves per cylinder operated by four chain-driven overhead cams.

Bore and stroke: 92mm (3.61in) x 91mm (3.60in)

Displacement: 4605cc (281ci)

Compression ratio: 9.8:1

Induction system: Multipoint fuel injection with Kenne Bell twin-screw whipple supercharger

Maximum power: 392bhp at 5800rpm

Maximum torque: 405lb-ft at 4500rpm

Top speed: 227km/h (141mph)

0–96km/h (0–60mph): 4.3 sec.

TRANSMISSION
Three-speed automatic

BODY/CHASSIS
Steel chassis with steel body

SPECIAL FEATURES

Even the boot has been upholstered in matching fabrics.

RUNNING GEAR
Steering: Rack-and-pinion

Front suspension: A-arms with coil springs and telescopic shock absorbers

Rear suspension: Live rear axle with leaf springs and telescopic shock absorbers

Brakes: Discs, 27.9cm (11in) dia. (front),22.8cm (9in) dia. (rear)

Wheels: Alloy, 43.2cm (17) x 17.8cm (7in) (front); 43.2cm (17in) x 20.3cm (8in) (rear)

Tires: Toyo 215/45ZR17 (front), 245/45ZR17 (rear)

DIMENSIONS
Length: 4.47m (176.0in)

Width: 1.8cm (71.0in)

Height: 1.28m (50.3in)

Wheelbase: 274cm (108.0in)

Track: 149cm (58.6in) (front and rear)

Weight: 1070kg (2358lb)

Ford **MUSTANG GT/CS**

Greater competition within the ponycar ranks resulted in a drop in Mustang sales for 1968. Ford sought to rectify the situation with a spate of limited-edition models, like the GT/CS.

California Special

'...rich, creamy torque.'

'Compared to the 1964 Mustangs, the GT/CS places more emphasis on brawn and refinement. It is still unmistakably a Mustang, but take it out on the motorway and it demonstrates a different character than its forebears. With a heavy front weight bias, it will understeer through hard turns, but the trade-off is the grunt of the big-block 6391cc (390ci), which delivers an almost endless supply of rich, creamy torque.'

Safety was becoming important by 1968, evidenced by the padded dash and wheel.

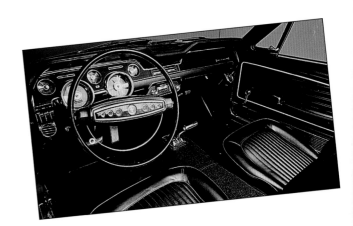

Milestones

1964 On April 17, Ford displays its new sporty Mustang at the New York World's Fair. Two bodystyles (coupe and convertible) are offered, as are engines ranging from a 2786cc (170ci) six to a 4736cc (289ci) hi-po V8 – with performance and luxury options.

The coupe was by far the most popular 1964 Mustang.

1966 Late in the year, the revised 1967 Mustang goes on sale. The big news is the arrival of a fastback and the availability of a big-block V8. Sales are down, yet still strong, with 472,121 Mustangs finding owners.

Mustang adopted a bigger, heavier look for 1967.

1968 A special promotional model, the GT/CS goes on sale. It has Shelby-style taillights, unique side treatment and a plain grill with twin driving lights.

UNDER THE SKIN

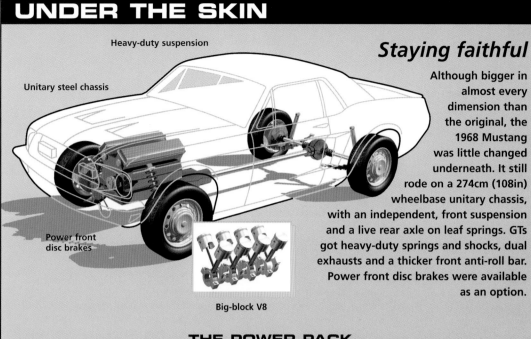

Heavy-duty suspension

Unitary steel chassis

Power front disc brakes

Big-block V8

Staying faithful

Although bigger in almost every dimension than the original, the 1968 Mustang was little changed underneath. It still rode on a 274cm (108in) wheelbase unitary chassis, with an independent, front suspension and a live rear axle on leaf springs. GTs got heavy-duty springs and shocks, dual exhausts and a thicker front anti-roll bar. Power front disc brakes were available as an option.

THE POWER PACK

More cubes

One of the major reasons for the increase in power for 1967 was to make the Mustang's engine bay big enough to accommodate big-block V8s. The first of these to be fitted was the 6391cc (390ci) mill. This engine is a member of the FE series of big-blocks, featuring, among other things, a cast-iron block and heads, a five-main-bearing crankshaft, hydraulic valve lifters and a dual-plane, cast-iron, intake manifold topped by a Holley four-barrel carburetor. The engine's greatest asset lies in its big, fat torque curve, for although it packs only 280bhp, it cranks out a mighty 403lb-ft at just 2600rpm.

A rare treat

The 1968 California Special was one of several special-edition Mustangs in the early years, and bore a resemblance to the High Country Special that year. Not many of these cars were sold new, and finding a fully optioned car would be quite a feat.

This GT/CS came loaded with options.

Ford MUSTANG GT/CS

CS stands for California Special, and as its name suggests, this limited-edition Mustang was a regional promotional model. It featured all the GT performance and handling features, plus a few of its own.

Big 390 V8
In many ways, the 390 was the ideal engine for the Mustang in 1968. It's smooth, tractable and packs a substantial wallop, thanks to its incredible 403lb-ft of torque.

Hardtop styling
To order the GT/CS, you had to start with the base hardtop coupe and then add the GT package and California Special trim option. The latter included special side scoops, Shelby-style taillights, a plain grill and special emblems.

Floating front calipers
A notable improvement of the 1968 Mustangs were floating calipers on the optional front disc brakes. These provide more balanced power compared to fixed calipers.

Safety features

The 1968 Mustang has an energy-absorbing dash and steering column, dual circuit brakes and a double-laminated windshield.

Heavy-duty suspension

The GT equipment includes uprated suspension, which in 1960s Detroit consisted of stiffened springs and shocks, plus a beefier front anti-roll bar.

Dual exhaust

1968 GTs also got a standard dual exhaust system, with (for just this year) quad tips protruding through the rear valance.

Specifications

1968 Ford Mustang GT/CS

ENGINE

Type: V8

Construction: Cast-iron block and heads

Valve gear: Two valves per cylinder operated by a single V-mounted camshaft with pushrods and rockers

Bore and stroke: 103mm (4.05in) x 96mm (3.78in)

Displacement: 6391cc (390ci)

Compression ratio: 10.5:1

Induction system: Single Holley four-barrel downdraft carburetor

Maximum power: 280bhp at 4400rpm

Maximum torque: 403lb-ft at 2600rpm

Top speed: 193km/h (120mph)

0–96km/h (0–60mph): 7.5 sec

TRANSMISSION

C6 Cruise-O-Matic three-speed automatic

BODY/CHASSIS

Steel unitary chassis with steel body panels

SPECIAL FEATURES

These side scoops are found only on 1968 CS, HCS and Shelby Mustangs.

A neat option were the turn signal repeaters in the bonnet scoops.

RUNNING GEAR

Steering: Recirculating-ball

Front suspension: Unequal-length A-arms, coil springs, telescopic shock absorbers and anti-roll bar

Rear suspension: Live axle, semi-elliptic leaf springs and telescopic shock absorbers

Brakes: Discs (front), drums (rear)

Wheels: 35.6cm (14in) x 17.8cm (7in) stamped steel

Tires: Goodyear Polyglas E70-14

DIMENSIONS

Length: 4.66m (183.6in)

Width: 1.75m (68.9in)

Height: 1.3m (51.2in)

Wheelbase: 274cm (108.0in)

Track: 149cm (58.5in) (front and rear)

Weight: 1195kg (2635lb)

Ford MUSTANG GT

Although the Mustang enjoyed a performance renaissance during the 1980s, it did not have the same romance as the original. For 1994, an all-new retro-styled car arrived, which has become progressively more sophisticated.

'...truly refined performance.'

'Compared to third-generation Mustangs, the current GT has much better ergonomics and feels tighter with no rattling or squeaking. The 4.6l (281ci) modular V8, however, does not have as much torque and doesn't feel as fast as the 5.0l (305ci) engine it replaced. Handling is noticeably better than the previous model and with much less understeer. Braking is excellent and safe, with standard ABS and four-wheel discs. The current 4.6l (281ci) Mustang GT offers truly refined performance.'

A twin-cowl dashboard layout is a retro touch that harks back to the original Mustang.

Milestones

1993 In the last month of the year the fourth-generation Mustang is launched in 3.8l (232ci) V6 or 5.0l (305ci) V8 forms, and in coupe or convertible body styles. The hatchback version is no longer offered.

Third-generation 5.0l (305ci) were very powerful and had the same performance as 1960s muscle cars.

1994 The Mustang celebrates its 30th birthday and a 240bhp Cobra version joins the range.

1995 A new modular 4.6l (281ci) V8 engine arrives for 1996. All Mustangs get new taillights; the GT gets 43.2cm (17in) wheels.

The Mustang is heavily facelifted for 1999.

1998 Responding to criticisms of lack of power, the GT gets an additional 10bhp. A standard value performance package is also offered to help boost flagging sales.

UNDER THE SKIN

Live rear axle

Unitary construction

MacPherson strut front suspension

Modular V8

Old hat

Although substantially revised for 1994, the current Mustang shares characteristics of the 1979–1993 'Fox' platform, with a conventional front engined, rear-drive format. The front suspension uses modified MacPherson struts on lower 'A'-arms, with a standard front anti-roll bar. The rear is a 22.3cm (8.8in) live axle that features both horizontal and vertical shocks to reduce axle tramp.

THE POWER PACK

Modular-mania

Known as the SN95, the current Mustang's base engine is a 3.8l (232ci) V6. Early fourth-generation GTs were powered by the venerable 5.0l (305ci) V8, although for 1996 this was replaced by a version of Ford's overhead-cam 'Modular V8.' Displacing 4.6l (281ci), this engine has an alloy block and cylinder heads, with a single overhead cam layout and a composite intake manifold. In current trim it puts out the same power as the old 5.0l (305ci) unit – 225bhp – but with less torque.

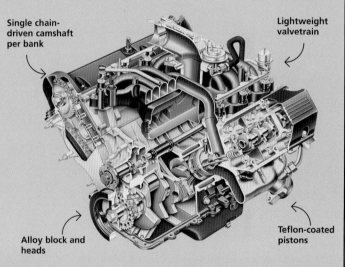

Single chain-driven camshaft per bank

Lightweight valvetrain

Alloy block and heads

Teflon-coated pistons

5l (305ci) is best

Although the 4.6l (281ci) is undeniably sophisticated, many prefer the 1994–1995 5.0l (305ci) cars. The old pushrod V8 is still satisfying and simpler to maintain. Best of all, there is an abundance of speed equipment to make these cars go even faster.

Many enthusiasts prefer the older 5.0l (305ci) Mustangs.

Ford **MUSTANG GT**

The GT was essentially a sport appearance package on the original Mustang and, since 1982, has been the mainstream performance variant. Current GTs are often loaded with options, although they still offer plenty of power.

Choice of body styles

Current Mustangs come in either two-door coupe or convertible forms. In the interests of torsional rigidity, the hatchback style, as seen on the 1979–1993 model, was discontinued.

Modern V8 engine

The Mustang underwent something of a revolution in 1996 when the old pushrod V8 was replaced by a modern overhead-cam unit. The engine, although smaller in displacement (4.6l/281ci versus 5.0l/305ci), comes close to duplicating the power of the 5.0l (305ci) engine it replaces.

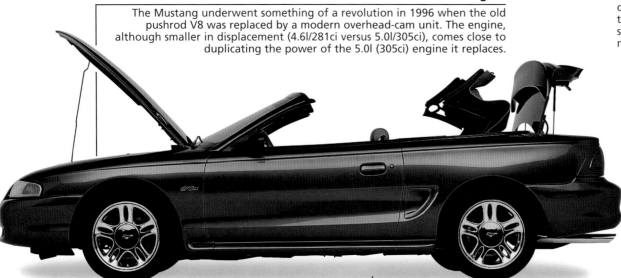

Luxury equipment

Cruise control, twin airbags, air-conditioning, tilt steering and foglights are popular optional equipment. Power windows, door locks, mirrors and lumbar support are all standard on the Mustang GT.

Quadrashock rear suspension

Since 1985, all factory V8-powered Mustangs have had an extra pair of rear shocks, mounted horizontally, to reduce axle wind-up under hard, standing-start acceleration.

Retro-styling

When Ford consulted enthusiasts on how the fourth-generation Mustang should look, many wanted a return to the original 1965. Thus, the current car features retro touches such as side scoops and triple taillights and the pony emblem in the grill. However, it remains contemporary and aerodynamically efficient.

Four-wheel disc brakes

Braking was always a problem on late third-generation cars. However, the current Mustang is fitted with four-wheel ABS-assisted disc brakes, which are a great improvement.

Five-speed transmission

All Mustangs can be ordered with the Borg-Warner T-45 five-speed manual transmission, with two sets of final-drive ratios: 2.73 or 3.08:1. Many buyers specify the optional 4R70W four-speed automatic, which is remarkably refined.

Specifications

1998 Ford Mustang GT

ENGINE

Type: V8

Construction: Alloy block and heads

Valve gear: Two valves per cylinder operated by a single overhead camshaft per bank

Bore and stroke: 91mm (3.60in) x 91mm (3.60in)

Displacement: 4.6l (281ci)

Compression ratio: 9.0:1

Induction system: Sequential electronic fuel injection

Maximum power: 225bhp at 4400rpm

Maximum torque: 285lb-ft at 3500rpm

Top speed: 227km/h (141mph)

0–96km/h (0–60mph): 6.3 sec

TRANSMISSION

Borg-Warner T-45 five-speed manual

BODY/CHASSIS

Integral chassis with two-door steel convertible body

SPECIAL FEATURES

A strut tower brace helps to improve body stiffness.

A large rear spoiler is standard with the Mustang GT package.

RUNNING GEAR

Steering: Rack-and-pinion

Front suspension: MacPherson struts with coil springs and shock absorbers

Rear suspension: Live axle with coil springs and quad shock absorbers

Brakes: Discs (front and rear)

Wheels: Alloy, 43.2cm (17in) dia.

Tires: Goodyear Eagle 245/45 ZR17

DIMENSIONS

Length: 4.61m (181.5in)

Width: 1.82m (71.5in)

Height: 1.25m (53.0in)

Wheelbase: 257cm (101.2in)

Track: 152cm (60.0in) (front), 149cm (58.6in) (rear)

Weight: 1544kg (3462lb)

Ford **MUSTANG BOSS 302**

Released as a limited production special in 1969, the Mustang Boss 302 proved highly successful both on the road and on the track. The owner of this car took the concept a stage further and transformed a tired Boss 302 into his interpretation of what a Trans Am racer should be.

'...goes where you want.'

'Climb into the high-back bucket seat, strap yourself in and savour the competition-style interior. The highly-tuned 4949cc (302ci) V8 is lumpy at idle, but on the move it propels the Mustang like a scalded cat, pulling hard in all four gears. Tug the steering wheel and the Boss responds instantly, going exactly where you want. There is virtually no body roll through corners and the huge brakes slow the Boss quickly.'

Except for the equipment necessary for competition, the interior is mostly stock.

Milestones

1969 Ford releases

a larger, curvier Mustang with more emphasis on performance. A special limited edition Trans Am racer, the Boss 302, debuts mid-year. Ford enters race-prepared examples in the Trans Am Championship and they finish second to the Penske/Donohue Camaro Z28s.

First-generation Mustangs share components with the Falcon.

1970 All Mustangs

are given a mild facelift with single headlights and a revised tail panel, and road-going Boss 302s receive hydraulic valve lifters. On the track, the cars prove more competitive than ever. Boss driver Parnelli Jones and Ford win the driver and constructor's championships.

Ford's main rival in the Trans Am wars was the Camaro Z28.

1971 A new Boss

351 replaces the 302. Ford decides to retire from racing mid-year and no Bosses are built after 1971.

UNDER THE SKIN

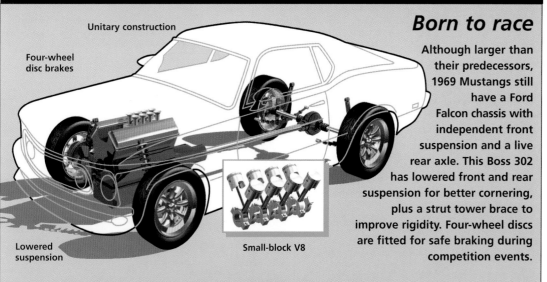

Unitary construction

Four-wheel disc brakes

Lowered suspension

Small-block V8

Born to race

Although larger than their predecessors, 1969 Mustangs still have a Ford Falcon chassis with independent front suspension and a live rear axle. This Boss 302 has lowered front and rear suspension for better cornering, plus a strut tower brace to improve rigidity. Four-wheel discs are fitted for safe braking during competition events.

THE POWER PACK

Exotic Boss

Available for only two seasons, the high-performance Boss 302 is perfectly suited to vintage road racing. This car has been tuned up considerably and features a roller camshaft, forged steel crank and connecting rods, ACCEL injection, braided hoses plus a special baffled oil pan and eight Autolite in-line carburettors atop a Doug Nash-modified Hilborn intake manifold. It has a power output of 400bhp and 343lb-ft of torque, making this Mustang a serious race contender.

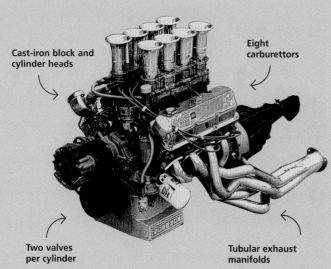

Cast-iron block and cylinder heads

Eight carburettors

Two valves per cylinder

Tubular exhaust manifolds

Highly prized

Road racing is gaining in popularity in the US. The Boss 302 is a milestone Mustang in its own right and highly competitive in this form. Consequently, both street and racing versions are very much in demand by collectors and enthusiasts.

Boss 302s are still seen at road racing events across the US.

Ford **MUSTANG BOSS 302**

This one-of-a-kind, pristine Boss 302 road racer combines a high-tech chassis and suspension with some very exotic and rare engine and drivetrain components.

Reworked engine

Standard Boss 302s are rated at 290bhp, but this one, with its multiple-carburetor free-flowing cylinder heads and exhaust manifolds, is rated at an impressive 400bhp.

Interior alterations

This Boss retains the original high-back bucket seats, but four-point harnesses, a Mallory tachometer and Grant steering wheel have been added.

Big wheels and tyres

During the 1969 season, the factory Boss 302s ran with Minilite wheels. A set of these classic wheels, which have been chromed and shod with modern Goodyear tyres, are fitted to this racer.

Stock body

Despite the radical internal modifications the body remains fairly stock, with no spoilers or unnecessary additions.

Lowered suspension
For better handling and stability, this Boss has been lowered with relocated control arms and reversed-rolled rear leaf springs.

Original paint
The policy of keeping the exterior appearance of this 302 as original as possible even extends to the paintwork. It is painted in Calypso Coral, a factory available colour on Boss 302s in 1969. The black stripes however, have been added by the owner.

Uprated transmission
A Ford 22.8cm (9in) rear end with a 4.11:1 set of gears sends the power to the rear wheels. A 5.43:1 Detroit Locker rear end can be installed if required.

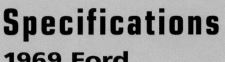

Specifications
1969 Ford Mustang Boss 302

ENGINE

Type: V8

Construction: Cast-iron block and heads

Valve gear: Two valves per cylinder operated by a single camshaft via pushrods and rockers

Bore and stroke: 102mm (4in) x 76mm (3in)

Displacement: 4949cc (302ci)

Compression ratio: 10.5:1

Induction system: Eight Autolite carburettors giving 2850cfm

Maximum power: 400bhp at 6500rpm

Maximum torque: 343lb-ft at 4300rpm

Top speed: 206km/h (128mph)

0–96km/h (0–60mph): 6.5 sec

TRANSMISSION

Borg-Warner T-10 four-speed manual

BODY/CHASSIS

Steel monocoque with two-door body

SPECIAL FEATURES

Eight carburettor stacks poke through the bonnet.

RUNNING GEAR

Steering: Recirculating ball

Front suspension: Unequal length wishbones with coil springs, telescopic shocks and anti-roll bar

Rear suspension: Live axle with multi-leaf springs, telescopic shocks and anti-roll bar

Brakes: Power discs (front and rear)

Wheels: Minilite spoked magnesium, 20.3cm (8in) x 38.1cm (15in)

Tyres: Goodyear P225/50 ZR15

DIMENSIONS

Length: 4.75m (187in)

Width: 1.83m (72in)

Height: 1.19m (47in)

Wheelbase: 274cm (108in)

Track: 168cm (66in) (front), 157cm (61.8in) (rear)

Weight: 1456kg (3209lb)

Ford MUSTANG BOSS 351

Based on the newly redesigned SportsRoof, the Boss 351 superseded the previous Boss 302 and 429 versions. It was larger and less distinctive in appearance, but was quicker, less temperamental and still offered fine handling for a large muscle car of the period.

'...great all-round performer.'

'Compared to its predecessor, the Boss 351 is a great all-round performer. It offers quicker off-the-line acceleration and enjoys high speed cornering, although it still remains susceptible to oversteer. The massive size of the Boss 351 means it feels a little unwieldy in traffic, plus the harsh ride and low-set driving position can be tiring, but muscle-era Mustang performance does not come much more user friendly than this.'

The 1971 model was the first Mustang not to use a dual cowl dashboard layout.

Milestones

1969 With its 'Total Performance' campaign in full swing, Ford releases two limited-production special Mustangs, the Boss 302 and 429. The 302 is built to satisfy Trans Am rules and has a high-revving 4949cc (302ci) Windsor V8. A big-block version, the 429, uses a 'semi-Hemi' V8 and is designed as a homologation special so the race-prepared Talladegas can run these engines in NASCAR.

A total of 8641 Boss 302s were built between 1969 and 1970.

1970 The Boss 302 continues in production, but the 351 Cleveland V8 engine is developed with canted valve heads. A larger Mustang on a 2.5cm (1in) longer wheelbase arrives for 1971, and a Boss 351 replaces both previous Bosses.

In 1971, the biggest-engined Mustang was the Mach 1 429 CJ.

1971 With Ford having pulled out of racing, the Boss 351 is dropped halfway through the model year.

UNDER THE SKIN

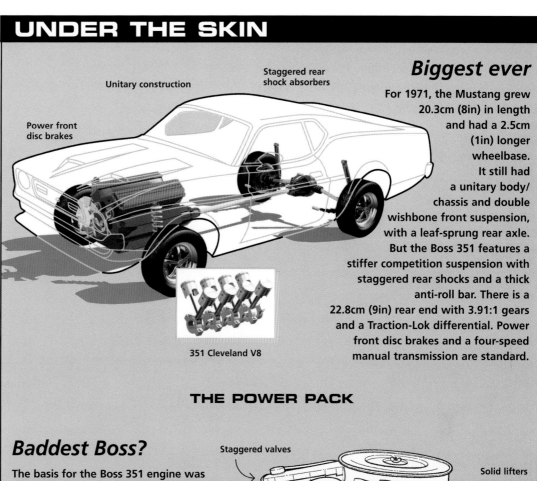

Unitary construction

Staggered rear shock absorbers

Power front disc brakes

351 Cleveland V8

Biggest ever

For 1971, the Mustang grew 20.3cm (8in) in length and had a 2.5cm (1in) longer wheelbase. It still had a unitary body/chassis and double wishbone front suspension, with a leaf-sprung rear axle. But the Boss 351 features a stiffer competition suspension with staggered rear shocks and a thick anti-roll bar. There is a 22.8cm (9in) rear end with 3.91:1 gears and a Traction-Lok differential. Power front disc brakes and a four-speed manual transmission are standard.

THE POWER PACK

Baddest Boss?

The basis for the Boss 351 engine was the 5752cc (351ci) Cleveland V8. This cast-iron unit has canted-valve cylinder heads and huge ports in the intake manifold. For the Boss, the connecting rods were shot-peened and Magna-fluxed for strength, and forged aluminum pistons were specified, as was an aggressive camshaft with solid lifters. Atop the intake is a 750cfm four-barrel carburettor. The result is an incredibly robust and powerful engine that cranks out 330bhp.

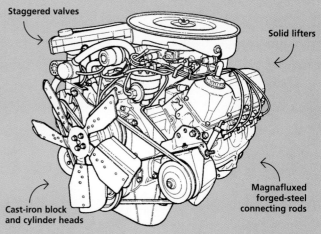

Staggered valves

Solid lifters

Magnafluxed forged-steel connecting rods

Cast-iron block and cylinder heads

Final fling

While the Boss 351 isn't as popular as the Boss 302 or 429, it still has strong collectible status. The large Boss 351 was also one of the quickest cars to come out of Detroit in 1971. Only 1806 Boss 351s were built before it was dropped.

Although collectible, Boss 351s are cheaper than earlier muscle Mustangs.

Ford MUSTANG BOSS 351

Ford released its largest ever Mustang in 1971, and the tip of the performance sword was the Boss 351. It was arguably the last of the true muscle Mustangs and today appeals to a generation of car enthusiasts.

Cleveland V8

The Boss 351 came with a 330bhp, 5752cc (351ci) Cleveland V8. It has large angled valves and huge ports, allowing it to breathe better than the 351 Windsor. It is strengthened to run safely at high rpm and high power.

Four-speed transmission

All 351s were equipped with a Hurst-shifted Borg-Warner T10 four-speed and a 22.8cm (9in) differential with 3.91:1 final drive. This made it the quickest-accelerating Mustang in 1971.

Live axle

The 1971 Boss 351 has a heavy duty 22.8cm (9in) rear axle and semi-elliptic leaf springs. Performance models have staggered rear shocks (one behind and one in front of the axle) to help reduce wheelspin off the line. Boss 351s also have a larger-diameter anti-roll bar.

Flat rear window

One of the main styling features of the 1971 model year SportsRoof Mustangs was a near-horizontal rear deck. Unfortunately, it hindered rearward vision somewhat.

Wishbone front suspension

The double wishbone front suspension features stiffer springs and shock absorbers and a massive front anti-roll bar. The suspension had been strengthened for the earlier Boss 302 with reinforcement to the shock housings and larger-diameter wheel spindles to withstand cornering forces.

Front discs

Boss 351s came standard with large, vented front disc brakes and smaller drums at the rear. They could stop the 351 in about 76m (250ft) from 129km/h (80mph).

Polyglas tyres

Back in 1971, very few cars had radials, and so Boss 351s ran on bias-ply tyres. This one has the optional Goodyear Polyglas GTs and Magnum 500 wheels, which give it good at-the-limit handling.

Colour-coded graphics

The air-scooped bonnet includes a colour-coded center section. Dark-coloured cars have this painted silver, while light-coloured cars have it painted semi-gloss black. This reduces glare from the sunlight bouncing off the bonnet and into the driver's direct line of sight.

Specifications

1971 Ford Mustang Boss 351

ENGINE

Type: V8

Construction: Cast-iron block and heads

Valve gear: Two valves per cylinder operated by a single camshaft via pushrods, solid valve lifters and rockers

Bore and stroke: 102mm (4.0in) x 76mm (3.0in)

Displacement: 5752cc (351ci)

Compression ratio: 11.0:1

Induction system: Autolite four-barrel carburettor

Maximum power: 330bhp at 5400rpm

Maximum torque: 370lb-ft at 4000rpm

Top speed: 187km/h (116mph)

0–96km/h (0–60mph): 5.8 sec

TRANSMISSION

Borg-Warner T10 four-speed manual

BODY/CHASSIS

Steel unitary chassis with two-door 2+2 SportsRoof body

SPECIAL FEATURES

351 RAM AIR

Ram Air induction was standard on Boss 351s and optional on Mach 1s.

RUNNING GEAR

Steering: Recirculating ball

Front suspension: Double wishbones with coil springs, telescopic shock absorbers and anti-roll bar

Rear suspension: Live axle with semi-elliptic leaf springs, angled telescopic shock absorbers and anti-roll bar

Brakes: Vented discs, 28.7cm (11.3in) dia. (front), drums, 25.4cm (10in) dia. (rear)

Wheels: Pressed-steel discs, 17.8cm (7in) x 38.1cm (15in)

Tyres: Goodyear Polyglas GT, F60-15

DIMENSIONS

Length: 4.81m (189.5in)

Width: 1.88m (74.1in)

Height: 1.28m (50.1in)

Wheelbase: 277cm (109.0in)

Track: 156cm (61.5in) (front), 155cm (61.0in) (rear)

Weight: 1610kg (3550lb)

Ford **MUSTANG BOSS 429**

The Boss 429 Mustang was built to satisfy Ford's need to qualify at least 500 production vehicles with its new engine for NASCAR racing. Rather than putting the engine in the mid-size Torinos it ran for stock car racing, Ford put the engine in the sleek and exciting Mustang fastback instead.

'...a rippling mass of power.'

'Those who expected the Mustang Boss 429 to be a Corvette® killer were disappointed by its true intent. With a semi-hemi engine that offered high-revving performance, the Boss 429 was a rippling mass of power, but was somewhat disappointing behind the wheel. It's at 6000rpm and above where the 429 NASCAR engine makes its power, so it's not much of a street dominator. It's hard to imagine why Ford made such a car. But the Boss 429 was actually a successful homologation exercise.'

All Boss 429s were treated with plush interiors and an 8000rpm tachometer.

Milestones

1969 The Mustang

is redesigned with a sleeker body. Performance models include 857 Boss 429s, built to sanction Ford's new NASCAR 429 V8 engine. Once the Boss 429s were homologated for NASCAR, race-prepared Torinos known as Talladegas used the massive V8s. Ford took the title away from Dodge's Hemi Daytonas with more than 30 wins in the 1969 season, thanks to the brawny 429 engines.

The early Shelby GT350 was the forerunner of the Boss Mustang.

1970 Mild restyling

for the second, and last, year of the Boss 429 includes a new nose, a revised tail light panel, plus a black bonnet scoop. Minor engine modifications include solid lifters. Again, Ford uses the same combination for NASCAR. Unfortunately, Plymouth's aerodynamic Hemi Superbird proves to be more successful.

The fearsome 428 Cobrajets were more fun on the street than the Boss 429s.

UNDER THE SKIN

Traction Lok differential with 3.91:1 gears

Massive '429' bonnet scoop

Chin spoiler

Wider front track

Big-block V8

Not quite stock

The Boss 429 features an altered front suspension, with relocated shock absorbers, which results in a wider track. All Boss 429s were equipped with a 4-speed Top Loader transmission, Traction Lok differential, relocated battery, front and rear stabilizers, quicker power steering and power front disc brakes.

THE POWER PACK

Bred for racing

This 429 engine was a homologation exercise – at least 500 had to be built to allow it to race in NASCAR, so it was no ordinary engine. It has four-bolt mains, forged steel crankshaft, high (10.5:1) compression, semi-hemi combustion chambers (similar to Chrysler's Hemi), Holley 735cfm four-barrel carb, and headers. It could easily rev past 6000rpm. The big 429 engine was put in the restyled Mustang, and not the mid-size Torinos it was used in for NASCAR racing.

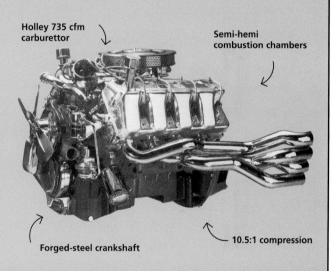

Holley 735 cfm carburettor

Semi-hemi combustion chambers

Forged-steel crankshaft

10.5:1 compression

Race-bred?

In 1969, muscle car fans thought Ford had built a car to run with the big-block Corvettes. They were saddened to learn that the car was made to homologate the engine for use in NASCAR racing. Despite being a rev-happy engine, the Boss 429 could run the ¼ mile in 14 seconds. It was the most expensive non-Shelby Mustang.

Solid lifters, which allow for higher rpm, were used in 1970 Boss 429s.

Ford **MUSTANG BOSS 429**

Built for just two model years, the Boss 429 is one of the rarest and most valuable of all Mustangs. The homologated high-performance Boss 429 engine, however, earned Ford 30 wins in the 1969 NASCAR season.

Deluxe interior
All 429s have a deluxe interior with full instrumentation, including an 8000rpm tachometer deeply inset into the dashboard and improved seats, but air conditioning was not an option.

Front spoiler
A functional front airdam was optional. At highway speeds, it offers little aerodynamic advantage, however.

Close-ratio transmission
A close-ratio, four-speed manual is the only transmission available on the Boss 429. Automatics weren't strong enough and couldn't handle the 429's torque.

Boot-mounted battery
The huge and heavy V8 leaves little room for anything else in the tightly packed engine bay, including the battery. Ford engineers were forced to relocate it to the boot.

Modified front suspension

As well as having the stiffest springs fitted to any Mustang up to that time, the Boss 429 has a thick, 24mm (15/16in) diameter, front anti-roll bar and revalved shocks.

7030cc (429ci) engine

The 429s cylinder heads were so wide that not only did the battery have to be mounted in the boot, but the shock towers had to be spread apart just to get the engine to fit.

Specifications

1969 Ford Mustang Boss 429

ENGINE

Type: V8

Construction: Cast-iron block and aluminum cylinder heads

Valve gear: Two valves per cylinder operated by a block-mounted camshaft

Bore and stroke: 110mm (4.36in) x 92mm (3.59in)

Displacement: 7030cc (429ci)

Compression ratio: 10.5:1

Induction system: Four-barrel carburettor

Maximum power: 375bhp at 5200rpm

Maximum torque: 450lb-ft at 3400rpm

Top speed: 190km/h (118mph)

0–96km/h (0–60mph): 6.8 sec

TRANSMISSION

Top Loader close-ratio manual transmission

BODY/CHASSIS

Steel-frame chassis with steel two-door fastback body

SPECIAL FEATURES

These distinctive side scoops are unique to the 1969 model Boss 429.

RUNNING GEAR

Steering: Recirculating ball

Front suspension: Upper and lower wishbones, coil springs, telescopic shocks and anti-roll bar

Rear suspension: Live axle with semi-elliptical leaf springs, staggered telescopic shocks and anti-roll bar

Brakes: Discs front, drums rear

Wheels: Magnum 500, 17.8cm (7in) x 38.1cm (15in)

Tyres: Goodyear Polyglas GT F60 x 38.1cm (15in)

DIMENSIONS

Length: 4.75m (187in)

Width: 1.83m (72in)

Height: 1.24m (49in)

Wheelbase: 274cm (108in)

Track: 151cm (59.3in) (front), 149cm (58.8in) (rear)

Weight: 1755kg (3870lb)

Ford MUSTANG COBRA

With its 235bhp and true muscle car performance, the 1993 Mustang Cobra was a fitting finale for the tremendously successful Fox-platform Mustang, which lasted an incredible 14 seasons with more than 2 million cars sold.

'...civilized performer.'

'It takes a second glance to distinguish the Cobra from a regular GT, but once the car is in motion, the differences begin to surface. A lighter clutch makes for faster shifting and the small-block V8 has a useful increase in both power and torque. An SVT altered chassis and suspension mean that the Cobra has better grip than its stock counterpart. When it comes to hard cornering, the Cobra is reminiscent of the Shelby Mustangs of the 1960s.'

The bland interior of the Cobra masks the exciting performance that can be unleashed.

Milestones

1987 The Mustang receives a facelift. All models get flush headlights, revised side glass and a new instrument panel. The series is reduced to just the LX and GT with two powerplants – a 2.3l (140ci) four and 5.0l (305ci) V8.

The two-door coupe was the most inexpensive model of the Mustang 5.0l (lineup in 1993.

1989 Instead of an option package, the LX 5.0L becomes a separate model.

1990 A driver's airbag and door map pockets are standard.

For 1996, the Mustang Cobra got a 305bhp, 4.6l (281ci) engine.

1991 LX 5.0Ls and GTs are fitted with bigger 40.6cm (16in) wheels as standard.

1993 A special Cobra model is released.

UNDER THE SKIN

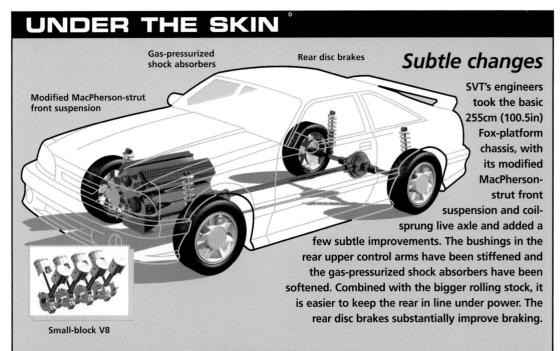

Modified MacPherson-strut front suspension

Gas-pressurized shock absorbers

Rear disc brakes

Small-block V8

Subtle changes

SVT's engineers took the basic 255cm (100.5in) Fox-platform chassis, with its modified MacPherson-strut front suspension and coil-sprung live axle and added a few subtle improvements. The bushings in the rear upper control arms have been stiffened and the gas-pressurized shock absorbers have been softened. Combined with the bigger rolling stock, it is easier to keep the rear in line under power. The rear disc brakes substantially improve braking.

THE POWER PACK

Legendary Powerplant

Possibly one of the most amazing traits of the 5.0L Mustang is its 4949cc (302ci), small-block V8. The little Windsor unit cranked out a credible 205bhp and 275lb-ft of torque in 1993, but for the Cobra more performance was needed. A bigger throttle body and mass air meter were coupled with Ford Motorsport GT40 free-breathing cylinder heads, 10.9kg (24lb) fuel injectors, stronger valve springs and a new intake plenum. A revised camshaft was specified with less overlap and roller rockers helped minimize valvetrain friction. The result was an additional 30bhp and 10lb-ft of torque, with 0–96km/h (0–60mph) taking just 5.8 seconds.

Collectible

Besides being the best-performing factory Fox Mustang, the 1993 model is also the most collectible. Including the 107 'R' models, only 5100 Cobras were built. They were sold at only 200 select SVT dealers. A clean, original Cobra can cost more than $20,000.

The limited availability of the Cobra has ensured its desirable status.

185

Ford MUSTANG COBRA

In many ways, the Cobra was a more subtle alternative to the GT. It boasts greater levels of performance and, at the same time, was more civilized. From the Dearborn factory, Cobras came with either red, black or teal paint.

Subtle styling changes

From the outside, the Cobra differs little from the GT. The front grill houses a running horse emblem, the side scoops have been eliminated and a new rear bumper and decklid spoiler fitted. The taillights are from the SVO.

Small-block V8 engine

Although power was increased only modestly from 205bhp to 235bhp, it translated into a useful amount of mid-range grunt that greatly helped in the acceleration department.

Traction-Lok rear

All Mustangs with automatic transmissions could be ordered with 3.27:1 gears. Cars with 5-speed transmissions could only get gears as steep as 3.07:1.

Revised suspension tuning

Although the modified MacPherson-strut and coil-sprung live axle was retained, SVT engineers fitted stiffer bushings in the upper control arms and actually softened damping rates. The result is a smoother ride and greater cornering stability.

Minimal interior changes

The only difference between the Cobra and the GT is a set of Cobra-embroidered floor-mats. The dashboard, gauges and seats are all unchanged, and, like the GT, all Cobras came with power windows and mirrors.

Specifications

1993 Ford Mustang Cobra

ENGINE

Type: V8

Construction: Cast-iron block and heads

Valve gear: Two valves per cylinder operated by a single V-mounted camshaft

Bore and stroke: 102mm (4.0in) x 76mm (3.0in)

Displacement: 5.0l (305ci)

Compression ratio: 9.0:1

Maximum power: 235bhp at 5000rpm

Maximum torque: 285lb-ft at 4000rpm

Top speed: 243km/h (151mph)

0–96km/h (0–60mph): 5.8 sec

Fuel system: Sequential multipoint electronic fuel injection

TRANSMISSION

Borg-Warner T-5 five-speed manual

BODY/CHASSIS

Steel unitary chassis with three-door hatchback body

SPECIAL FEATURES

The factory-fitted flip-open sunroof was available as an option.

RUNNING GEAR

Steering: Rack-and-pinion

Front suspension: MacPherson struts, lower A-arm, coil springs and anti-roll bar

Rear suspension: Live axle with coil springs, semi-trailing arms, telescopic shock absorbers (two longitudinally, two horizontally) and anti-roll bar

Brakes: Vented discs, 27.4cm (10.8in) (front), solid disc 25.7cm (10.1in) (rear)

Wheels: Cast aluminium, 43.2cm (17in) x 19cm (7.5in)

Tyres: Goodyear Eagle GT, P245/45 ZR17

DIMENSIONS

Length: 4.55m (179.3in)

Width: 1.76m (69.1in)

Height: 1.32m (52.1in)

Wheelbase: 255cm (100.5in)

Track: 144cm (56.6in) (front), 145cm (57.0in) (rear)

Weight: 1463kg (3225lb)

Ford **MUSTANG COBRA R**

The name Cobra is synonymous with high-performance Ford automobiles. In 1995, Ford's Special Vehicle Team (SVT) unveiled a very special Mustang, which was built to compete on the track. It was known as the Cobra R.

'...well-balanced.'

'Massive torque at low rpm is a good recipe, and that's what the Cobra R has. All the power you're going to get has come by 4800rpm, and so there is no point revving the big motor beyond that; however the torque comes along with instant throttle response. It is a hard ride on anything but a smooth surface, but it's worth it, as it turns a fine-handling Mustang into an excellent one – well-balanced and responsive with superb braking ability.'

The Cobra is equipped with only the absolute necessities, which does not include a radio.

Milestones

1993 Ford builds a limited edition homologation special – the Cobra R (R for race). All 107 cars were painted Vibrant Red and had a Cobra intake, strut tower brace, 33cm (13in) front brakes and no rear seat.

Among the last of the Fox generation Mustangs was the limited production Cobra R.

1995 In the never-ending war with the Camaro Z28, Ford SVT fit a heavily modified all-iron, pushrod, overhead-valve, 5752cc (351ci) V8 into the Mustang, which produces 300bhp. Only 250 of the limited edition Cobra Rs are built.

For 1998 the Mustang Cobra received R-type alloy wheels.

1996 Both the GT and Cobra receive a new 4.6l (281ci) V8 engine.

1998 The spirit of the Cobra R lives on in the standard 300bhp, 4.6l (281ci) Cobra, which is fitted with new R model type five-spoke alloy wheels.

UNDER THE SKIN

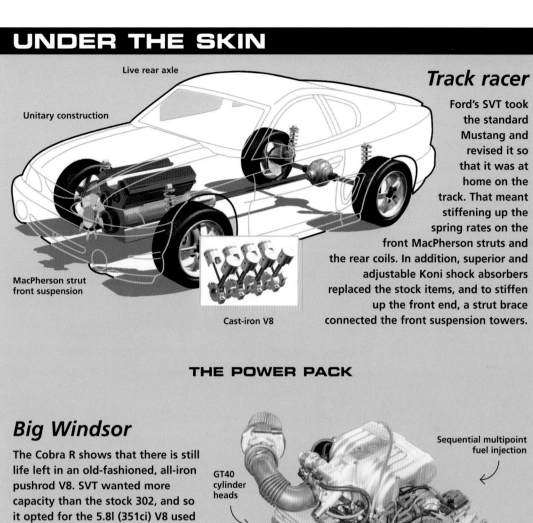

Live rear axle

Unitary construction

MacPherson strut front suspension

Cast-iron V8

Track racer

Ford's SVT took the standard Mustang and revised it so that it was at home on the track. That meant stiffening up the spring rates on the front MacPherson struts and the rear coils. In addition, superior and adjustable Koni shock absorbers replaced the stock items, and to stiffen up the front end, a strut brace connected the front suspension towers.

THE POWER PACK

Big Windsor

The Cobra R shows that there is still life left in an old-fashioned, all-iron pushrod V8. SVT wanted more capacity than the stock 302, and so it opted for the 5.8l (351ci) V8 used in the F150 Lightning truck. With a longer stroke and Ford Special Vehicle Operations (SVO) GT-40 cylinder heads and intake manifold, it puts out 300bhp at 4800rpm and an incredible 365lb-ft of torque at 3750rpm. On the street, few factory-stock cars can outdrag the muscular Cobra R.

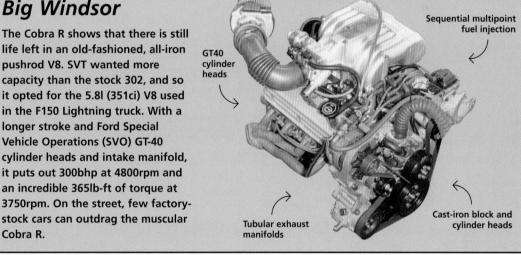

GT40 cylinder heads

Sequential multipoint fuel injection

Tubular exhaust manifolds

Cast-iron block and cylinder heads

Less is more

Ford commissioned SVT to build only 250 1995 Cobra Rs. All are Crystal White and have minimal sound-deadening and no air-conditioning or radio. Although they were built for racing, the Rs are fully street legal and command premium prices.

Despite being built as a racer, the Cobra is surprisingly usable.

Ford MUSTANG COBRA R

Produced by Ford's Special Vehicle Team as a limited production special and designed to compete in SCCA showroom stock racing, the Cobra R is the ultimate factory-stock SN95 Mustang.

Composite hood
The flat factory hood has been replaced with this lightweight high rise cowl induction piece. The extra clearance is needed to fit the taller intake manifold.

V8 engine
Ford's SVT chose the 5.8l (351ci) V8 to power the Cobra. Fitted with special cylinder heads, it produces an astounding 300bhp at 4800rpm.

Five-speed transmission
The extra torque from the bigger 5.8l (351ci) engine meant replacing the existing Borg-Warner five-speed with a stronger Tremec 3550 transmission, which also has five gears.

Low-profile tires
The extra stiff suspension springs ensure the low-profile, unidirectional 245/45 ZR17 BF Goodrich Comp T/As remain 'square' to the track, so that the maximum amount of rubber is in contact with the road.

Huge fuel load
The thirsty, high-powered V8 engine required a change to the fuel tank for racing. The standard tank was swapped for a custom fabricated fuel cell. It has more resistance to rupturing on impact and a larger capacity of 75.6l (20 gallons).

Adjustable brake balance

Braking in the Cobra R is excellent due to the combination of twin-piston calipers. What really sets it apart from a standard road car is the adjustable brake balance front to rear.

Specifications

1995 Ford Mustang Cobra R

ENGINE

Type: V8

Construction: Cast-iron block and heads

Valve gear: Two valves per cylinder operated by pushrods and rockers

Bore and stroke: 102mm (4.00in) x 89mm (3.50in)

Displacement: 5752cc (351ci)

Compression ratio: 9.2:1

Induction system: Electronic fuel injection

Maximum power: 300bhp at 4800rpm

Maximum torque: 365lb-ft at 3750rpm

Top speed: 241km/h (150mph)

0–96km/h (0–60mph): 5.5 sec

TRANSMISSION

Tremec 3550 five-speed manual

BODY/CHASSIS

Steel monocoque two-door coupe body

SPECIAL FEATURES

On all R models the foglights were removed to save weight, but the holes were left open. They feed air to a power steering and oil cooler.

A Cobra emblem on the injection plenum signifies that this is no run-of-the-mill Mustang.

RUNNING GEAR

Steering: Rack-and-pinion

Front suspension: Modified MacPherson struts with adjustable Koni inserts and anti-roll bar

Rear suspension: Live axle with upper and lower trailing links, coil springs, telescopic adjustable Koni shock absorbers and anti-roll bar

Brakes: Vented discs, 33cm (13.0in) dia. (front), 29.6cm (11.65in) dia. (rear)

Wheels: Alloy, 20.3cm (8in) x 43.2cm (17in)

Tires: BF Goodrich Comp T/A, 245/45 ZR17

DIMENSIONS

Length: 4.64m (182.5in)

Width: 1.82m (71.8in)

Height: 1.35m (53.2in)

Wheelbase: 257cm (101.3in)

Track: 152cm (60.0in) (front), 149cm (58.7in) (rear)

Ford MUSTANG MACH 1

1973 was the final year of the big, original-style Mustang. The pick of the range was the Mach 1. It looked sporty, had special interior trim, competition suspension and standard V8 power. It was one of the most popular of Ford's ponycar range.

'...sporty aspirations.'

'A standard 1973 Mustang is a long way from the original 1964 model. It became known as the Mustang that was bigger, heavier and plusher but not really as sporty as its forebearer. The Mach I, with its 4949cc (302ci) V8 changed that myth. It may not have a sense of urgency to it, but the Mach 1 offers adequate acceleration compared to other 1973 muscle missiles. The competition suspension virtually eliminates body roll, while ride comfort remains soft for a car with sporty aspirations.'

The Mach 1's sporty theme extends to the cabin, with extra gauges and tach as standard.

Milestones

1969 The very first Mach 1 performance SportsRoof model is launched by Ford in response to demand.

A matte-black bonnet section with an aggressive bonnet scoop were typical trademarks of the 1969 Mach 1.

1971 The Mustang grows in all dimensions, addressing previous criticisms of cramped passenger space on early ponycars. There is extra space under the bonnet, too. Among other options, the 429 Cobra Jet V8 is offered, packing all of 375bhp.

By 1974, in Mustang II guise, the Mach 1 was built for an environmentally conscious market.

1973 In its last year before it was replaced by the slimmer, more economical Mustang II (fitting, given the approaching fuel crisis), the Mustang is offered in a range of five variations, topped by the sporty Mach 1.

UNDER THE SKIN

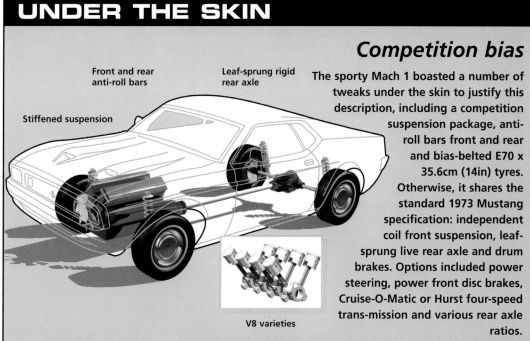

Front and rear anti-roll bars

Leaf-sprung rigid rear axle

Stiffened suspension

V8 varieties

THE POWER PACK

Competition bias

The sporty Mach 1 boasted a number of tweaks under the skin to justify this description, including a competition suspension package, anti-roll bars front and rear and bias-belted E70 x 35.6cm (14in) tyres. Otherwise, it shares the standard 1973 Mustang specification: independent coil front suspension, leaf-sprung live rear axle and drum brakes. Options included power steering, power front disc brakes, Cruise-O-Matic or Hurst four-speed trans-mission and various rear axle ratios.

Two-barrel terror

In the 1973 Mustang lineup, the Mach 1 was the only model to come with a standard V8. The base V8 was the 4949cc (302ci) overhead-valve unit, fitted with a Motorcraft two-barrel carburettor. It made 136bhp. For an extra $128, you could choose the 5752cc (351ci) Windsor V8 with the two-barrel carb and 156bhp, or the 5752cc (351ci) Cleveland with a two-barrel carb and 154bhp. Among further options was a four-barrel 5752cc (351ci) V8. It made more power and had large-port cylinder heads and a different intake manifold.

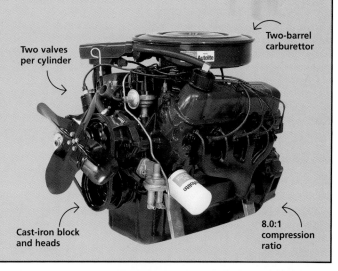

Two valves per cylinder

Two-barrel carburettor

Cast-iron block and heads

8.0:1 compression ratio

Best of breed

Although it was hardly recognizable as a first generation Mustang, the 1973 model, though restyled, was just that. While the Mach 1 isn't the most desirable of the early 1970 Mustangs – the earlier Boss 351 model takes the top honours here – it was still very fast and sporty.

Of all the 1973 Mustangs, the Mach 1 is the most collectable today.

Ford MUSTANG MACH 1

The Mach 1 line, which began in 1969, enhanced the sporty qualities of the Mustang, picking up on some of the themes of Carroll Shelby's modifications. The 1973 Mach 1 boasted a variety of enhancements.

Standard V8 power

All Mustangs for 1973 came with a six-cylinder engine as standard except the Mach 1, with its 4949cc (302ci) V8. Because it had an emissions-restricted output of 136bhp, ordering one of the optional V8 engines was an attractive choice.

Competition suspension

Justifying its reputation as the sporty member of the Mustang group, the Mach 1 received a standard competition suspension, with heavy-duty front and rear springs and revalved shock absorbers.

SportsRoof style

The Mach 1 was offered in one body style only, a fastback coupe known as the SportsRoof. This is characterized by a near-horizontal rear roof line, in contrast to the cut-away style of the Mustang hardtop coupe. The rear window is tinted on the Mach 1 and a rear spoiler was optional.

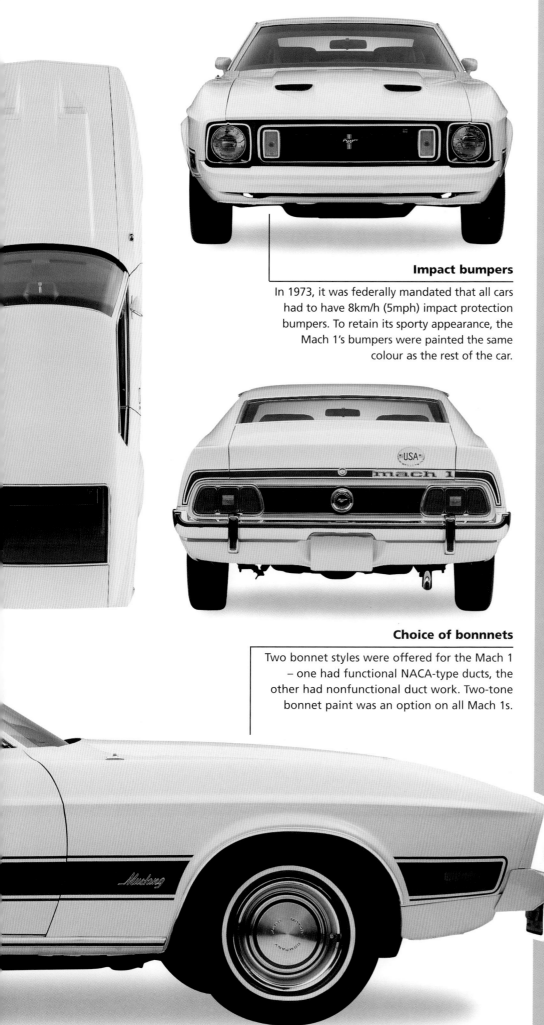

Impact bumpers

In 1973, it was federally mandated that all cars had to have 8km/h (5mph) impact protection bumpers. To retain its sporty appearance, the Mach 1's bumpers were painted the same colour as the rest of the car.

Choice of bonnnets

Two bonnet styles were offered for the Mach 1 – one had functional NACA-type ducts, the other had nonfunctional duct work. Two-tone bonnet paint was an option on all Mach 1s.

Specifications

1973 Ford Mustang Mach 1

ENGINE

Type: V8

Construction: Cast-iron block and heads

Valve gear: Two valves per cylinder operated by a single camshaft with pushrods and rocker arms

Bore and stroke: 102mm (4.00in) x 76mm (3.00in)

Displacement: 4949cc (302ci)

Compression ratio: 8.5:1

Induction system: Single Motorcraft two-barrel carburettor

Maximum power: 136bhp at 4200rpm

Maximum torque: 232lb-ft at 2200rpm

Top speed: 177km/h (110mph)

0–96km/h (0–60mph): 10 sec

TRANSMISSION

Three-speed automatic

BODY/CHASSIS

Unitary monocoque construction with steel two-door coupe body

SPECIAL FEATURES

Fold-down rear seats allow access to the boot from inside. It also permits more room to carry unusually long items.

RUNNING GEAR

Steering: Recirculating ball

Front suspension: Wishbones with lower trailing links, coil springs, shock absorbers and anti-roll bar

Rear suspension: Live axle with semi-elliptic leaf springs, shock absorbers and anti-roll bar

Brakes: Discs (front), drums (rear)

Wheels: Steel, 35.6cm (14in) dia.

Tires: E70 x 35.6cm (14in)

DIMENSIONS

Length: 4.8m (189.0in)

Width: 1.88m (74.1in)

Height: 1.29m (50.7in)

Wheelbase: 277cm (109.0in)

Track: 156cm (61.5in) (front), 151cm (59.5in) (rear)

Weight: 1402kg (3090lb)

Ford **MUSTANG SVO**

After a second energy crisis, most people believed that V8-powered cars were living on borrowed time. Nevertheless, the public again began clamouring for performance cars. Enter the 1984–1986 Mustang SVO, a GT with a European approach to performance.

'...the machine speaks for itself.'

'When Ford gave the slogan "The machine speaks for itself" to the SVO, it knew the turbo four banger would be a sophisticated, race-proven automobile for driving enthusiasts. All of its exterior modifications, from the dual rear wing to the hood scoop are all functional. The power delivery is smoother with next to no turbo lag. This car offers world-class performance and can rival the cornering ability of the Ferrari 308 and Porsche 944.'

SVO interiors boast items like a left foot rest, 8000rpm tachometer and a boost gauge.

Milestones

1981 Ford announces a new Special Vehicles Operation division, headed up by Michael Kranefuss. Its purpose is to build a new generation of performance cars, both for the street and track.

Early SVOs had a 175bhp engine and a single exhaust with twin outlets.

1984 The Mustang SVO,
a heavily re-engineered version of the Mustang Turbo GT, goes on sale. It has a turbocharged 2.3l (140ci) engine producing 175bhp. It is fast but expensive, at $14,521, and only a small number are sold.

V8-powered GTs got an SVO-inspired front end for 1987.

1985 Ford massages the turbo
four, resulting in 205bhp. The SVO also gets flush-mounted headlights and a drop in price, but petrol prices are falling, making V8s more desirable, and the car remains a slow seller. It is finally dropped after 1986.

UNDER THE SKIN

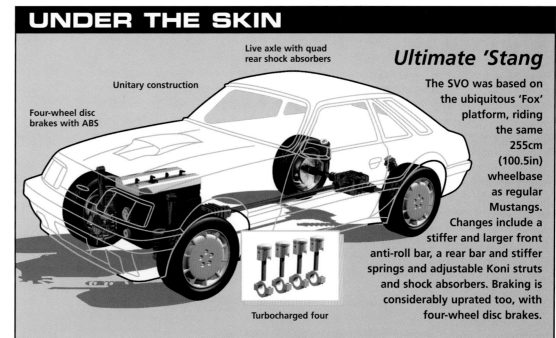

Unitary construction

Live axle with quad rear shock absorbers

Four-wheel disc brakes with ABS

Turbocharged four

Ultimate 'Stang

The SVO was based on the ubiquitous 'Fox' platform, riding the same 255cm (100.5in) wheelbase as regular Mustangs. Changes include a stiffer and larger front anti-roll bar, a rear bar and stiffer springs and adjustable Koni struts and shock absorbers. Braking is considerably uprated too, with four-wheel disc brakes.

THE POWER PACK

Less is more

Reflecting the times, the SVO was about getting the maximum amount of power from a small displacement engine. Ford took its 88bhp, 2.3l (140ci), four-cylinder unit, dropped the compression to 8.0:1 and added a Garrett T3 turbocharger. It then made a more respectable 145 bhp. With the addition of an air-to-air intercooler and electronically adjustable boost control, power further rose to 175bhp at 15 psi of boost. 205bhp and 240lb-ft of torque were available in the 1986 model – the SVO's last year.

Bosch electronic fuel injection

Air-to-air intercooler

Cast-iron block and cylinder head

8.0:1 compression ratio

Second series

Mustang SVOs can be split into two distinct series, the 1984 cars, and 1985½ and 1986 models. The latter examples have more usable power, a higher 3.73:1 rear end gear ratio and Koni dual shock absorbers on each side of the rear axle.

1985½ and 1986 models can be distinguished by flush-mounted headlights.

Ford MUSTANG SVO

The Mustang SVO showed the world that with a sophisticated fuel injection system, turbo and intercooler, a 2.3l (140ci) four-cylinder could make enough power to rival engines twice its size and still get 25mpg.

Distinguishing features

SVO variants can be distinguished from other 'Stangs by twin square headlights, rear wheel spats, grill-less front styling, functional bonnet scoop, bi-level deck-lid spoiler and unique taillight treatment.

2.3l (140ci) turbo

Built at Ford's Lima, Ohio plant, the 2.3l (140ci) single overhead-cam four put out 175bhp and 210lb-ft of torque. In 1985½, responding to criticism, Ford modified it to produce 205bhp and 240lb-ft.

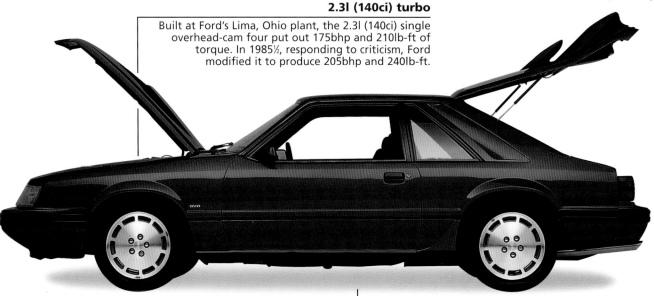

Five-speed transmission

Marketed as a serious driver's car, the SVO was only available with a Borg-Warner T-5, 5-speed, manual transmission and a Hurst short-throw shifter.

Suspension upgrades

SVOs were upgraded with Koni adjustable gas pressurized shock absorbers, recalibrated coil springs, front and rear anti-roll bars and close-ratio power steering. This contributed to its outstanding handling.

Four-wheel discs

To ensure that SVO's could stop as quickly as they accelerate, they were all equipped with four-wheel disc brakes. This didn't become standard again on regular Mustangs until 1994.

Driver-oriented interior

Interior equipment includes an 8000rpm tachometer, multi-adjustable sport bucket seats, leather-rimmed steering wheel, plus power door locks, mirrors and windows. Its pedals were also reconfigured to allow heel and toe downshifting.

Live rear axle

SVOs came with a 19cm (7.5in) live rear axle with a Traction-Lok differential and quad rear shocks. 3.73 gears were available in 1985½ and 1986.

Specifications

1986 Ford Mustang SVO

ENGINE
Type: In-line four-cylinder

Construction: Cast-iron block and head

Valve gear: Two valves per cylinder operated by a single overhead camshaft

Bore and stroke: 96mm (3.78in) x 80mm (3.13in)

Displacement: 2294cc (140ci)

Compression ratio: 8.0:1

Induction system: Bosch EFI with Garrett T3 turbocharger and air-to-air intercooler

Maximum power: 205bhp at 5000rpm

Maximum torque: 240lb-ft at 3000rpm

Top speed: 225km/h (140mph)

0–96km/h (0–60mph): 6.7 sec

TRANSMISSION
Borg-Warner T-5 five-speed manual

BODY/CHASSIS
Unitary steel chassis with steel three-door hatchback body

SPECIAL FEATURES

A unique bi-level deck lid spoiler distinguishes the SVO from the V8 GT.

Cast-aluminium wheels were standard, but tires changed to Goodyear Eagle GT 'Gatorbacks' in 1985.

RUNNING GEAR
Steering: Rack-and-pinion

Front suspension: MacPherson struts with lower control arms, telescopic shock absorbers and an anti-roll bar

Rear suspension: Live axle with horizontally and vertically mounted telescopic shock absorbers (two per side) and anti-roll bar

Brakes: Discs, 27.7cm (10.92in) dia. (front), 28.6cm (11.25in) dia. (rear)

Wheels: Cast-aluminum, 17.8cm (7in) x 40.6cm (16in)

Tires: Goodyear Eagle GT, P225/50 VR16

DIMENSIONS
Length: 4.59m (180.8in)

Width: 1.76m (69.1in)

Height: 1.32m (52.1in)

Wheelbase: 255cm (100.5in)

Track: 144cm (56.6in) (front), 145cm (57.0in) (rear)

Weight: 1377kg (3036lb)

Ford SALEEN MUSTANG S351

Steve Saleen starts from scratch and upgrades almost everything on the production Mustang. From all suspension components to major engine work, this is the ultimate street-racing Mustang.

'...gobs of power everywhere.'

'Knowing that Steve Saleen builds a Mustang race-ready hasn't prepared you for how hard-edged and unforgiving this Mustang really is. There's gobs of power everywhere, the suspension is punishingly hard and despite some impressive rubber, this thing is a handful if you don't pay attention. But on the right road or track at racing speeds of over 160km/h (100mph), you'll know you're behind the wheel of the ultimate race-bred pony car.'

The standard Mustang driving position is the best of the 'pony car' lot – as long as you're under 1.8m (6ft) tall.

Milestones

1984 Racing driver and builder Steve Saleen modifies his first Mustang, winning the 24-hour race at Mosport Park in Canada.

Steve Saleen races his own upgraded Mustangs with a good deal of success.

1988 Saleens win at Mosport for the third straight year, finishing 1-2-3.

1995 Bolting on the Vortech supercharger turns the 370bhp S351 into the SR, with 480bhp.

The S351 is built around a standard Ford Mustang V6 shell.

1996 Steve Saleen turns his attention to Ford's new 4.6l (281ci) overhead-cam V8, to produce the S281.

1997 S351 has even more power than the previous SR, with an incredible 495bhp produced from the redesigned V8. Steve Saleen's team embarks on a world tour, competing in the 24 Hours of Daytona and Le Mans, and at Silverstone in England – making the Saleen known worldwide.

UNDER THE SKIN

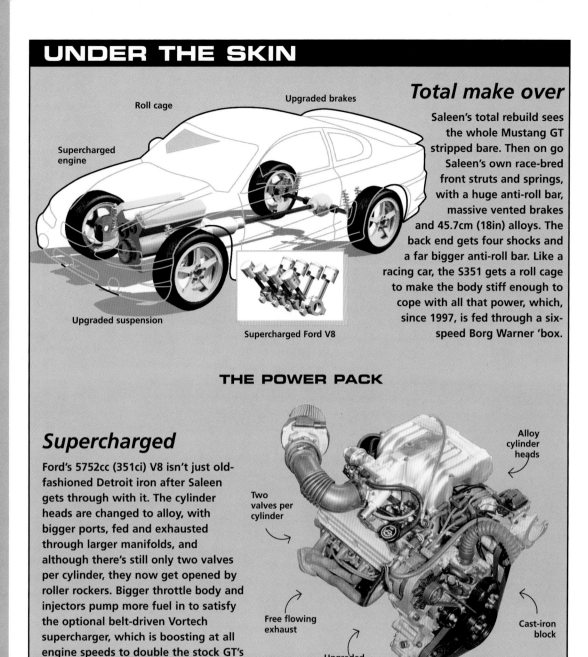

Roll cage

Upgraded brakes

Supercharged engine

Upgraded suspension

Supercharged Ford V8

Total make over

Saleen's total rebuild sees the whole Mustang GT stripped bare. Then on go Saleen's own race-bred front struts and springs, with a huge anti-roll bar, massive vented brakes and 45.7cm (18in) alloys. The back end gets four shocks and a far bigger anti-roll bar. Like a racing car, the S351 gets a roll cage to make the body stiff enough to cope with all that power, which, since 1997, is fed through a six-speed Borg Warner 'box.

THE POWER PACK

Supercharged

Ford's 5752cc (351ci) V8 isn't just old-fashioned Detroit iron after Saleen gets through with it. The cylinder heads are changed to alloy, with bigger ports, fed and exhausted through larger manifolds, and although there's still only two valves per cylinder, they now get opened by roller rockers. Bigger throttle body and injectors pump more fuel in to satisfy the optional belt-driven Vortech supercharger, which is boosting at all engine speeds to double the stock GT's power. Torque is also boosted.

Two valves per cylinder

Free flowing exhaust

Upgraded fuel injection

Alloy cylinder heads

Cast-iron block

Racing Saleen

The ultimate Saleen in 1997 was the SR Widebody with 510bhp, a huge rear wing for added downforce, massively flared wheel arches and a carbon-fibre bonnet. Steve Saleen's team races modified versions with much success in America and Europe.

Steve Saleen is a determined and successful racer.

Ford SALEEN MUSTANG S351

In its trademark bright Saleen Racing Yellow, the S351 looks like no stock Mustang. But it's not all for show – the S351 needs those big wheels, low-profile tyres, scoops and wings at the speed it's heading toward.

Five-speed Tremec

The faster you go, the more gears you need if you want all the ratios to make sense. This model had a five-speed, but starting in 1997, Saleens use a six-speed gearbox – like its Corvette and Viper rivals – which is made by Borg-Warner.

Reworked V8

Saleen installed aluminium Edelbrock cylinder heads in place of the original cast-iron type although they still have just two valves per cylinder. Saleen also remapped the fuel injection and made the exhaust bigger.

Low-profile tyres

With a stiff suspension, this car can use low profile tyres with minimal sidewall depth to ensure maximum grip. Low-profile front tyres improve steering feel because there is no lost motion due to sidewall flexing.

Wing scoops

Saleens have scoops everywhere – in the wings, bonnet and spoiler since cooling air needs to be fed to the large brakes to keep them working effectively.

Recaro seats

Although the interior is recognizably Mustang, there's one big improvement: the expensive Recaro sports seats holding you in place.

Specifications
1995 Saleen Mustang S351

ENGINE
Type: Ford V8
Construction: Cast-iron block, light alloy heads
Valve gear: Two valves per cylinder operated by single block-mounted camshaft via pushrods and roller rockers
Bore and stroke: 102mm (4in) x 89mm (3.5in)
Displacement: 5752cc (351ci)
Compression ratio: 9.5:1
Induction system: Multi-point electronic fuel injection
Maximum power: 371bhp at 5100rpm
Maximum torque: 380lb-ft at 3400rpm
Top speed: 285km/h (177mph)
0–96km/h (0–60mph): 4.5 sec

TRANSMISSION
Five-speed Tremec manual

BODY/CHASSIS
Ford Mustang GT unitized body with Saleen strengthening

SPECIAL FEATURES

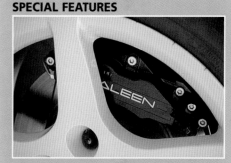

Larger brake discs and bigger calipers allow more force to be exerted on the brakes, dramatically improving stopping times.

RUNNING GEAR
Steering: Rack-and-pinion
Front suspension: Gas pressurized Saleen MacPherson struts with larger anti-roll bar
Rear suspension: Live axle with two vertical and two horizontal shocks
Brakes: Vented and grooved discs, 33cm (13in) dia. (front), 27.9cm (11in) dia. (rear)
Wheels: Speedline magnesium alloys, 45,7cm (18in) x 21.6cm (8.5in) (front), 45.7cm (18in) x 25.4cm (10in) (rear)
Tyres: BFG, 255/35 ZR18 (front), 285/35 ZR18 (rear)

DIMENSIONS
Length: 4.62m (182in)
Width: 1.82m (71.8in)
Height: 1.27m (50in)
Wheelbase: 257cm (101.3in)
Track: 156cm (61.6in) (front), 154cm (60.6in) (rear)
Weight: 1565kg (3450lb)

Huge brakes
Mustang GT's brakes are replaced by bigger, grooved and vented rotors. Pad area is increased too, with Saleen/Alcon big four-pot calipers gripping the disc.

New front suspension
Saleen racing struts with gas pressurized shocks and much stiffer coil springs replace the GT's softer settings and the front anti-roll bar is now 36mm (1.4in) thick.

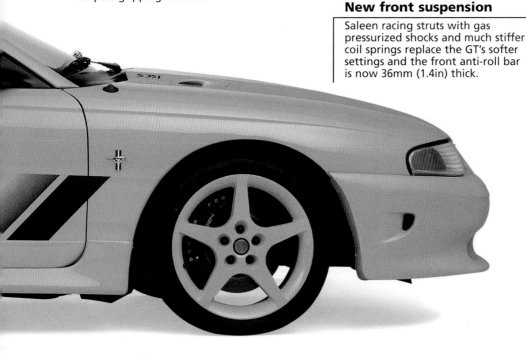

Ford **SHELBY MUSTANG GT350**

When dynamic Texan Carroll Shelby worked his magic on the best-selling Ford Mustang, he created a classic. The rare top-of-the-line 350bhp Shelby Mustang GT350 was a great champion – and you could rent the street-legal 306bhp version from Hertz for $35 a day!

'...tons of upper end power.'

'Rough...nasty...noisy...hard steering...I love it!" were the comments most testers made back in 1965, and it hasn't changed since. The special Detroit Locker limited slip differential makes loud ratcheting noises on slow corners, then locks with a bang when you hit the accelerator. The engine is smaller than most other American muscle cars of the time, but the GT350 is a winner at the track or on the street. Suspension is stiffer than the stock Mustang and really helps the car negotiate sharp turns. The high-performance 4736cc (289ci) offers lots of torque and tons of upper end power.'

With full instrumentation and a stripped-out interior, it is obvious that the GT350 means business.

Milestones

1964 Mustang introduced in April

and showrooms are mobbed. The first V8 comes slightly later, followed by a bigger V8, then a 271bhp version (code name 'K'), which is the basis for the GT350.

The Mustang was launched in 1964 as a 'pony' car.

1965 Shelby

American takes time out from building Cobras to produce 100 GT350s and qualifying them to run as SCCA sports cars. They win four out of five of the B-Production regional wins in 1965, and take the overall championship that year and in 1966 and 1967.

1966 Hertz Rent-a-Car

buys about 1000 GT350Hs (for Hertz), painted with gold stripes – most have automatic transmissions. There are stories about people renting them, racing them, then returning the Rent-a-Racers with brakes smoking and tyres worn out.

Hertz gained publicity from renting Shelby Mustangs.

UNDER THE SKIN

New suspension

Engine is mounted in the front, driving through a special Borg Warner T-10 four-speed transmission to a heavy-duty rear axle, taken from a Ford Galaxie station wagon. The Mustang monocoque is steel with Shelby adding a rear seat replacement panel and fibreglass bonnnet (with air scoop). Shelby added a wooden steering wheel – a sports car must-have at the time.

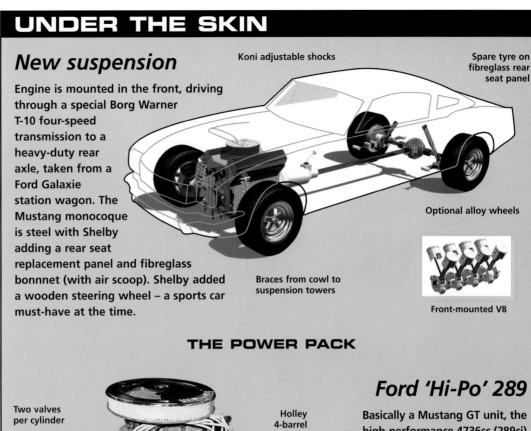

Koni adjustable shocks

Spare tyre on fibreglass rear seat panel

Optional alloy wheels

Braces from cowl to suspension towers

Front-mounted V8

THE POWER PACK

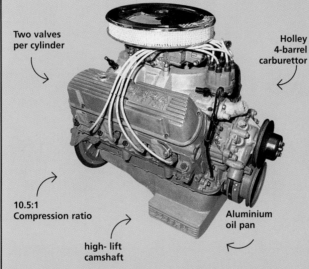

Two valves per cylinder

Holley 4-barrel carburettor

10.5:1 Compression ratio

Aluminium oil pan

high- lift camshaft

Ford 'Hi-Po' 289

Basically a Mustang GT unit, the high-performance 4736cc (289ci) Ford small block started at 271bhp before Shelby began working on it, a substantial improvement on the 101bhp of the first six-cylinder Mustangs. The engine of the GT350 street car with a Holley four-barrel carburettor developed 306bhp, and the mighty GT350R had another 44bhp. The main modifications were a higher compression ratio, high-lift cam, larger valves, and improved breathing with the performance carburettor.

The GT350R

Only 37 examples of the 'R' (for race) version were built. With a stout 350bhp engine and stripped interior, it won championships in the Sports Car Club of America's (SCCA) hot B-Production class against Corvettes, Ferraris, Cobras, Lotuses and E-type Jaguars.

GT350R has a fibreglass apron that increased airflow to the radiator.

Ford SHELBY MUSTANG GT350

Ford's Mustang was selling well, but it lacked the high-performance image of the Corvette. So Ford asked Carroll Shelby to develop the GT350, which beat the Corvette on the race track and outperformed it on the road.

High performance 289 V8

Shelby modified Ford's 'Hi-Po' version of the small-block V8 with 10.5:1 compression ratio, improved valve timing and better breathing. This gave 306bhp at 6000rpm.

Rear-exiting exhaust system

The original GT350s had side-exiting exhausts, which were noisy and not permitted in some states. 1966 models were given a conventional rear-exiting exhaust system.

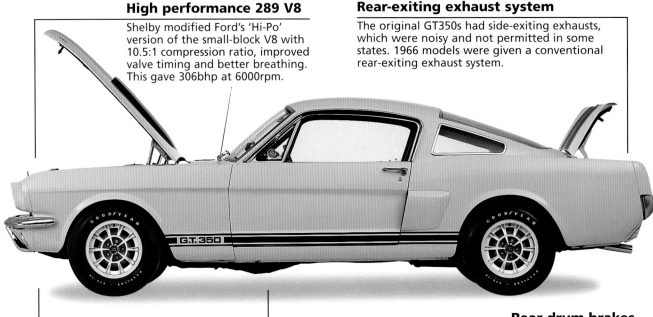

Optional Cragar alloy wheels

Conventional steel wheels were standard wear on the GT350, but many owners opted for the lighter Cragar alloys approved by Shelby.

Functional side scoops

The 1966 GT350 had side scoops that fed air to the rear brakes, distinguishing it from the standard fastback Mustang.

Rear drum brakes

The GT350's extra performance dictated the use of Kelsey-Hayes front discs, but drums were retained at the rear.

Acrylic rear quarter windows

On the 1966 models, the standard Mustang fastback louvers were replaced by acrylic windows to make the car lighter.

The standard Mustang front suspension was improved for the GT350 with stiffer springs, revalved Koni shocks and relocated control arms.

Custom fuel cap

The 1966-model GT350s were given their very own fuel cap in the middle of the rear of the car, carrying the Cobra logo.

Limited slip differential

Early Shelbys were fitted with the Detroit Locker limited slip differential to improve cornering traction and eliminate wheelspin.

Specifications
1966 Ford Shelby Mustang GT350

ENGINE
Type: V8

Construction: Cast-iron block and heads, aluminium intake manifold, tubular steel exhaust manifolds

Valve gear: Two valves per cylinder operated by single block-mounted camshaft via pushrods and rockers

Bore and stroke: 102mm (4.02in) x 73mm (2.87in)

Displacement: 4736cc (289ci)

Compression ratio: 10.5:1

Induction system: Holley four-barrel carburettor

Maximum power: 306bhp at 6000rpm

Maximum torque: 329lb-ft at 4200rpm

Top speed: 217km/h (135mph)

0–96km/h (0–60mph): 5.7 sec

TRANSMISSION
Borg Warner T-10 four-speed with close-ratio gears and aluminium case

BODY/CHASSIS
Standard steel Mustang fastback body with Shelby grill; fibreglass bonnet, removed rear seat, Mustang monocoque with subframes

SPECIAL FEATURES

Goodyear tyres were the performance rubber to have on your 1960s muscle car.

RUNNING GEAR
Front suspension: Wishbones, coil springs, Koni shocks and anti-roll bar

Rear suspension: Live axle with semi-elliptic leaf springs, Koni shocks and traction control arms

Brakes: Kelsey-Hayes disc brakes 28.7cm (11.3in) dia. (front), drums (rear)

Wheels: Steel 6in) x 35.6cm (14in) or magnesium alloy 17.8cm (7in) x 35.6cm (14in)

Tyres: Goodyear Blue Dot 775-14

DIMENSIONS
Length: 4.61m (81.6in)

Width: 1.73m (68.2in)

Height: 1.4m (55in)

Wheelbase: 274cm (108in)

Track: 144cm (56.5in) (front), 145cm (57in) (rear)

Weight: 1266kg (2792lb)

Ford SHELBY MUSTANG GT500

Softer, roomier and more practical than the original stark GT350, the GT500 still boasted masses of brute strength with over 350bhp and a gigantic 420lb-ft of torque from its 7014cc (428ci) V8.

'...so much power and torque.'

'With so much power and torque available, anyone can get stunning performance from the GT500, particularly with the automatic. There are two surprises in store: you expect it to be faster than a 15.6-second ¼ mile suggests, but you don't expect it to handle as well as it does. Despite the huge engine making it front heavy, the power steering makes sure the GT500 goes where you want it to. The ride isn't bad for a late-'60s muscle car and the engine isn't very temperamental, although it does throw out an awful lot of heat, making the air conditioning option a must.'

The dashboard has a special 225km/h (140mph) speedometer and 8000rpm tachometer as well as plenty of extra gauges.

Milestones

1965 First Shelby GT350s appear as 1966 models, but sell slowly.

1966 Efforts to make it more of a street car lead to the specifications being toned down: The exhaust is quieter, the limited slip differential is an option and Koni shocks are left off.

1968 was the first year you could get a GT500 convertible.

1967 The last year before Ford takes over building the Shelby Mustang. The GT350 is restyled and the bigger engined GT500 is introduced.

1968 GT500 is joined by the GT500KR (King of the Road). It has a 7014cc (428ci) engine – the Cobra Jet rather than the Police unit.

Ford's own Mach 1 Mustang killed off the GT500.

1969 Whole Mustang range is restyled, including the GT500 to the big, flatter looking Mach 1 style.

UNDER THE SKIN

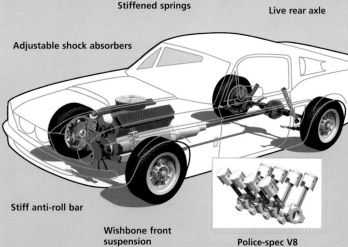

Stiffened springs

Live rear axle

Adjustable shock absorbers

Stiff anti-roll bar

Wishbone front suspension

Police-spec V8

Suspension improvements

Like all performance Mustangs, the GT500 had a straightforward front V8 engine driving a live rear axle. Shelby's improvements saw the springs stiffened and Gabriel adjustable shock absorbers added, and a stiff anti-roll bar at the front. The modification that lowered the pivot for the front upper wishbone was so good Ford adopted it on the stock Mustang.

THE POWER PACK

Simply big

Don't confuse the 7014cc (428ci) unit installed in the GT500 with the fierce 427 engine in Shelby's Cobras. The 428 has a different bore and stroke and, although it shares the same all-iron pushrod V8 layout, it is a less sophisticated design, and less powerful. It was designed for lower engine speeds and for long sustained use, often in the police chase cars in which it was used. Later, the police-spec unit was replaced with the Cobra Jet version, which was rated with an extra 5bhp but no increase in torque.

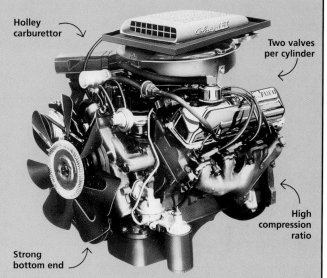

Holley carburettor

Two valves per cylinder

High compression ratio

Strong bottom end

Early or open?

Although the GT500 continued until the 1970 model year, by that stage there was very little to set it apart from the rest of the Mustang range. So if you're after one of the big-engined Shelby Mustangs, it's best to go for an earlier, more subtle car or one of the rare convertibles, which are highly collectible and often faked.

The rarest of the GT500s is the factory convertible.

Ford SHELBY MUSTANG GT500

If bigger was better, the GT500 was the best of the Shelby Mustang line. There was no way you could have added a bigger engine to the car, and that made sure it was the most powerful of all.

Fibreglass bonnet

A new fibreglass bonnet with functional air scoops helps to accommodate the big engine and also reduces the car's weight.

Power steering

With so much weight over the nose and with wide tyres, power steering was a very good idea. In fact you had no choice – it was a standard feature, as were the power brakes and shoulder harnesses.

Front heavy

That huge cast-iron V8 naturally made the GT500 front heavy, with a weight distribution of 58 per cent front and 42 per cent rear. It was just as well that the bonnet was fibreglass.

V8 engine

With the GT500, Shelby went for the biggest engine he could fit in the bay, the Police Interceptor type 7014cc (428ci) V8. It filled the engine compartment so fully you couldn't even see the spark plugs.

Wide tyres

The GT500 needed to put as much rubber on the road as possible to cope with its power. Shelby opted for Goodyear Speedway E70-15s, a popular choice for muscle cars of the era that were rated at 225km/h (140mph).

Alloy wheels

Steel wheels were a standard feature, but these Shelby alloys were available as an option. They are very desirable today.

Adjustable shocks

The standard shocks were thrown out and replaced by Gabriel adjustables. However, the car left the Shelby works with what was considered the optimum settings.

Unique tail lights

The back of the car was distinguished from the standard Mustang fastback by different tail lights, two very wide ones replacing the two sets of triple lights. Above the lights, the trunk lid was another Shelby fibreglass part.

Specifications
1967 Ford Shelby Mustang GT500

ENGINE

Type: V8

Construction: Cast-iron block and heads

Valve gear: Two valves per cylinder operated by single block-mounted camshaft via pushrods, rockers and hydraulic lifters

Bore and stroke: 105mm (4.13in) x 101mm (3.98in)

Displacement: 7014cc (428ci)

Compression ratio: 10.5:1

Induction system: Two Holley four-barrel carburettors

Maximum power: 355bhp at 5400rpm

Maximum torque: 420lb-ft at 3200rpm

Top speed: 212km/h (132mph)

0–96km/h (0–60mph): 7.0 sec

TRANSMISSION

Ford Cruise-O-Matic three-speed automatic or four-speed manual

BODY/FRAME

Unitary steel with two-door coupe body

SPECIAL FEATURES

The bonnet scoops added by Shelby were changed with each model year. They became more prominent after these rather subtle scoops on this 1967 car.

RUNNING GEAR

Steering: Recirculating ball

Front suspension: Double wishbones with adjustable Gabriel shock absorbers and 25mm (1in) dia. anti-roll bar

Rear suspension: Live axle with semi-elliptic leaf springs

Brakes: Discs, 27.8cm (11.3in) dia. (front), drums, 25.4cm (10in) dia. (rear)

Wheels: Shelby alloy, 17.8cm (7in) x 38.1cm (15in)

Tyres: E70-15 (front and rear)

DIMENSIONS

Length: 4.74m (86.6in)

Width: 1.8m (70.9in)

Height: 1.24m (49in)

Wheelbase: 274cm (108in)

Track: 147cm (58in) (front and rear)

Weight: 1597kg (3520lb)

Ford TORINO TALLADEGA

In the late 1960s Ford and Chrysler were waging war in NASCAR. In 1969 Ford revealed its aero-styled Torinos, which cleaned up in the year's stock car racing by collecting 30 victories. To satisfy homologation rules, at least 500 road-going versions had to be built. The result was the Ford Talladega.

'...the car was lethal.'

'Though sedate-looking, the Torino Talladega was the answer to watching the taillights of quicker Mopars and Chevrolets. Its nose was tapered and stretched 12.7cm (5in), and a flush mounted grill replaced the stock Torino piece. In street trim, the Talladega, named after NASCAR's fastest super-speedway, used a 335bhp 7014cc (428ci) Cobra Jet engine with a Drag Pack oil cooler. On the street, the car was dangerous; in NASCAR trim, it was deadly.'

Talladegas have basic interiors, but they are equipped with full instrumentation.

Milestones

1968 Ford restyles

its Fairlane model with swoopier styling. A new top-of-the-line Torino, including a GT fastback and convertible, joins the line up. The latter can be ordered with a 6391cc (390ci) or 7014cc (428ci) V8 big-block engine.

The Torino made its debut as a top-of-the-range Fairlane in 1968.

1969 In response to

the Dodge Charger 500 built for NASCAR racing, Ford releases the Talladega for NASCAR using the 427 engine at first, but switched to the semi-hemi Boss 429 engines after enough were homologated into the Mustang. Ford's aero-aces trounced the Charger 500 and the even more slippery winged Daytonas by winning 30 races that season.

Restyled 1970 Torinos had smoother styling.

1970 A redesigned

Talladega was disappointing in testing, so Ford retained the 1969 cars for NASCAR. Though successful the previous year, the Fords were no match for Plymouth's winged Superbirds.

UNDER THE SKIN

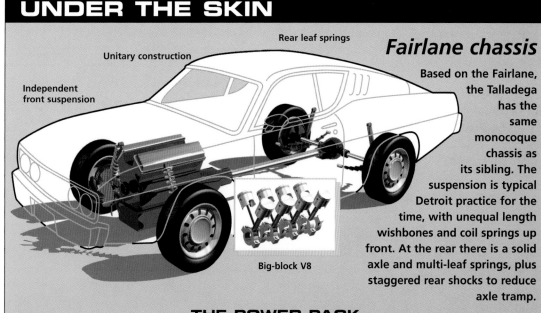

Rear leaf springs

Unitary construction

Independent front suspension

Big-block V8

Fairlane chassis

Based on the Fairlane, the Talladega has the same monocoque chassis as its sibling. The suspension is typical Detroit practice for the time, with unequal length wishbones and coil springs up front. At the rear there is a solid axle and multi-leaf springs, plus staggered rear shocks to reduce axle tramp.

THE POWER PACK

Motown muscle

All production Talladegas are powered by Ford's stout 7014cc (428ci) Cobra Jet big-block V8s. Underrated at 335bhp, this engine was Ford's ace in the late 1960s horsepower race. The engines all had 10.6:1 compression, steel cranks, stronger con rods and received fuel from a Holley four-barrel 735cfm carburettor. While this was the street engine, the NASCAR competition version used the sinister Boss 429 semi-hemi engine that was homologated the same year in the Boss 429 Mustang.

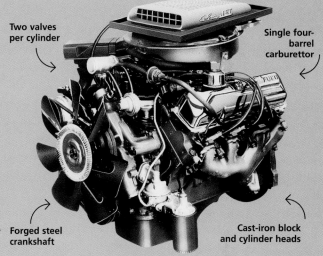

Two valves per cylinder

Single four-barrel carburettor

Forged steel crankshaft

Cast-iron block and cylinder heads

Two of a Kind

While Ford built only 745 Talladegas, its crosstown brother, Mercury, made similar modifications to 353 of its 1969 Cyclones and called it the Spoiler II. Its body was slightly longer and lower to the ground and included a rear spoiler and unique badging.

Cyclone IIs were offered with a 5752cc (351ci) V8, but a 7014cc (428ci) was optional.

Ford **TORINO TALLADEGA**

Through the use of aerodynamics and the Boss 429 engine, the purpose-built Talladegas accomplished its mission – to take the 1969 NASCAR championship. Once again, Ford's 'Total Performance' campaign shines through.

Cobra Jet power

The standard engine is the monster 7014cc (428ci) Cobra Jet unit. It was factory rated at 335bhp for insurance reasons, but the true output is probably somewhere in the region of 450bhp. In race trim, the engine of choice was the Boss 429 that was homologated for racing in the Mustang Boss 429.

Handling suspension

All Talladegas are equipped with a 'handling' suspension, which basically consists of stiffer springs and shocks plus a thick front anti-roll bar.

Rocker Panel Modifications

The rocker panels were raised over 25mm (1in) so the NASCAR prepared cars could be lowered while being in full compliance with the ride height requirements.

Traction-Lok rear

Ford's Traction-Lok differential, with a 3.25:1 final-drive ratio, was the only rear gearing available. It makes the Talladega surprisingly capable at high-speed cruising, although all-out acceleration suffers as a result.

Lack of ornamentation

The exterior of the Talladega is very plain and does not have any nameplates. Instead, it carries 'T' motifs on the fuel cap and above the door handles.

Nose modifications

The Talladega was based on the Fairlane SportsRoof but with some aerodynamic advantages. The nose was stretched more than 12.7cm (5in) and brought closer to the ground. It also features a flush mounted grill and a narrowed Fairlane bumper.

Staggered rear shocks

Like many Detroit cars of the era, the Talladega has a solid axle and rear leaf springs. Staggered shocks are used to prevent severe axle tramp during hard acceleration.

Lightweight interior

To keep weight to a minimum, the Talladega uses a base interior, with a standard vinyl front bench seat and column shifter for the C6 automatic transmission.

Specifications

1969 Ford Torino Talladega

ENGINE

Type: V8

Construction: Cast-iron block and heads

Valve gear: Two valves per cylinder operated by a single camshaft via pushrods and rockers

Bore and stroke: 105mm (4.13in) x 101mm (3.98in)

Displacement: 7014cc (428ci)

Compression ratio: 10.6:1

Induction system: Single Holley four-barrel carburettor

Maximum power: 335bhp at 5200rpm

Maximum torque: 440lb-ft at 3400rpm

Top speed: 209km/h (130mph)

0–96km/h (0–60mph): 5.8 sec

TRANSMISSION

Ford C-6 Cruise-O-Matic

BODY/CHASSIS

Steel monocoque with two-door fastback body design

SPECIAL FEATURES

'T' (for Talladega) emblems are carried in the coach stripe on each side.

RUNNING GEAR

Steering: Recirculating ball

Front suspension: Unequal length wishbones with coil springs, telescopic shocks and anti-roll bar

Rear suspension: Live axle with semi-elliptical multi-leaf springs and staggered telescopic shocks

Brakes: Discs (front), drums (rear)

Wheels: Ford slotted chrome steel, 35.6cm (14in) dia.

Tyres: Goodyear Polyglas F70-14

DIMENSIONS

Length: 5.33m (209.8in)

Width: 2.14m (84.4in)

Height: 1.5m (59.1in)

Wheelbase: 295cm (116in)

Track: 164cm (64.7in) (front), 157cm (62in) (rear)

Weight: 1604kg (3536lb)

Mercury COUGAR GT-E

Introduced as a 1967 model, the Cougar was more of a refined boulevard cruiser than an all-out muscle car. However, for its sophomore year it turned into a real fire-breather when it was equipped with a 6997cc (427ci) V8.

'...tremendous torque.'

'If you thought that early Cougars were little more than puffed-up Mustangs, the GT-E will undoubtedly change your mind. It does boast upscale appointments, but nail the throttle and be prepared to hold on for dear life. The big 427 packs a tremendous dose of torque and traction is good, thanks to a fairly substantial curbweight and long wheelbase. The Cougar isn't the handling champ of all time, but it won't disappoint.'

As the GT-E was based on the XR-7 model, it has a fully loaded interior.

Milestones

1967 Mercury gets its own
pony car, the Cougar. It shares components with the Ford Mustang but rides on a longer 282cm (111in) wheelbase and comes standard with V8 power. It was offered in base, GT, or XR-7 form, and some 150,893 Cougars are built.

The Eliminator supplanted the GT-E as the Hi-Po Cougar in 1969–1970.

1968 Changes are few, but
the GT option is dropped. In its place is a special GT-E model, an XR-7 with a 6997cc (427ci) V8 and heavy-duty suspension. 358 are built before the 7014cc (428ci) engine replaces the 6998cc (427ci) mid-year. In all, 602 GT-Es are built.

The last of the real muscle Cougars was the 1971 429 CJ.

1969 The Cougar is heavily
facelifted and the performance model is now called the Eliminator.

UNDER THE SKIN

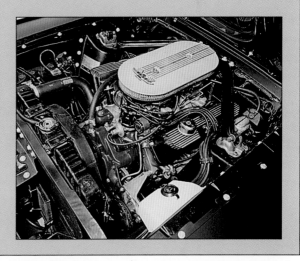

Unitary body/chassis

Front disc brakes

Live rear axle

Large-bore FE V8

Mustang Merc

The GT-E shares its underpinnings with the Mustang. The Cougar boasts a unitary chassis with a separate front subframe to carry the engine, transmission and front suspension. Up front are a set of double wishbones with coil springs, while at the rear is a live axle suspended on leaf springs. GT-E models have heavy-duty suspensions to handle the added weight of the 427/428 engine and a thicker front anti-roll bar. Front disc brakes could be specified.

THE POWER PACK

Fearsome 427

When the Cougar was launched in 1967, the mainstream performance model – the GT – was available with a 320bhp, 6391cc (390ci) engine. But for 1968, things got even wilder. The magical number 427 appeared on the option sheet. This was the side-oiler engine, so named because it has a different block to the original 427 with the oil galley mounted on the left side to reduce engine wear. The cast-iron FE-series engine in the Cougar GT-E has a forged-steel crank, cross-bolted main-bearing caps, a 10.9:1 compression ratio and a dual-plane intake with a single four-barrel carburettor. Dual quad setups could be ordered.

Most power

The Cougar GT-E is among the most underrated 1960s muscle machines, but it also ranks as one of the most powerful Cougars ever built. Fitted with either the 6997cc (427ci) or (7014cc) 428ci engine, it is a terrific buy today and still has a lot of power.

The sultry though sinister Cougar GT-Es were only built in 1968.

Mercury **COUGAR GT-E**

It may have been almost indistinguishable from other Cougars, but the GT-E was in a different league altogether. With 6997cc (427ci) and 460lb-ft of torque, it was arguably one of the quickest factory ponycars in 1968.

6997cc (427ci) V8
It was the hallowed 6997cc (427ci) that made the Cougar into a real screamer. Its 460lb-ft of torque put the GT-E firmly in the true muscle car league.

Unitary chassis
Like most Ford Motor Company products of the time, the Cougar features unitary construction almost identical to the popular Mustang.

Automatic transmission
Unlike the 428 Mustangs, all Cougar GT-Es came with automatic transmissions in the shape of Ford's proven C6 Cruise-O-Matic unit. Even so, the car could run high 14s with a super tuning and an experienced drive behind the wheel.

Hardtop styling
Although its little brother – the Mustang – had a choice of bodystyles, all Cougars in 1967 and 1968 were exclusively two-door coupes. A convertible arrived for 1969.

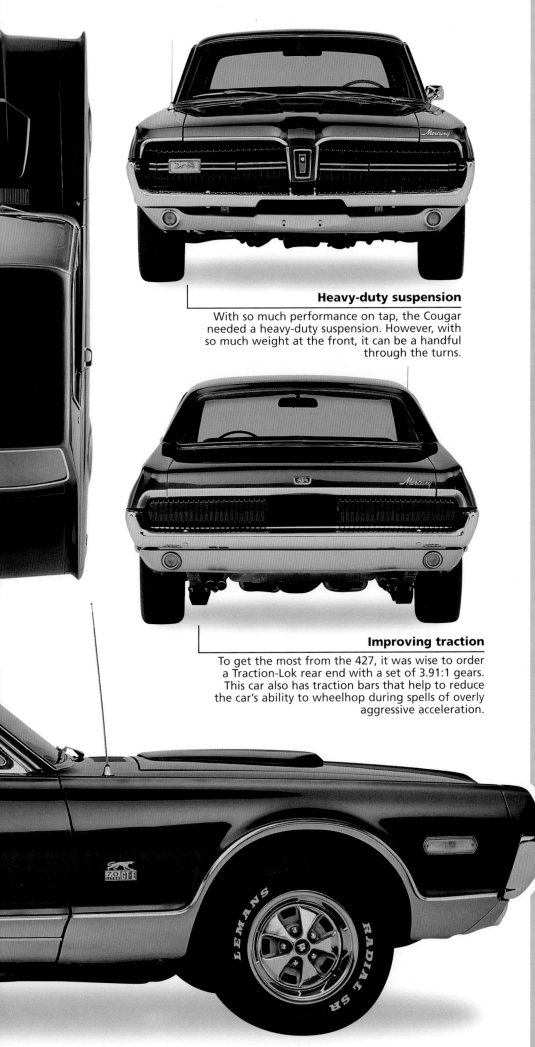

Heavy-duty suspension

With so much performance on tap, the Cougar needed a heavy-duty suspension. However, with so much weight at the front, it can be a handful through the turns.

Improving traction

To get the most from the 427, it was wise to order a Traction-Lok rear end with a set of 3.91:1 gears. This car also has traction bars that help to reduce the car's ability to wheelhop during spells of overly aggressive acceleration.

Specifications

1968 Mercury Cougar GT-E

ENGINE
Type: V8

Construction: Cast-iron block and heads

Valve gear: Two valves per cylinder operated by a single V-mounted camshaft with pushrods and rockers

Bore and stroke: 107mm (4.23in) x 96mm (3.78in)

Displacement: 6997cc (427ci)

Compression ratio: 10.9:1

Induction system: Two Holley 652-cfm four-barrel carburettors

Maximum power: 390bhp at 5600rpm

Maximum torque: 460lb-ft at 3200rpm

Top speed: 206km/h (128mph)

0–96km/h (0–60mph): 7 sec

TRANSMISSION
C6 Cruise-O-Matic three-speed automatic

BODY/CHASSIS
Steel unitary chassis with two-door coupe body

SPECIAL FEATURES

An overhead console with twin map lights could be ordered.

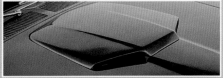

The bonnet scoop is a distinguishing feature of the GT-E.

RUNNING GEAR
Steering: Recirculating-ball

Front suspension: Unequal-length wishbones with coil springs, telescopic shock absorbers and anti-roll bar

Rear suspension: Live axle with semi-elliptic leaf springs and telescopic shock absorbers

Brakes: Discs (front), drums (rear)

Wheels: Styled steel, 35.6cm (14in) x 15.2cm (6in)

Tyres: Goodyear Polyglas, G60-14

DIMENSIONS
Length: 4.83m (190.3in)

Width: 1.87m (73.6in)

Height: 1.39m (54.6in)

Wheelbase: 282cm (111.0in)

Track: 155in (61.2in) (front), 153cm (60.3in) (rear)

Weight: 1440kg (3174lb)

Mercury COUGAR ELIMINATOR

A true performance Cougar emerged in 1969 and continued through 1970. Available with a long list of sports options, it posed a considerable threat to the muscle cars established both on the street and at the drag strip. Despite its potential, the Eliminator is often overlooked by enthusiasts today.

'...a gentleman's muscle car.'

'With its wood-rimmed steering wheel and full instrumentation, the Cougar appears to be a gentleman's muscle car. Starting up the monster 7014cc (428ci) engine reveals a totally different character. The big engine demands high-octane fuel and concentration on the open road. Its greatest asset is the huge amount of mid-range torque. A drag racer's dream, it is enough to humble any would-be challenger. It's quick enough to run the ¼ mile in 14.1 seconds.'

This Eliminator has base model trim and is fitted with vinyl seats instead of leather ones.

Milestones

1967 Two years after
Mustang, Mercury launches its own pony car, the Cougar. It features a distinctive front end with a razor-style grill and hidden headlights. Initially, it is offered only as a hardtop.

Mercury's other 1969 muscle car was the Cyclone. This one is a Spoiler II.

1969 After minor updates
for 1968, the Cougar is restyled the following year and a convertible is now offered. A high performance model, the Eliminator, is launched mid-year and is available with a host of extra performance options, and was painted with 'high impact' exterior colours such as yellow blue, and orange.

The Cougar share the 302 and 428 engines with the Mustang.

1970 The Eliminator
returns for its second and final season. Its body restyling is more refined than the 1969 model. Just over 2000 cars are sold and the model is dropped after only two years of production.

UNDER THE SKIN

Mustang stretch

Essentially a stretched Mustang, the Cougar has independent front suspension with double wishbones, coil springs, telescopic shocks and an anti-roll bar. At the rear are twin semi-elliptical leaf springs, and staggered heavy-duty shocks are fitted to limit wheel hop during a brisk standing start.

Live rear axle

Wishbone front suspension

Unitary construction

Front disc brakes

Big-block V8

THE POWER PACK

Snake bite

The Eliminator was available with a 4949cc (302ci) V8 or a 7014cc (428ci) Cobra Jet V8 (identical to the Mustang engine shown here). The 7014cc (428ci) came with or without a ram air system. The engine has a modified crankshaft, stronger connecting rods, and, if the Drag Pak was specified, the owner received an oil cooler and 4.30:1 gears. Headers, dual quads and quadruple Weber carbs could be ordered from dealers to make the Eliminator more of a street terror than it already was.

Ram-air induction

Four-barrel carburettor

Heavy duty connecting rods

Oil cooler

Street racer

Since the Eliminator is longer and heavier than the Mustang, it is able get more grip and harness the power from the mighty 7014cc (428ci) V8. Though the engine had a factory rating of 335bhp, it actually made closer to 410. The lower rating was to fool insurance companies.

The 1970 Eliminator is offers more refined body panels than the 1969 car.

Mercury **COUGAR ELIMINATOR**

This is Mercury's version of the high-performance Mustang. More refined than its baby brother, it still keeps the Ford heritage with bright paint, side stripes, spoilers, a bonnet scoop, and big block power.

Staggered shocks

Axle tramp can be a serious problem with smaller-sized performance Fords from this era, especially those with big engines. The Cougar Eliminator has staggered rear shock absorbers to help overcome this problem.

'High Impact' paintwork

'High Impact' exterior colours was the order of the day in 1970. The Cougar was available in bright blue, yellow and Competition Orange, as seen here.

Cobra Jet engine

The Eliminator is available with either the 290bhp Boss 302 or the stout 7014cc (428ci) Cobra Jet with a conservatively rated 335bhp. This example is powered by the larger 7014cc (428ci), often thought of as one of the finest muscle car engines ever produced.

Interior trim

Although more luxurious than the Mustang, the Eliminator is a base model Cougar and has vinyl upholstery. Full instrumentation is standard and includes a tachometer.

Drag Pak

This Eliminator is garnished with the legendary 'Drag Pak' option, which includes the 428 Super Cobra Jet engine, an oil cooler, and ultra-low rear-end gearing (3.91:1 or 4.30:1). This makes the Cougar one of the fastest accelerating muscle cars.

Restyled front

For 1970, the Cougar received a revised front grill with vertical bars and a more pronounced nose. The tail panel was also slightly altered.

Sequential turn indicators

The rear indicators, which are also combined with the brake lights, flash in sequence when the driver flicks the lever. These are also found on contemporary Shelby Mustangs.

Specifications

1970 Mercury Cougar Eliminator

ENGINE
Type: V8

Construction: Cast-iron block and heads

Valve gear: Two valves per cylinder operated by pushrods and rockers

Bore and stroke: 102mm (4.0in) x 89mm (3.5in)

Displacement: 7014cc (428ci)

Compression ratio: 10.6:1

Induction system: Four-barrel carburettor

Maximum power: 335bhp at 5200rpm

Maximum torque: 440lb-ft at 3400rpm

Top speed: 171km/h (106mph)

0–96km/h (0–60mph): 5.6 sec

TRANSMISSION
C-6 Cruise-O-Matic

BODY/CHASSIS
Steel monocoque two-door coupe body

SPECIAL FEATURES

The headlights are concealed behind special 'flip-up' panels.

A rear Cougar spoiler is standard Eliminator equipment.

RUNNING GEAR
Steering: Recirculating ball

Front suspension: Unequal length wishbones with coil springs, telescopic shocks and anti-roll bar

Rear suspension: Semi-elliptical multi-leaf springs with staggered rear telescopic shocks

Brakes: Discs (front), drums (rear)

Wheels: Styled steel, 12.7cm (5in) x 35.6cm (14in)

Tyres: F60-14 Goodyear Polyglas GT

DIMENSIONS
Length: 4.87m (191.6in)

Width: 197m (77.6in)

Height: 1.34m (52.8in)

Wheelbase: 282cm (111in)

Track: 152cm (60in) (front), 152cm (60in) (rear)

Weight: 1715kg (3780lb)

Mercury CYCLONE

Essentially an upmarket Falcon, the Mercury Comet was seen by young people as a grocery getter, but it could be ordered in Cyclone GT trim. Packing a solid-lifter 4736cc (289ci) V8 and four-speed transmission, it was light and could run rings around the more popular 6997cc (427ci) equipped cars.

'...iron-fisted performer.'

'It may look like a run-of-the-mill compact both inside and out, but take the Comet Cyclone for a drive and you'll soon get a different picture. The iron-fisted, small-block V8 performer packs a punch, particularly in mid range and coupled with the four-speed Top Loader. You feel confident enough to take on bigger, more powerful cars at the stop light. The Cyclone's unitary construction, and 271bhp engine made this feather-weight flyer a joy to drive.'

Comet Cyclones have slightly plusher interiors than contemporary Falcon Sprints.

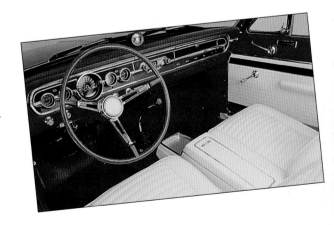

Milestones

1960 A compact Mercury makes its debut.
Named Comet, it is similar to the new Ford Falcon but has squarer sheet metal, plus the sedans and coupes have a longer, 290cm (114in) wheelbase. It is quite popular in its first season, with more than 116,000 being sold.

Ford's version of the Cyclone was the Falcon Futura Sprint.

1964 Styling is squared up and a V8 becomes available in Comets.
Arriving at midyear is a Cyclone GT with a 210bhp, 4736cc (289ci) V8 as its base engine. Offered as a hardtop, 7454 cars are built.

The Final Cyclone, launched in 1970, packed up to 370bhp.

1965 Stacked headlights are a feature
of all Comets this year and the Cyclone GT version returns, with standard 289 V8s packing up to 271bhp. 12,347 are sold. Comets are upsized for 1966.

UNDER THE SKIN

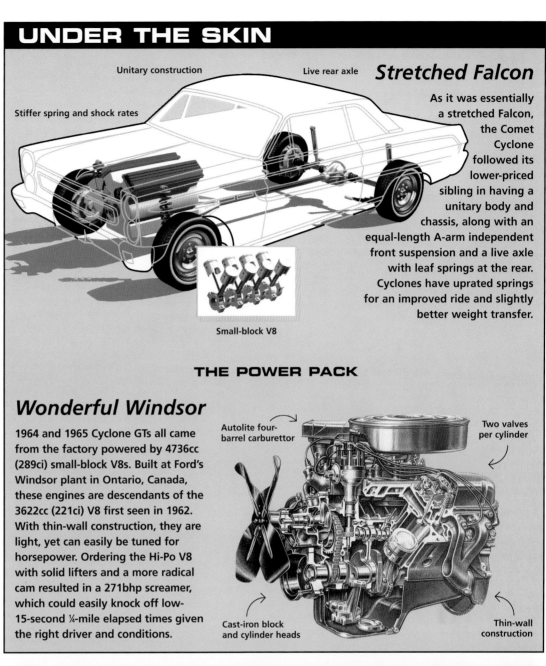

Unitary construction

Live rear axle

Stiffer spring and shock rates

Small-block V8

Stretched Falcon

As it was essentially a stretched Falcon, the Comet Cyclone followed its lower-priced sibling in having a unitary body and chassis, along with an equal-length A-arm independent front suspension and a live axle with leaf springs at the rear. Cyclones have uprated springs for an improved ride and slightly better weight transfer.

THE POWER PACK

Wonderful Windsor

1964 and 1965 Cyclone GTs all came from the factory powered by 4736cc (289ci) small-block V8s. Built at Ford's Windsor plant in Ontario, Canada, these engines are descendants of the 3622cc (221ci) V8 first seen in 1962. With thin-wall construction, they are light, yet can easily be tuned for horsepower. Ordering the Hi-Po V8 with solid lifters and a more radical cam resulted in a 271bhp screamer, which could easily knock off low-15-second ¼-mile elapsed times given the right driver and conditions.

Autolite four-barrel carburettor

Two valves per cylinder

Cast-iron block and cylinder heads

Thin-wall construction

Fireball

One of the lesser-known muscle cars, both then and now, the Comet Cyclone was built only in small numbers and can be tough to track down today. Nevertheless, simple, robust mechanicals, neat styling and ample go make it an attractive classic.

1965 Cyclones are preferred over later variants because of their simple styling.

Mercury **CYCLONE**

Not the best promoted or the fastest, the 1965 Cyclone nevertheless showed that the Lincoln-Mercury division was serious about the muscle market. The Cyclone led to some of the quickest factory hot rods ever built.

Small-block exclusive
Officially, the Comet Cyclone came with a 200bhp, 4736cc (289ci) V8 in 1965, which was adequate but no drag strip performer. Those who knew how to play with the options list, however, got the Hi-Po 289. With solid valve lifters and a four-barrel Autolite carburettor, it turned the Mercury compact into a bona fide junior muscle car.

Drum brakes
Braking ability on most cars in 1965 was not a strong point, though Cyclones could be ordered with sintered metallic linings or front disc brakes for those concerned about bringing it to a halt.

Optional gearing
In the 1960s, several axle ratios were offered on Cyclones. Ordering ultra-steep 4.11:1 cogs made these little Mercs into high-14-second-¼-mile cars with a good tune-up and an experienced driver at the wheel.

Hardtop styling
All of the 19,801 first-generation Comet Cyclones built were two-door hardtops. The Merc's counterpart at Ford Division, the Falcon Futura Sprint, was offered in both hardtop and convertible forms. When the Comet grew to intermediate size for the 1966 model year, a convertible variation was added to the option list.

GTO cues

Pontiac's stylish GTO was a hot seller, and other makes tried image copy its design in an attempt to stimulate demand for their own hot offerings. The 1965 Cyclone pays homage to the GTO with its stacked headlights and full-width rear grill/taillight assembly.

Bias-ply tyres

Traction can be a problem due to the tyre technology of the day. With rock-hard bias-plys, it is easy to spin the wheels in every gear, and good launches require considerable skill.

Plush interior

Costing $346 more than a Falcon Sprint, it was only natural that the Comet had a more upmarket interior. Among the options were tinted glass, padded sun visors, bucket seats, power windows and, being the 1960s, even seatbelts!

Specifications

1965 Mercury Comet Cyclone

ENGINE

Type: V8

Construction: Cast-iron block and heads

Valve gear: Two valves per cylinder operated by a single camshaft with pushrods and solid valve lifters

Bore and stroke: 102mm (4.00in) x 73mm (2.87in)

Displacement: 4737cc (289ci)

Compression ratio: 10.5:1

Induction system: Autolite four-barrel downdraft carburettor

Maximum power: 271bhp at 6000rpm

Maximum torque: 312lb-ft at 3400rpm

Top speed: 200km/h (124mph)

0–96km/h (0–60mph): 7.4 sec

TRANSMISSION

Four-speed manual

BODY/CHASSIS

Steel unitary chassis with two-door coupe body

SPECIAL FEATURES

This car has the Hi-Po 289, identified by the Super Cyclone air cleaner.

Wheel covers cunningly look like reverse chrome steel rims.

RUNNING GEAR

Steering: Recirculating ball

Front suspension: Unequal-length A-arms, coil springs and telescopic shock absorbers

Rear suspension: Live axle, semi-elliptic leaf springs and telescopic shock absorbers

Brakes: Discs (front), drums (rear)

Wheels: Pressed steel, 35.6cm (14in) dia.

Tyres: G70-14

DIMENSIONS

Length: 4.96m (195.3in)

Width: 1.85m (72.9in)

Height: 1.36m (53.5in)

Wheelbase: 290cm (114.0in)

Track: 140cm (55.0in) (front), 142cm (56.0in) (rear)

Weight: 1358kg (2994lb)

Mercury CYCLONE SPOILER

Mercury redesigned its intermediates for 1970, which spelled big changes for the Cyclone. Besides the smoother, more flowing contours, it got a new engine. Packing a massive amount of torque, it could run rings around rival muscle cars.

'...unique and distinctive style.'

'A four-speed with a Hurst shifter, high-back bucket seats and acres of black vinyl greet you when you take your place behind the wheel. Being a Mercury, the Cyclone rides extremely well on the highway. The Cyclone also has a unique and distinctive style. The steering may feel light and the Spoiler can feel a little unwieldy around sharp corners, but in a straight line it really goes. Accelerating hard from 32km/h (20mph), the force is incredible.'

A three-spoke steering wheel and a Hurst shifter complete the businesslike cockpit.

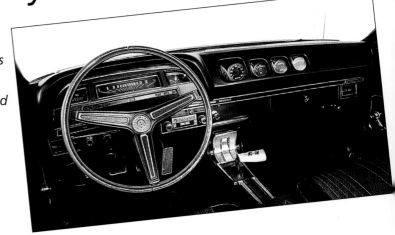

Milestones

1968 The midsize Mercury gets new styling
and a new name – the Montego. A semi-sporty Montego – the GT – is offered, but only 334 are built.

A limited-edition spoiler for 1969 was the Dan Gurney Special.

1969 A new Cyclone CJ appears,
fitted with a standard 7014cc (428ci) V8 producing 335bhp. A Spoiler version also arrives but has a standard 5752cc (351ci) small-block V8.

Ford's Torino Cobra is a close relative of the Cyclone Spoiler.

1970 Midsize Mercs are rebodied
and get a longer wheelbase. The Cyclone now comes in three different trims: base, GT and Spoiler. The 351 and 390 are offered in lesser Cyclones, but the 370bhp 429 is standard in the Spoiler. 13,490 Cyclones are built.

1971 The Cyclone returns with
few changes. Production plummets to 3084 in this, its final year.

UNDER THE SKIN

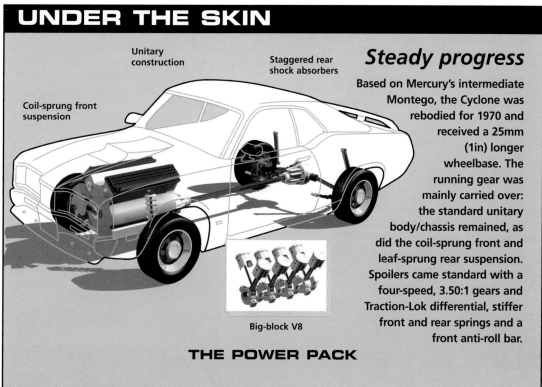

Unitary construction

Staggered rear shock absorbers

Coil-sprung front suspension

Big-block V8

Steady progress

Based on Mercury's intermediate Montego, the Cyclone was rebodied for 1970 and received a 25mm (1in) longer wheelbase. The running gear was mainly carried over: the standard unitary body/chassis remained, as did the coil-sprung front and leaf-sprung rear suspension. Spoilers came standard with a four-speed, 3.50:1 gears and Traction-Lok differential, stiffer front and rear springs and a front anti-roll bar.

THE POWER PACK

Thunder torque

For 1970, the hallowed 7014cc (428ci) engine was replaced by a new unit, a 7030cc (429ci) big-block V8, which came standard in the Cyclone GT and Spoiler. The Spoiler is fitted with the 370bhp version with standard Ram Air induction, solid lifters and a Rochester Quadrajet four-barrel carburettor. Although it packs considerable horsepower, this engine's greatest asset is its torque – 450lb-ft at 3400rpm. Properly tuned, a Cyclone Spoiler was more than a match for some of the competition's hottest iron.

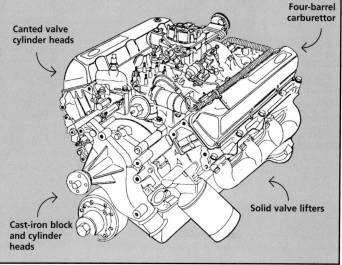

Four-barrel carburettor

Canted valve cylinder heads

Cast-iron block and cylinder heads

Solid valve lifters

Unspoiled

The most desired car among the second-generation Cyclones is the 1970 Spoiler, with its Ram Air V8. Add a few other options, such as the Drag Pak with lower rear gearing and the Hurst shifted four-speed, and good ones can cost $15,000.

Cyclone Spoilers are still undervalued muscle cars.

Mercury CYCLONE SPOILER

In 1970, Mercury really came together, launching its best-ever muscle car. The Cyclone Spoiler had its own distinctive style, packing a wallop, which made it a real threat on the street no matter who was driving it.

Luxury interior

The Cyclone boasts a plusher cabin than the closely related Ford Torino. This includes hounds-tooth vinyl seats and a dash with all auxiliary controls angled toward the driver.

Thunder Jet engine

The canted valve-head 7030cc (429ci) came with standard Ram Air in the Spoiler, producing 370bhp and 450lb-ft of earth-moving torque. It made the Spoiler a strong runner, especially on the street, which is what counted most of all.

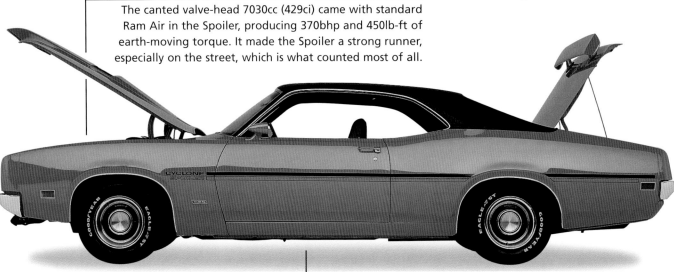

Drag Pak

The Drag Pak option gives the Spoiler even more straight line grunt. This adds an engine oil cooler, stronger bearings and main caps, plus steeper rear axle ratios in the form of 3.91:1 or 4.30:1 cogs.

Swoopy styling

Like its relative the Ford Torino, the Cyclone was rebodied for 1970 with smoother, more flowing lines. A distinctive feature is the projecting snout with gunsight grill treatment. This gave rise to the nickname 'Coffin Nose' and wasn't universally well received. At 5.33m (209.9in) overall, the Cyclone is one of the larger 1970 muscle intermediates.

Safety emphasis

Ford was one of the first US manufacturers to seriously market safety features. The Cyclone boasts such items as dual hydraulic braking systems with warning light, glare-reducing dashboard, energy-absorbing steering wheel and column, standard front and rear lap belts, safety rimmed wheels and corrosion-resistant brake lines.

Hidden headlights

By the late 1960s, hideaway headlights were popular in Detroit. The Cyclone's quad circular units are hidden behind flip-up grill panels operated by vacuum tubes. A second set of running lights is mounted astride the grill.

Heavy-duty suspension

In an effort to give the car a more balanced enthusiast flavour, a heavy-duty suspension was standard on the Spoiler. This included stiffer springs, shocks and a front anti-roll bar.

Specifications

1970 Mercury Cyclone Spoiler

ENGINE

Type: V8

Construction: Cast-iron block and heads

Valve gear: Two valves per cylinder operated by a single camshaft with pushrods and rockers.

Bore and stroke: 111mm (4.36in) x 91mm (3.59in)

Displacement: 7030cc (429ci)

Compression ratio: 11.3:1

Induction system: Rochester Quadrajet four-barrel carburettor

Maximum power: 370bhp at 5400rpm

Maximum torque: 450lb-ft at 3400rpm

Top speed: 212km/h (132mph)

0–96km/h (0–60mph): 7 sec

TRANSMISSION

Borg-Warner T-10 four-speed manual with Hurst shifter

BODY/CHASSIS

Steel unitary chassis with two-door fastback body

SPECIAL FEATURES

The protruding front end contains a distinctive 'gunsight'-type grill.

RUNNING GEAR

Steering: Recirculating ball

Front suspension: Unequal-length A-arms with coil springs, telescopic shock absorbers and anti-roll bar

Rear suspension: Live axle with semi-elliptic leaf springs and telescopic shock absorbers

Brakes: Discs (front), drums (rear)

Wheels: Steel, 17.8cm (7in) x 35.6cm (14in)

Tyres: Goodyear Polyglas, G60-14

DIMENSIONS

Length: 5.33m (209.9in)

Width: 1.96m (77.3in)

Height: 1.33m (52.2in)

Wheelbase: 297cm (117.0in)

Track: 154cm (60.5in) (front), 152cm (60.0in) (rear)

Weight: 1711kg (3773lb)

Oldsmobile 4-4-2 W30

While the 1968 4-4-2 had plenty of power with its 6555cc (400ci) V8 engine, this stock-looking Oldsmobile street machine has been modified with a 7456cc (455ci) V8 that makes the kind of power found only in the limited edition Hurst-modified cars.

'...fast and fun street machine.'

'The 1968 Oldsmobile 4-4-2 came with a W-30 360bhp 6555cc (400ci) engine with the new, forced-air option. This custom example, however, has a full-size 7456cc (455ci) Rocket motor with added performance parts, similar to the Hurst/Olds introduced that same year. With a 410bhp under the bonnet and a convertible top, this 4-4-2 is a fast and fun street machine. It accelerates like a rocket and handles better than most cars of its era.'

The interior remains relatively stock, but the engine under the hood is a different story.

Milestones

1964 The 4-4-2
nameplate debuts as a package option on the mid-size F-85™.

1965 The 4-4-2 engine
is a destroked and debored 6965cc (425ci) V8, creating the new 6555cc (400ci) V8.

Early 4-4-2s have more square bodywork than the later cars.

1967 Tri-power
induction is offered for one year and the engine makes 360bhp.

1968 A restyled body
gives the 4-4-2 a more elegant look. 3000 modified versions known as the Hurst/Olds are offered with 455 engines.

The 1970 W-30 came with a big 455 V8 and fibreglass bonnet.

1970 A 7456cc
(455ci) engine becomes available with Oldsmobile's "select fit" parts. The W-30 455 makes 370bhp, but its 14.3-second, quarter-mile time suggests this car made more power. These cars had fibreglass bonnets and plastic fender liners.

UNDER THE SKIN

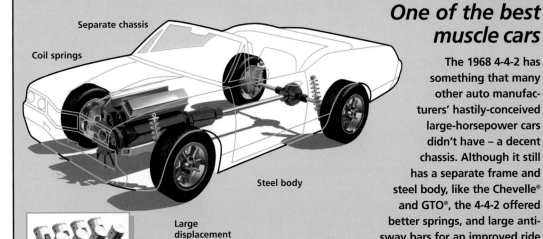

Separate chassis

Coil springs

Steel body

Large displacement engine

Toronado™ V8

One of the best muscle cars

The 1968 4-4-2 has something that many other auto manufacturers' hastily-conceived large-horsepower cars didn't have – a decent chassis. Although it still has a separate frame and steel body, like the Chevelle® and GTO®, the 4-4-2 offered better springs, and large anti-sway bars for an improved ride and handling.

THE POWER PACK

Full-size V8

After 1965 the first '4' in 4-4-2 stood for the size of the standard 6555cc (400ci) engine. Oldsmobile destroked and debored its full-size 425 V8 engine just for the 4-4-2. For 1966, Olds™ offered a tri-carburettor, boosting power to 360bhp (right). In 1970, its size was increased again to 7456cc (455ci). It was the biggest and most powerful engine Olds ever offered. The owner of the model featured here has replaced the factory 6555cc (400ci) V8 engine with a 7456cc (455ci) Rocket motor that makes 410bhp thanks to special modifications.

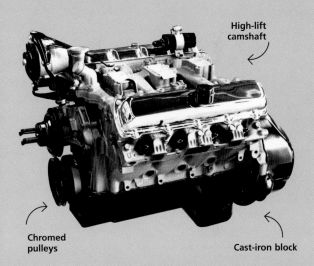

High-lift camshaft

Chromed pulleys

Cast-iron block

Convertible

The new 1968 range of 4-4-2 models updated the earlier cars. At the top of the new range, above the hardtop coupe, was the convertible. It offered incredible value for this type of car, not to mention loads of fun with the top down in the summer.

The convertible top and stock wheels give this 4-4-2 a stealthlike look.

Oldsmobile 4-4-2 W30

The 4-4-2 was one of the best muscle cars of the 1960s. It has incredible performance and, unlike many of its rivals, it also has the agility and braking to match the speed.

Custom paint
The bodywork has been sprayed with a base coat of Infinity White paint, followed by a clear coat to give a deep, high gloss finish.

4-4-2 badging
By 1968, the 4-4-2 nameplate had become familiar and sought-after property. Badging in the grill announced that you were driving something special.

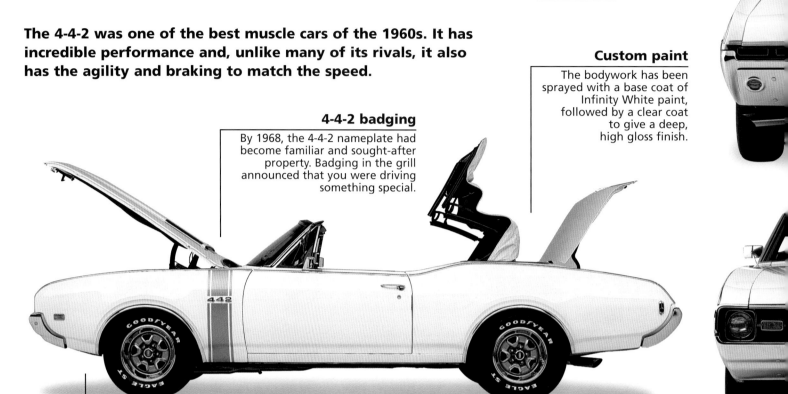

Uprated wheels and tires
The 1968 4-4-2 had 35.6cm (14in) diameter wheels, but the owner of this car has chosen to upgrade to 381.cm (15in) Super Stock II rims, shod with Goodyear Eagle ST tyres.

Improved cabin
As well as a 1970 Gold Madrid interior, this particular car features full GM and AutoGauge instruments and a 'Rallye' steering wheel.

Heavy-duty suspension
The rear end has been beefed up by replacing the stock coil springs with heavy-duty springs from a station wagon. Modern polyurethane bushings and 48mm ($1\frac{7}{8}$in) thick front and rear anti-roll bars have also been added to tighten the suspension further.

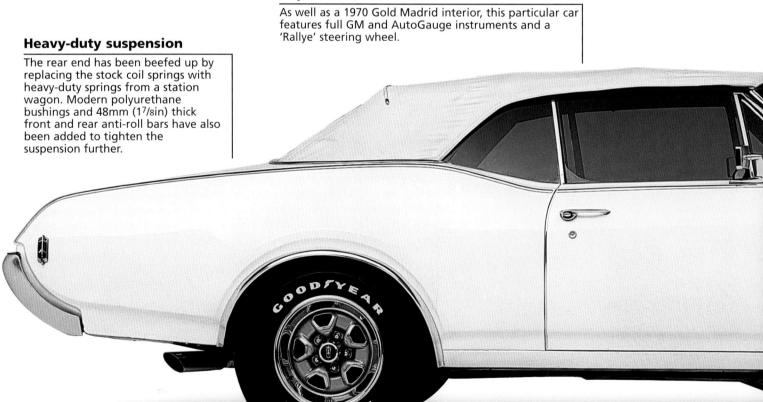

Sharp steering

To improve handling, the owner installed a quick-ratio steering box. This means the wheel has to be turned less when cornering.

Big 455 V8

Although the 455 V8 engine was not offered in the 1968 4-4-2, it was available in a special edition called the Hurst/Olds. It became standard for all 4-4-2 models in 1970.

Specifications

Oldsmobile 4-4-2 W30 Convertible

ENGINE

Type: V8

Construction: Cast-iron cylinder block and cylinder heads

Valve gear: Two valves per cylinder operated by a single camshaft

Bore and stroke: 105mm (4.12in) x 108mm (4.25in)

Displacement: 7456cc (455ci)

Compression ratio: 10.5:1

Induction system: Four-barrel carburettor

Maximum power: 410bhp at 5500rpm

Maximum torque: 517lb-ft at 3500rpm

Top speed: 248km/h (154mph)

0–96km/h (0–60mph): 6.8 sec

TRANSMISSION

Turbo HydraMatic 350 three-speed automatic

BODY/CHASSIS

Separate chassis with two-door convertible steel body

SPECIAL FEATURES

The interior has been taken from a 1970 Oldsmobile and features Gold Madrid vinyl upholstery.

On this modified car, the exhaust tips exit behind the rear tyres rather than out of the back as on the standard 4-4-2s.

RUNNING GEAR

Steering: Recirculating ball

Front suspension: Wishbones with coil springs, shocks, and anti-roll bar

Rear suspension: Rigid axle with coil springs, shocks, and anti-roll bar

Brakes: Discs front, drums rear

Wheels: Super Stock II, 38.1cm (15in) dia.

Tyres: Goodyear Eagle ST

DIMENSIONS

Length: 5.12m (201.6in)

Width: 1.94m (76.2in)

Height: 1.24m (52.8in)

Wheelbase: 284cm (112in)

Track: 150cm (59.1in) (front), 150cm (59.1in) (rear)

Curb weight: 1764kg (3890lb)

Oldsmobile **HURST/OLDS**

In 1983, 15 years after the appearance of the first Hurst/Olds, a special anniversary version was released. With a tuned 5031cc (307ci) V8, uprated suspension, bigger tyres and limited production run, it was destined to become a future collectible.

'...takes to curves.'

'Like previous Hurst/Olds cars, this one lets you shift between first and second manually, for a quick snap off the line. The high-output V8, combined with relatively short gearing, gives adequate 0–96km/h (0–60mph) performance. A special suspension means that this H/O takes to curves with much more confidence than previous versions. At highway speeds the car feels comfortable and composed, though the steering may be a little light for some tastes.'

The unusual Hurst Lightning Rod shifter came standard in all 1983 Hurst/Olds models.

Milestones

1978 Oldsmobile's intermediate Cutlass™
is downsized to a 275cm (108.1in) wheelbase and sheds over 181kg (400lb). It still proves a success and 527,606 are sold.

The Hurst/Olds burst onto the scene in 1968, packing a 455 V8.

1979 The Hurst/Olds appears
as a limited edition package on the Cutlass Supreme coupe. All 2499 cars come with two-tone black and gold paint, plus a 5735cc (350ci) V8.

1983 An eighth incarnation of
the Hurst/Olds appears. Only available in two-tone black and silver, it has a tweaked V8 and suspension; 3000 are sold.

The 307 V8 was standard in 1983 Custom Cruiser™ wagons.

1984 With reversed silver
and black paint, the H/O makes its final showing. A reborn 4-4-2 replaces it for 1985.

UNDER THE SKIN

Body-on-frame construction

Live rear axle

Stiffer coil springs front and rear

Small-block V8

Cutlass based

All Hurst/Olds models were built from the mid-size Cutlass two-door versions. Though smaller than previous editions, the car still retained a separate steel perimeter chassis and a front-engined, rear-drive format. Improvements over the standard Cutlass include thicker front and rear anti-roll bars, stiffer springs and shocks, quicker steering, shorter gearing and large 38.1cm (15in) x 17.8cm (7in) wheels.

THE POWER PACK

High output 307

By 1983, engine choices on the Cutlass had been whittled down to a Buick-built 3785cc (231ci) V6, a 5031cc (307ci) V8 or a 5735cc (350ci) diesel V8. In keeping with its sporty tradition, the 15th Anniversary Hurst/Olds had a V8 engine, but the 5031cc (307ci) unit was tweaked. It has a performance Delco ignition, an electronically controlled Rochester Quadrajet carburettor, stiffer valve springs and a low restriction cat-back dual exhaust. This boosted power from 140bhp to 180bhp.

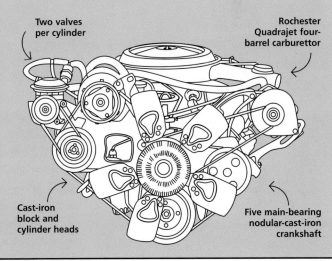

Two valves per cylinder

Rochester Quadrajet four-barrel carburettor

Cast-iron block and cylinder heads

Five main-bearing nodular-cast-iron crankshaft

Hurst handler

Although all Hurst/Olds models gain collector interest, the 1983 version stands out as being an anniversary commemorative edition. Although it may not pack the same punch as previous incarnations, it handles better and is more practical to drive every day.

The 1983 Hurst/Olds places more emphasis on balance than acceleration.

Oldsmobile HURST/OLDS

As Detroit came to terms with emissions regulations in the early 1980s, performance cars began to make a comeback. The 1983 Hurst/Olds exemplified the breed, being able to handle and go fast in a straight line.

Aero styling

In 1981, Cutlass coupes were fitted with a raked-back nose cap, which improved drag coefficient. The 1983 Hurst/Olds went a stage further and has an air dam integrated into the lower bumper to smooth airflow under the car.

Tuned small-block V8

Back in 1983, the biggest Oldsmobile engine was the 5031cc (307ci) V8. Not content with the standard 140bhp mill, engineers fitted a fortified version, with high-energy ignition, a four-barrel carburettor and low restriction exhaust. The result was an extra 40bhp.

Lightning Rod shifter

To say the least, the three-handled shifter was unique. The lever closest to the driver operated like a traditional automatic transmission with park, reverse neutral, drive and overdrive. If this lever was left in drive. the transmission would operate in a normal fashion. The other two shifters were a neat performance option. The shifter furthest from the driver only engaged first and second, while the middle shift lever brought the 2004R automatic from second to third.

Performance rear gearing

A standard set of 3.73:1 rear gears gives the Hurst/Olds considerable snap off the line by early-1980s standards. A limited-slip differential was offered as an option to further improve traction.

Two-tone paint

All 1983 Hurst/Olds were painted black, with silver on the lower body and bumpers. When the car reappeared in 1984, the colour pattern was reversed.

Superlift shocks

Superlift self-levelling air shock absorbers are fitted at the rear, but Oldsmobile recommended that pressure should not exceed 90psi.

Specifications

1983 Oldsmobile Hurst/Olds

ENGINE

Type: V8

Construction: Cast-iron block and heads

Valve gear: Two valves per cylinder operated by a single camshaft with pushrods and rocker arms.

Bore and stroke: 97mm (3.80in) x 99mm (3.89in)

Displacement: 5031cc (307ci)

Compression ratio: 8.0:1

Induction system: Single GM Rochester Quadrajet four-barrel carburettor

Maximum power: 180bhp at 4000rpm

Maximum torque: 245lb-ft at 3200rpm

Top speed: 193km/h (120mph)

0–96km/h (0–60mph): 8.4 sec

TRANSMISSION

GM 2004R four-speed automatic

BODY/CHASSIS

Separate steel chassis with two-door coupe body

SPECIAL FEATURES

The Hurst Lightning Rods shifter permits first and second, and second and third to be engaged manually.

All 1983 Hurst/Olds have a subtle bonnet bulge, hinting at the car's performance.

RUNNING GEAR

Steering: Recirculating ball

Front suspension: Unequal length A-arms with coil springs, telescopic shock absorbers and anti-roll bar

Rear suspension: Live axle with coil springs, telescopic shock absorbers and anti-roll bar

Brakes: Discs (front), drums (rear)

Wheels: Steel Rallye, 17.8cm (7in) x 38.1cm (15in)

Tyres: Goodyear Eagle GT, 225/60 VR15

DIMENSIONS

Length: 5.08m (200.0in)

Width: 1.82m (71.6in)

Height: 1.45m (57.1in)

Wheelbase: 275cm (108.1in)

Track: 132cm (51.8in) (front and rear)

Weight: 1603kg (3535lb)

Oldsmobile **RALLYE 350**

Due to rocketing insurance premiums on big-block muscle cars, manufacturers began offering alternatives. One of the best-balanced was the small-block powered Oldsmobile Cutlass Rallye 350, offered only for the 1970 model year.

'...similar to a 4-4-2.'

'Sitting behind the wheel, the Rallye 350 seems similar to a 4-4-2. When you drive away, however, the difference really becomes apparent. The small-block Cutlass feels slightly better balanced and more agile – easier to coax through sharp corners at high speeds. It may not have earth-shattering torque, but the willing small-block has a decent amount of power and sounds as deadly as its big-cubed brother. With less weight over the front wheels, the Cutlass also stops better than a 4-4-2.'

A four-spoke steering wheel indicates that this was intended to be more than a straightline screamer.

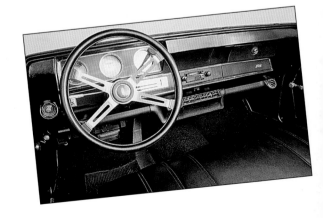

Milestones

1970 All GM intermediates
get new styling, including the Oldsmobile Cutlass. The 4-4-2 returns, now with standard 7456cc (455ci) power, but is joined by a small-block derivative, the Cutlass W31™, with a 325bhp, 5735cc (350ci) engine. A further small-block muscle car, the Rallye 350, arrives. It has Sebring yellow paint and a standard 310bhp 5735cc (350ci) engine.

Oldsmobile's standard muscle car was the 4-4-2; this is a 1968 model.

1971 Both the W31 and Rallye 350
are dropped. The most powerful 5735cc (350ci) V8 offered on the Cutlass cranks out just 260bhp.

The limited-edition Hurst/Olds was based on the Cutlass.

1972 The 4-4-2 reverts
to an option package with a standard 350 instead of a 455. The Hurst/Olds makes a welcome return and is selected to pace the Indy 500.

UNDER THE SKIN

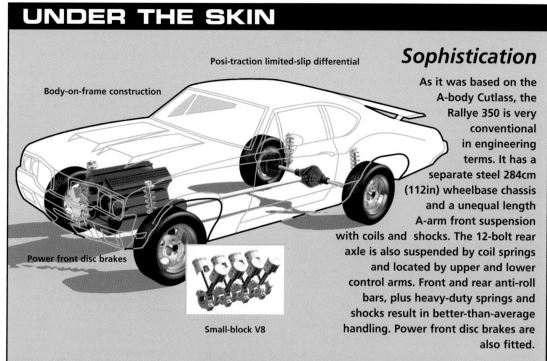

Posi-traction limited-slip differential

Body-on-frame construction

Power front disc brakes

Small-block V8

Sophistication

As it was based on the A-body Cutlass, the Rallye 350 is very conventional in engineering terms. It has a separate steel 284cm (112in) wheelbase chassis and a unequal length A-arm front suspension with coils and shocks. The 12-bolt rear axle is also suspended by coil springs and located by upper and lower control arms. Front and rear anti-roll bars, plus heavy-duty springs and shocks result in better-than-average handling. Power front disc brakes are also fitted.

THE POWER PACK

Rowdy Rallye 350

Oldsmobile's 5735cc (350ci) V8 appeared for 1968 as an enlarged version of the 5401cc (330ci) small-block. Used mainly in standard Cutlass sedans, coupes and wagons, its moment of glory arrived in 1970. The Rallye 350 package Oldsmobile specified the L34 version of its small-block, with a 10.3:1 compression ratio and a Rochester four-barrel Quadrajet carburettor. Rated at 310bhp and with 390lb-ft of torque, it could propel the Rallye 350 through the ¼-mile in 15.2 seconds. A second hi-po small-block, the 325bhp W31, was available for the Cutlass in 1970, but it was not installed in the Rallye 350.

W-45

Undoubtedly the most sought-after of all 1970 Oldsmobiles is the 4-4-2 W30, but the small-block cars – the Rallye 350 in particular – deserve a look. All Rallye 350s have Sebring Yellow paint, and with 390lb-ft of torque they have quite a punch, too.

Just 3547 Rallye 350s were built for 1970.

Oldsmobile **RALLYE 350**

Arguably one of the most handsome GM intermediates of 1970, the Cutlass was also one of the most sophisticated and driveable, especially in Rallye 350 form.

Dual exhaust

Like any true muscle car, the Rallye 350 has full-length dual exhaust pipes. Smog equipment consists of a PCV valve, which was recommended to be replaced every 19,300km (12,000 miles).

V8 engine

The peppy little 5735cc (350ci) V8, with 310bhp and 390lb-ft of torque, made the Rallye 350 more than a match for other big-block muscle cars. This is because of its lighter weight and lower torque, which enable the bias-ply tyres to hook up more effectively.

TH350 Automatic

The base transmission on the Cutlass range was a three-speed manual, though in order to get the most from the free-revving L34 small-block, the optional four-speed was perhaps the best choice. A TurboHydramatic three-speed automatic could be specified, with either a column or floor-mounted shifter.

Independent front suspension

Like most Detroit cars of the time, the Cutlass has independent unequal length A-arm front suspension. To improve handling, Rallye 350s have anti-roll bars front and back, plus heavy-duty springs and shocks.

Sebring Yellow paint

The Rallye 350 was available in only one colour – Sebring Yellow. All of the cars have yellow bumpers, sport mirrors and Rally wheels, and black stripes on the bonnet and around the back window, outlined in orange and black.

Two body styles

As an option package on the Oldsmobile F-85 Cutlass two-door, the Rallye 350 could be ordered either as a pillared coupe (seen here) or as a hardtop. One small flaw with the pillared coupe is that the vent windows cannot be fully opened because of the twin sport mirrors.

Specifications

1970 Oldsmobile Cutlass Rallye 350

ENGINE

Type: V8

Construction: Cast-iron block and heads

Valve gear: Two valves per cylinder operated by a block-mounted camshaft

Bore and stroke: 103mm (4.06in) x 86mm (3.38in)

Displacement: 5735cc (350ci)

Compression ratio: 10.25:1

Induction system: Single Rochester four-barrel carburettor

Maximum power: 310bhp at 4600rpm

Maximum torque: 390lb-ft at 3200rpm

Top speed: 196km/h (122mph)

0–96km/h (0–60mph): 7.0 sec

TRANSMISSION

TH 350 Automatic

BODY/CHASSIS

Body on frame construction; all steel

SPECIAL FEATURES

The body-coloured front and rear bumpers are unique to Rallye 350s.

The bonnet is identical to that on the 4-4-2 W30™ and includes bonnet locks.

RUNNING GEAR

Steering: Recirculating ball

Front suspension: Unequal length A-arms with coil springs, telescopic shock absorbers and anti-roll bar

Rear suspension: Live axle with upper and lower control arms, coil springs, telescopic shock absorbers and anti-roll bar

Brakes: Discs (front), drums (rear)

Wheels: Stamped-steel, 35.6cm (14in) x 15.2cm (6in)

Tyres: Goodyear Polyglas, G-70 14

DIMENSIONS

Length: 5.16m (203.2in)

Width: 1.94m (76.2in)

Height: 1.34m (52.8in)

Wheelbase: 284cm (112.0in)

Track: 150cm (59.0in) (front and rear)

Weight: 1621kg (3574lb)

Plymouth BARRACUDA

The Barracuda was the result of Chrysler's determination not to be left out of the 'pony car' market. Plymouth took an existing compact platform from the Valiant, added unique bodywork and options, and there it was – Chrysler's very own version of the Mustang.

'...exhilarating experience.'

'The 1967 Barracuda was part of the new wave of smaller, more powerful cars that swept across the US during the mid-to-late 1960s. Chrysler followed the trend by providing an exhilarating driving experience, combining compact dimensions with awesome power. The Barracuda has decent handling characteristics. However, with legendary 6276cc (383ci) V8 grunt, it can be quite a handful when driven at the limit. Nonetheless, it's high on the fun factor.'

The Barracuda's large steering wheel dominates the cabin and is typical of the era.

Milestones

1964 The Plymouth Barracuda
is launched on April 1st, two weeks before the Ford Mustang. Though it appears mid-1964, it is branded a 1965 model. It features folding rear seats, which are novel for the time.

Modified Cudas became a common site on drag strips.

1967 The Barracuda undergoes
its first major restyle, which includes a 5cm (2in) wheelbase extension. Convertible and hardtop coupe models are also introduced.

The Road Runner was Plymouth's full-size muscle car.

1970 Lower, wider and shorter,
the Barracuda begins the new decade with a total redesign. The legendary Hemi engine is now available.

1974 Production of the Barracuda
comes to an end – a victim of the fuel crisis and emissions controls.

UNDER THE SKIN

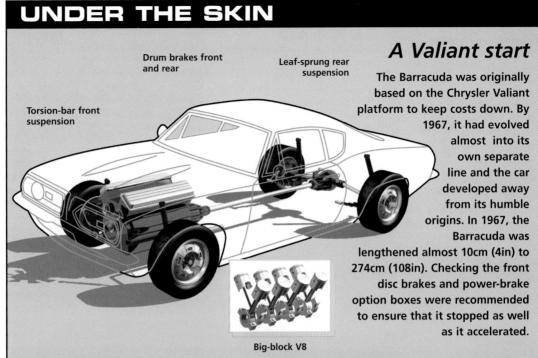

Drum brakes front and rear

Leaf-sprung rear suspension

Torsion-bar front suspension

Big-block V8

A Valiant start
The Barracuda was originally based on the Chrysler Valiant platform to keep costs down. By 1967, it had evolved almost into its own separate line and the car developed away from its humble origins. In 1967, the Barracuda was lengthened almost 10cm (4in) to 274cm (108in). Checking the front disc brakes and power-brake option boxes were recommended to ensure that it stopped as well as it accelerated.

THE POWER PACK

Solid performance
The big-block, 6276cc (383ci) engine dates back to 1960, when the Golden Commando unit, complete with 'Ram Induction' was created for the Fury/Sport Suburban models. It is a simple design with a cast-iron block and cylinder heads. Hemi-engined Plymouths may have offered the ultimate in power output, but with Carter four-barrel carburettors, the 6276cc (383ci)-equipped Barracuda pumps out 280bhp and an impressive 400lb-ft of torque at 2400rpm. The 6276cc (383ci) is a very flexible motor and can be easily tuned or modified with components from other Chrysler engines.

Formula S
Starting in 1968, Barracudas were available with a performance option package called 'Formula S.' These cars were available with a four-speed manual transmission, dual exhaust, anti-roll bars, wider tyres and, of course, Formula S badging.

The stylish lines of the Barracuda are some of the finest seen on a Plymouth.

Plymouth **BARRACUDA**

The Barracuda, with the Mustang, is in many ways the quintessential pony car. It offered the buyer a practical car that could be driven every day, yet had great performance potential – especially with the 6276cc (383ci) engine.

Engine options

In 1967, buyers could choose either the base 145bhp, 3687cc (225ci) slant-six engine or the 4474cc (273ci) or 6276cc (383ci) V8. The following year, Plymouth offered another V8, the 5572cc (340ci), to fill the gap between the earlier engines.

Transmission choices

Barracudas may have come as standard with a three-speed manual, but the options list also included a four-speed manual, as well as a TorqueFlite three-speed automatic transmission.

Restyled rear window

Although the first-generation Barracuda sported a distinctive wraparound rear window, the styling cue could not entirely disguise its Valiant origins. New bodystyles for 1967 included a convertible and a hardtop.

Stretched chassis

For 1967, the Barracuda's wheelbase was stretched by 5cm (2in) and the car grew by about 10cm (4in) overall. It still remained in proportion, however, and the motoring press universally applauded its modest, yet distinctive, good looks.

Sporty options

Buyers could specify a range of options to give the car a sporty feel, from cosmetic items – such as bucket seats, consoles and stripes – to real performance hardware – like a Sure-Grip differential or the 6276cc (383ci) V8 engine.

Specifications

1967 Plymouth Barracuda

ENGINE

Type: V8

Construction: Cast-iron block and heads

Valve gear: Two valves per cylinder operated by a single camshaft

Bore and stroke: 108mm (4.25in) x 86mm (3.38in)

Displacement: 6276cc (383ci)

Compression ratio: 10.0:1

Induction system: Carter four-barrel carburettor

Maximum power: 280bhp at 4200rpm

Maximum torque: 400lb-ft at 2400rpm

Top speed: 193km/h (120mph)

0–96km/h (0–60mph): 7.0 sec

TRANSMISSION

Three-speed manual/four-speed manual or three-speed auto

BODY/CHASSIS

Unitary construction with steel body panels

SPECIAL FEATURES

The rear seats fold down to create cavernous luggage space.

The race inspired style of the fuel- filler cap is unique to the Barracuda.

RUNNING GEAR

Steering: Worm-and-roller

Front suspension: A-arms with torsion bars and telescopic shock absorbers

Rear suspension: Live axle with semi-elliptic leaf springs and telescopic shock absorbers

Brakes: Drums (front and rear)

Wheels: Steel, 35.6cm (14in) dia.

Tyres: Firestone wide ovals, D70 x 35.6cm (14in)

DIMENSIONS

Length: 4.9m (192.8in)

Width: 1.77m (69.6in)

Height: 1.34m (52.7in)

Wheelbase: 274cm (108.0in)

Track: 146cm (57.4in) (front), 141cm (55.6in) (rear)

Weight: 1334kg (2940lb)

Plymouth HEMI 'CUDA

As a muscle car legend, there are few cars to rival a 1970 Hemi 'Cuda. It has classic, well-proportioned good looks and an engine that is just as famous as the car itself. Despite its relative rarity, some owners feel the need to build themselves a better Hemi 'Cuda.

'...the definitive Plymouth.'

'The Hemi 'Cuda is the definitive Plymouth muscle car. It combines a great looking body style with the fearsome Hemi powerplant. Slip behind the steering wheel of this modified 'Cuda and prepare for an adventure. Off the line, it is obvious that this engine has been modified. Next you notice that the huge modern tyres grip fantastically. Power-shifting into second causing the rear tyres to screach reveals this Hemi 'Cuda's explosive acceleration.'

This 'Cuda retains a stock interior, including a pistol grip shifter and multiple gauges.

Milestones

1964 The Barracuda is launched
as Plymouth's retaliation to Ford's successful Mustang. It is built on the Valiant platform and has fastback coupe styling. Top engine option is the 4474cc (273ci) V8.

The 1967 GTX was just one of Plymouth's many Hemi powered muscle cars.

1967 A more powerful 6276cc
(383ci) V8 gives the Barracuda more performance.

1968 The Hemi engine
is finally fitted to a small number of 'Cudas.

The Duster was Plymouth's entry level muscle car for 1970.

1970 The 'Cuda is restyled
with Chrysler's new E-body. The Hemi is now a real production option, and 652 hardtops and 14 convertibles are manufactured.

1971 The Hemi engine
is retained for one final year. Power remains at 425bhp and 490lb-ft of torque.

UNDER THE SKIN

Solid as a rock

Based on Chrysler's E-body, the 'Cuda uses a steel monocoque. The front suspension uses double wishbones with torsion bar springing. The rear is more conventional with a semi-elliptic leaf-sprung live rear axle. This car has Koni adjustable shock absorbers in place of the standard Chrysler units. DIsc brakes are in the front, while drums are in the rear.

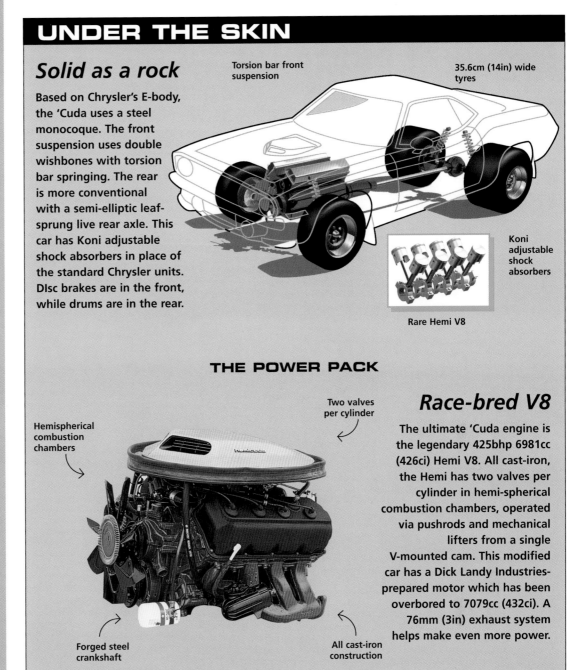

Torsion bar front suspension

35.6cm (14in) wide tyres

Koni adjustable shock absorbers

Rare Hemi V8

THE POWER PACK

Hemispherical combustion chambers

Two valves per cylinder

Forged steel crankshaft

All cast-iron construction

Race-bred V8

The ultimate 'Cuda engine is the legendary 425bhp 6981cc (426ci) Hemi V8. All cast-iron, the Hemi has two valves per cylinder in hemi-spherical combustion chambers, operated via pushrods and mechanical lifters from a single V-mounted cam. This modified car has a Dick Landy Industries-prepared motor which has been overbored to 7079cc (432ci). A 76mm (3in) exhaust system helps make even more power.

King 'Cuda

Of all the Barracuda range, the 1970 Hemi 'Cuda is the pick of the bunch. Its race-bred engine and rarity make it a real collector's piece, popular with purists and performance freaks alike. Not many are modified, as they command higher prices in stock condition.

This car is finished in the original factory colour of Lime Light.

Plymouth HEMI 'CUDA

Lime Light green was only one of the factory optioned 'High Impact' colours available for the 1970 'Cuda. If you have an engine as powerful as this one, why not have a paint scheme that's equally outrageous?

Hemi V8

The Hemi V8 was so called because of its hemispherical combustion chambers. These promote more efficient combustion of the air/fuel mixture. It was one of the most powerful engines ever put in any muscle car.

Low ratio back axle

The lowest standard axle ratio available was 4.10:1. This car has an even lower 4.56:1 ratio axle for more urgent acceleration.

Torsion bar front suspension

The 'Cuda uses double wishbone front suspension sprung by longitudinally-mounted torsion bars. Adjustable Koni shock absorbers are used on this car.

Drag racing tires and wheels

For looks and performance, 35.6cm (14in) wide Weld Racing Pro-Star alloy wheels and super-sticky Mickey Thompson tyres have been added to this wild Hemi 'Cuda.

Hardtop body

This, like most Hemi 'Cudas, has a two-door hardtop body. There were only 14 Hemi convertibles made in 1970.

Bonnet-retaining pins

These race-style bonnet-retaining pins were actually factory fitted with the shaker bonnet, which came as standard equipment on the Hemi 'Cuda.

Custom tail pipes

Even with the free-flow system fitted to this car, the owner has managed to retain the neat feature of having the twin tail pipes exiting through the rear valance.

Limited-slip differential

The 'Cuda has a Chrysler 'Sure-Grip' limited-slip differential as standard equipment.

Specifications
1971 Plymouth Hemi 'Cuda

ENGINE
Type: V8

Construction: Cast-iron block and heads

Valve gear: Two valves per cylinder actuated by a single camshaft via mechanical lifters and pushrods

Bore and stroke: 108mm (4.25in) x 95mm (3.75in)

Displacement: 7079cc (432ci)

Compression ratio: 10.25:1

Induction system: Twin Carter AFB four-barrel carburettors

Maximum power: 620bhp at 6500rpm

Maximum torque: 655lb-ft at 5100rpm

Top speed: 220km/h (137mph)

0–96km/h (0–60mph): 4.3 sec

TRANSMISSION
Chrysler A-833 four-speed manual

BODY/CHASSIS
Steel monocoque two-door coupe body

SPECIAL FEATURES

This Hemi 'Cuda has the popular shaker bonnet. The Shaker was often a different colour from the bodywork.

RUNNING GEAR
Steering: Recirculating ball

Front suspension: Double wishbones with longitudinal torsion bars, Koni adjustable telescopic shock absorbers and anti-roll bar

Rear suspension: Live axle with semi-elliptic leaf springs, Koni adjustable shock absorbers

Brakes: Discs (front), drums (rear)

Wheels: Weld Racing Pro-Star, 38.1cm (15in) x 17.8cm (7in) (front), 38.1cm (15in) x 35.6cm (14in) (rear)

Tyres: P225/70R-15 General (front), 18.5-31 Mickey Thompson (rear)

DIMENSIONS
Length: 4.74m (186.7in)

Width: 1.9m)74.9in)

Height: 1.29m (50.9in)

Wheelbase: 274cm (108in)

Track: 152cm (59.7in) (front), 154cm (60.7in) (rear)

Weight: 1789kg (3945lb)

Plymouth 'CUDA 383

Few Detroit muscle machines have the same impact as the E-body Plymouth 'Cuda. With a 6276cc (383ci) V8 under the bonnet, lightning acceleration and flamboyant paint, its styling is obviously well mated to its performance.

'...retina-scorching hue.'

'Chrysler products of the early 1970s – especially E-bodies – have a magic all their own. Slide yourself into the seat, turn the key and grab the Pistol Grip shifter. Floor the throttle and the rear spins violently as the tyres fight for traction. To optimize the power band, shift the transmission when the engine reaches 5000rpm. The 'Cuda jolts off the line and pulls extremely hard, even in 6276cc (383ci) guise. With its meaty-sounding exhaust and retina-scorching hue, it really turns heads.'

A three-spoke rim-blow steering wheel and Rally-pack gauges were standard on 'Cudas.

Milestones

1968 Plymouth squeezes
a 6276cc (383ci) V8 into the compact A-body 'Cuda, but the results are disappointing. ETs are slower than the 340-equipped cars.

The 1970 'Cuda 440 introduced the new body shape.

1969 Riding a new E-body
platform, the Barracuda now has enough room for a large displacement V8. The top 'Cuda performance version is offered with a 6276cc (383ci), 7210cc (440ci) or Hemi V8. It can run 14.4-second ETs. Only 19,515 'Cudas are built for 1970.

Dodge produced the Challenger in 1970 – its own version of the Barracuda.

1971 A new grill, with quad
headlights, front fender vents and revised side graphic, highlight this year's 'Cuda. The 6276cc (383ci) engine is detuned to 300bhp, and because of falling demand, the 'Cuda 383 is axed for 1972.

UNDER THE SKIN

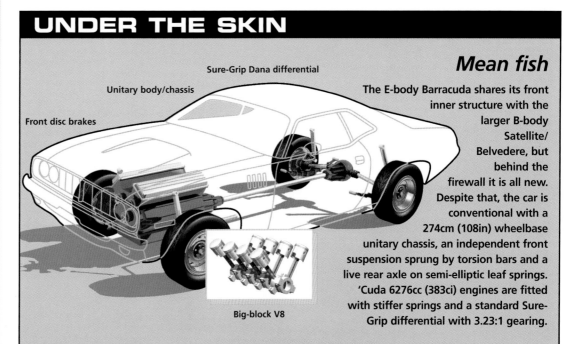

Sure-Grip Dana differential

Unitary body/chassis

Front disc brakes

Big-block V8

Mean fish

The E-body Barracuda shares its front inner structure with the larger B-body Satellite/Belvedere, but behind the firewall it is all new. Despite that, the car is conventional with a 274cm (108in) wheelbase unitary chassis, an independent front suspension sprung by torsion bars and a live rear axle on semi-elliptic leaf springs. 'Cuda 6276cc (383ci) engines are fitted with stiffer springs and a standard Sure-Grip differential with 3.23:1 gearing.

THE POWER PACK

383 Motorvation

For 1970, Barracuda engines started with the lowly 3687cc (225ci) Slant Six, but with the performance-oriented 'Cuda, something more was required to satisfy muscle car aficionados. The solution was to make the big-block 6276cc (383ci) the standard engine. It is essentially the same as that in the Road Runner, featuring parts from the 440 including the cylinder heads, exhaust manifolds, camshaft and windage tray. Heavy-duty valve springs were also specified. Fuel is delivered with a single Carter four-barrel carburettor and a low-restriction air cleaner. Rated at 300bhp and 410lb-ft of torque, the 6276cc (383ci) V8 could haul the 'Cuda to 96km/h (60mph) in less than 8 seconds.

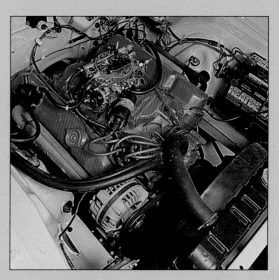

Tough lives

On the street, the E-body 'Cuda was one of the cars to beat. Many cars led hard lives and with poor quality control, many did not last long, either. Today, however, enthusiasts and collectors are buying up 'Cudas and restoring them to their former glory.

1971 was the second and last year for the formidable 'Cuda 383.

Plymouth 'CUDA 383

Chrysler was at the forefront of building factory street rods in the early 1970s and the 'Cuda was one of the most shining examples. High-impact colours, like Lemon Twist, made a statement on the street.

Big 6276cc (383ci) V8

Using parts from the bigger 7210cc (440ci) turned the 6276cc (383ci) into a street racer's dream. Smooth, streetable and affordable, it enabled E-bodies to turn in mid-14-second, ¼-mile elapsed times on street tyres.

Plenty of room

The 'Cuda shared its front subframe with the bigger B-body cars, and thus had ample room for big engines. It could be optioned with all the hard-hitters, right up to the fire-breathing Hemi. Only 115 Hemi 'Cudas were built in 1971.

Torsion bar front suspension

Chrysler's proven torsion-bar front suspension was still in widespread use in 1971 and was simple, strong and delivered an excellent ride. In the early 1970s, most serious racers cranked the bars up a few notches to help weight transfer during hard launches.

Dana differential

All 'Cudas came with a Sure-Grip differential with 3.23:1 gears. Shorter 3.55, 3.90 and 4.10 ratios were optional.

Specifications
1971 Plymouth 'Cuda 383

ENGINE
Type: V8

Construction: Cast-iron block and heads

Valve gear: Two valves per cylinder operated by a single V-mounted camshaft with pushrods and rockers

Bore and stroke: 108mm (4.25in) x 86mm (3.375in)

Displacement: 6276cc (383ci)

Compression ratio: 9.5:1

Induction system: Carter AFB four-barrel carburettor

Maximum power: 300bhp at 4800rpm

Maximum torque: 410lb-ft at 3400rpm

Top speed: 193km/h (120mph)

0–96km/h (0–60mph): 7.8 sec

TRANSMISSION
Four-speed manual

BODY/CHASSIS
Steel unitary chassis with steel bodywork

SPECIAL FEATURES

Non-functional fender vents are only seen on 1971 model 'Cudas.

The four-speed transmission includes this standard and unique Pistol Grip shifter.

RUNNING GEAR
Steering: Recirculating-ball

Front suspension: Unequal-length A-arms with longitudinal torsion bars, telescopic shock absorbers and anti-roll bar

Rear suspension: Live axle with semi-elliptic leaf springs, telescopic shock absorbers and anti-roll bar

Brakes: Discs (front), drums (rear)

Wheels: Steel Rallye, 35.6cm (14in) x 17.8cm (7in)

Tyres: Goodyear Polyglas, F70-14

DIMENSIONS
Length: 4.74m (186.6in)

Width: 1.82m (71.8in)

Height: 1.3m (51.4in)

Wheelbase: 275cm (108.1in)

Track: 137cm (53.8in) (front and rear)

Weight: 1576kg (3475lb)

High-impact colors

Chrysler's high-impact colour option was unique in the early 1970s. Colours included Tor Red, In-Violet, Vitamin C Orange, Go-Mango, Plum Crazy, Curious Yellow and Lemon Twist, which is painted on this example.

Dual-scoop hood

Performance-oriented 'Cudas got a standard steel bonnet with twin integral scoops. The bonnet could be equipped with bonnet pins to keep it from lifting at speed.

Plymouth **DUSTER 340**

At the end of the 1960s, the Chrysler Corporation attempted to create a new entry-level muscle car. This was achieved by combining the powerful 5572cc (340ci) V8 with a light, two-door version of the Plymouth Valiant bodyshell to create the high-performance Duster 340.

'...a budget street racer.'

'The Duster 340, Plymouth's budget muscle machine, is in essence a down-sized Road Runner. The 5572cc (340ci) V8 provides smooth power delivery and is capable of embarrassing drivers of other high-performance cars. Combined with a Torqueflite automatic transmission, it makes the Duster a perfect low-cost street racer. Standard front disc brakes provide exceptional stopping power, and the torsion bar suspension is extremely rugged.'

Like all Plymouth cars, the Duster's interior is simple but very functional.

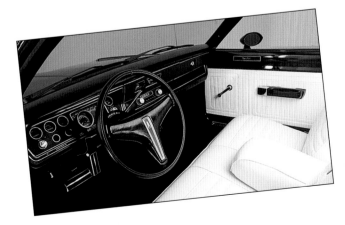

Milestones

1970 Plymouth

division introduces its Valiant-based Duster 340, with a swoopy coupe body and a high-power V8. With 275bhp and a $3300 list price, it is one of the best muscle car bargains of the year.

In 1971 Dodge introduced a Duster clone, the Demon 340.

1971 Performance

is unchanged, but the appearance is updated with the addition of a vertical bar grill, vivid graphics and an optional bonnet with huge '340' script.

The Challenger T/A was also powered by a 5572cc (340ci) V8, but it used three two barrels.

1972 New power

and emissions regulations take their toll and power is at 230bhp.

1974 The Duster

340 is replaced by the Duster 360 with a larger V8 producing 245bhp. Performance Dusters are retired after 1976.

UNDER THE SKIN

Live rear axle
Standard front disc brakes
Torsion bar front suspension
Small-block V8

Classic Chrysler

Like other Chrysler cars of the period, the Duster has monocoque construction, with torsion bar suspension at the front mounted on a separate subframe and a live rear axle suspended by leaf springs. Stiffer spring rates, a front anti-roll bar and E70 x 356cm (14in) tyres improve handling. It is the only one of Plymouth's performance cars to have standard front disc brakes.

THE POWER PACK

Hi-po exclusive

Unlike the 5211cc (318ci) V8, the high-revving 5572cc (340ci) is exclusively a high performance engine. For use in the Duster 340, it is fitted with a Carter AVS four-barrel carburettor, has a high 10.5:1 compression ratio – requiring it to run on premium fuel – and a high-lift camshaft. Optional dual exhausts and aggressive rear gears help to further enhance performance. Factory rated at 275bhp, the V8 propels the Duster to 96km/h (60mph) in just 6.0 seconds and gives elapsed times of 14.7 seconds at 94.3 mph.

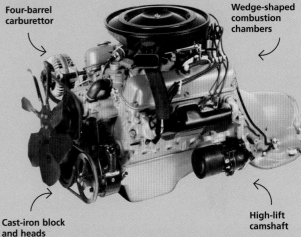

Four-barrel carburettor
Wedge-shaped combustion chambers
Cast-iron block and heads
High-lift camshaft

A good buy

The original Duster 340s are the most understated. 1971 editions retain all the performance credentials, but feature louder graphics. After 1971, performance is noticeably reduced, but today, at around $5000 a good Duster 340 is an excellent buy.

In their day, the Duster 340s were a good muscle car buy.

Plymouth DUSTER 340

Although sometimes viewed as little more than a coupe version of the Valiant, the Duster 340 combined light weight, Mopar V8 power and heavy-duty suspension at a very attractive price.

V8 engine

The 5572cc (340ci) V8 is one of Detroit's most tractable small-blocks of the muscle car era. With hydraulic lifters and a single four-barrel carburettor, it is easy to tune and its 275bhp was more than adequate for street races.

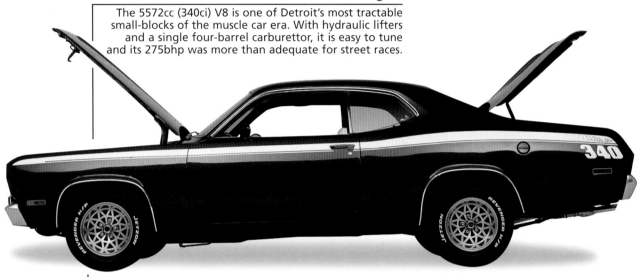

Performance tyres

The Duster 340 came with standard Goodyear Polyglas E70 x 35.6cm (14in) tyres and Rallye wheels, although this example has been fitted with period aftermarket wheels and later Jetzon Revenger 38.1cm (15in) radials.

Optional transmissions

The standard transmission is a three-speed manual, but a four-speed or the excellent TorqueFlite automatic were available as options.

Loud graphics

From 1971, the Duster 340 was given larger side stripes with a 340 script carried on the rear quarter panels. Two different bonnets were available – one with fake scoops and the other with a large 340 script.

Rear axle ratios

At the rear, the live axle is suspended by leaf springs. Standard rear gearing is 3.23:1, although shorter gears and a Sure Grip limited-slip differential were also available.

Power steering

In base form, the Duster 340 has manual steering, although the optional power set-up at extra cost was a sensible choice. Very light by today standards, it nevertheless makes the Duster easy to manoeuvre, especially at lower speeds.

Specifications
1971 Plymouth Duster 340

ENGINE
Type: V8

Construction: Cast-iron block and heads

Valve gear: Two valves per cylinder operated by a single camshaft via pushrods, rockers and hydraulic lifters

Bore and stroke: 102mm (4.03in) x 84mm (3.30in)

Displacement: 5572cc (340ci)

Compression ratio: 10.5:1

Induction system: Single Carter four-barrel carburettor

Maximum power: 275bhp at 5000rpm

Maximum torque: 340lb-ft at 3200rpm

Top speed: 193km/h (120mph)

0–96km/h (0–60mph): 6 sec

TRANSMISSION
Three-speed TorqueFlite automatic

BODY/CHASSIS
Unitary steel construction with two-door coupe body

SPECIAL FEATURES

An optional matt-black bonnet introduced in 1971 includes '340' in large script.

RUNNING GEAR
Steering: Recirculating ball

Front suspension: Double wishbones with longitudinal torsion bars, telescopic shocks and anti-roll bar

Rear suspension: Live axle with semi-elliptic leaf springs and telescopic shocks

Brakes: Ventilated discs, 26.7cm (10.5in) dia. (front), drums, 22.8cm (9in) dia. (rear)

Wheels: Cragar, 13.9cm (5.5in) x 38.1cm (15in)

Tyres: Jetzon Revenger, 178cm (70in) x 38.1cm (15in)

DIMENSIONS
Length: 4.88m (192in)

Width: 1.82m (71.6in)

Height: 1.34m (52.7in)

Wheelbase: 274cm (108in)

Track: 146cm (57.5in) (front), 141cm (55.5in) (rear)

Weight: 1588kg (3500lb)

Plymouth GTX

In the early 1960s, Plymouth built its reputation by selling high-performance cars. 1967 marked the first year it decided to combine performance with style. The sinister yet lavish GTX was the finished product and was built to combat the Pontiac GTO.

'...ready, willing and able.'

'Unlike the 1965 race Hemi, the street version is content to be driven around town and not just on the race track. When the pedal meets the floorboard, however, the engine screams to life and, with 490ft-lb of ready, willing and able torque, it shreds the rear tyres in any gear. But this is no bare bones street racer. It comes with standard bucket seats and luxury trimmings including a centre console. Whether on the street or at the drag strip, this Plymouth goes fast with class.'

This lavish GTX is equipped with standard front bucket seats and a deluxe interior.

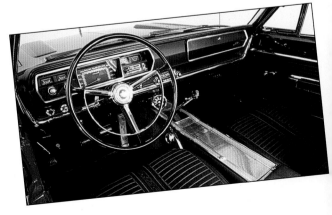

Milestones

1967 The GTX name appears
on a mid-size Belvedere hard-top coupe and convertible powered with the big 7210cc (440ci) V8 or the legendary 6981cc (426ci) Hemi. As a top-line model, it boasts a deluxe interior, bonnet scoops and stripes.

Arriving for 1968, the Road Runner was a bare bones GTX.

1968 Chrysler intermediates
are rebodied with crisp, smoother styling. NASCAR wins are numerous.

1969 Power refinements
are the order of the day with an 'Air Grabber' hood and a larger assortment of rear gear ratios ranging from 3.54 to 4.10.

The GTX still had big-block power in its final season.

1971 The last GTX built
has a new body and wider rear track. The 426 Hemi is still available, although few are installed.

UNDER THE SKIN

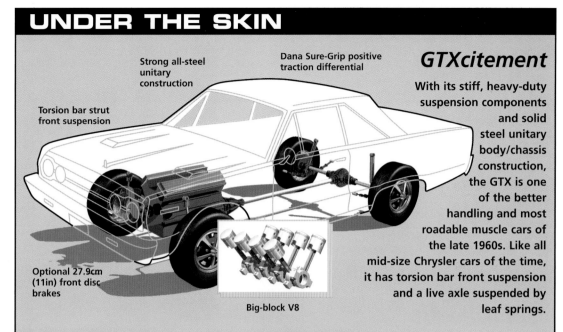

Strong all-steel unitary construction

Dana Sure-Grip positive traction differential

Torsion bar strut front suspension

Optional 27.9cm (11in) front disc brakes

Big-block V8

GTXcitement

With its stiff, heavy-duty suspension components and solid steel unitary body/chassis construction, the GTX is one of the better handling and most roadable muscle cars of the late 1960s. Like all mid-size Chrysler cars of the time, it has torsion bar front suspension and a live axle suspended by leaf springs.

THE POWER PACK

Hemi Hauler

Making its debut in 1964, the race Hemi (show here), was too radical to be used on the street. Chrysler offered a street version of the 426 Hemi that used lower 10.25:1 compression pistons and a milder cam than the race version for smoother, lowrpm use. It also uses an in-line rather than cross ram intake manifold topped with dual Carter four-barrel carburettors and not the race prepped Holleys.

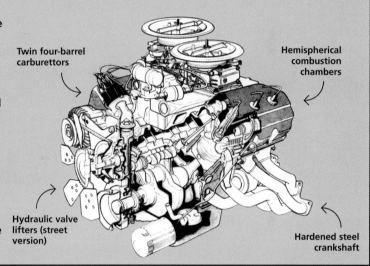

Twin four-barrel carburettors

Hemispherical combustion chambers

Hydraulic valve lifters (street version)

Hardened steel crankshaft

Guerrilla Power

Although the standard 440-powered GTX was a considerable threat, the optional Hemi engine turned the car into a legend. Although some drivability was sacrificed, few other cars could touch a Hemi GTX. Only 720 were built in 1967.

The Hemi engine makes for fearsome acceleration.

Plymouth GTX

The Hemi GTX was targeted at hard-core speed freaks who wouldn't skimp on comfort. It was a direct competitor of the GTO. At the track and on the street, it continuously trounced all over Pontiac's fastest.

Elegant styling

The 1967 GTX has a very elegant, in-motion style, thanks to the squared-off hardtop's forward-leaning C-pillars. For 1968, the GTX received a new body, leaving the first-year edition with a style of its own.

Hemi V8

Beneath the chromed air cleaner lies one of the most potent V8s ever built. The 6981cc (426ci) Hemi engine has hydraulic lifters and twin Carter four-barrel carburettors.

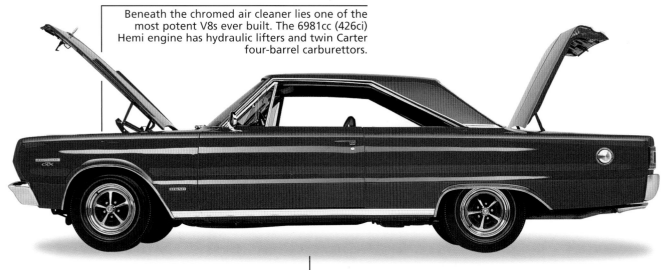

Traditional suspension

Continuing the Chrysler tradition, the GTX's front suspension consists of conventional upper A-arms and lower control arms attached to the chassis via torsion bars, heavy-duty tubular shock absorbers and an anti-roll bar. The rear is comprised of a solid axle suspended by heavy-duty tubular shock absorbers and leaf springs.

Deluxe interior

The thickly padded bucket seats and centre console with folding arm rest came as standard on the GTX, but a floor-mounted automatic shifter was optional. Styling is simple and instrumentation comprehensive, although the 241km/h (150mph) speedometer hints at the performance potential.

Sporty wheels

Fitted as standard are 35.6cm (14in) steel wheels finished in black with chrome trim. These are shod with racy-looking 20.9cm (8.25in) x 35.6cm (14in) Red Streak bias-ply tyres.

Heavy-duty brakes

Four-wheel, heavy-duty drum brakes were standard GTX equipment, although optional 27.9cm (11in) front discs were a wise choice considering the GTX's sprinting ability.

Three-speed transmission

The rugged, heavy-duty TorqueFlite three-speed automatic transmission features modified shift points to better utilize the Hemi's power curve. A four-speed manual was optional.

Specifications
1967 Plymouth GTX 426 Hemi

ENGINE

Type: V8

Construction: Cast-iron block and heads

Valve gear: Two valves per cylinder operated by a single camshaft, pushrods and rocker arms

Bore and stroke: 108mm (4.25in) x 95mm (3.75in)

Displacement: 6981cc (426ci)

Compression ratio: 10.25:1

Induction system: Twin Carter four-barrel carburettors

Maximum power: 425bhp at 5000rpm

Maximum torque: 490lb-ft at 4000rpm

Top speed: 204km/h (127mph)

0–96km/h (0–60mph): 4. sec

TRANSMISSION

TorqueFlite three-speed automatic

BODY/CHASSIS

Unitary steel body construction

SPECIAL FEATURES

Twin non-functional bonnet scoops and stripes are GTX exclusives.

The number 426 signifies that this example is equipped with the ultimate muscle motor – the 6981c (426ci) Hemi. With this engine, 13-second ¼-mile ETs are easily obtainable.

RUNNING GEAR
Steering: Recirculating ball

Front suspension: Adjustable torsion bars with upper and lower control arms, telescopic shock absorbers and anti-roll bar

Rear suspension: Live rear axle with telescopic shock absorbers and leaf springs

Brakes: Drums, 27.9cm (11in) (front and rear)

Wheels: 35.6cm (14in) x 15.2cm (6in)

Tyres: 20.9cm (8.25in) x 35.6cm (14in)

DIMENSIONS

Length: 5.09m (200.5in)

Width: 1.74m (68.6in)

Height: 1.32m (52.1in)

Wheelbase: 295cm (116in)

Track: 151cm (59.5in) (front), 149cm (58.5in) (rear)

Weight: 1603kg (3535lb)

Plymouth ROAD RUNNER

By the late 1960s, many muscle cars were beyond the financial reach of their would-be buyers. To corner this segment of the market, Plymouth offered the Road Runner. It was a no-frills coupe with a 6276cc (383ci) V8 engine as standard power. The result proved to be an instant sales success, and owners were well respected on the street.

'...back to the basics.'

'Getting back to the basics is what the Road Runner is all about. It is all business, from the steel wheels to the rubber floormats. The 6276cc (383ci) is a strong engine and thrives at low rpm. With the four-speed shifter in your right hand and your foot on the gas, its acceleration is unreal. Because it was a bare-bones muscle car, its weight was kept as low as possible for an even better power-to-weight ratio. With 335bhp, this was a car that really lived up to its name.'

The 1968 model is the Road Runner in its purest form with a no-frills interior.

Milestones

1968 With a growing number of enthusiasts wanting a no-frills factory hot rod, Plymouth decides to take the plunge and offer the Road Runner – a two-door coupe with a standard 6276cc (383ci) V8. Chrysler pays Warner Bros. $50,000 to use the Road Runner name. Projected sales are 2500, but in the end, 44,589 are sold.

The Super Bee was Dodge Division's equivalent to the Road Runner.

1969 The Road Runner goes upmarket, adding a convertible to the range. Mid-year, a 7210cc (440ci) Six-Barrel joins the 6276cc (383ci) and 6981cc (426ci) Hemi options.

The sporty Road Runner was extensively revamped for 1971.

1970 A new loop-type grill and revised taillights mark the 1970 edition. 38.1cm (15in) Rallye wheels are now a popular option.

UNDER THE SKIN

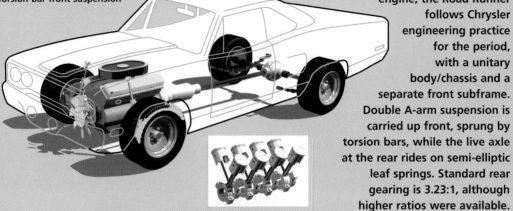

Unitary body and chassis

Four-wheel drum brakes

Torsion-bar front suspension

Big-block V8

Belvedere based

Essentially a two-door Belvedere fitted with a huge engine, the Road Runner follows Chrysler engineering practice for the period, with a unitary body/chassis and a separate front subframe. Double A-arm suspension is carried up front, sprung by torsion bars, while the live axle at the rear rides on semi-elliptic leaf springs. Standard rear gearing is 3.23:1, although higher ratios were available.

THE POWER PACK

Big block brawler

While other muscle cars relied on increasingly complex engines for propulsion, Plymouth decided that simplicity was essential to the Road Runner. For maximum effect and to keep costs down, the division decided to install the 6276cc (383ci) big-block as the standard engine. This cast-iron V8 had been in production since the 1950s, but for the Road Runner it received some upgrades. The heads, exhaust manifolds, camshaft, heavy-duty valve springs, and crankshaft windage tray are all from the 7210cc (440ci). With a four-barrel carburettor and a low-restriction air cleaner, it makes 335bhp at 5200rpm.

Hemi first

The first-generation Road Runner is an undisputed muscle car classic, and the first-year (1968) model is its purest form. Collectors prefer the 426 Hemi-engined cars. They can easily run 13-second ¼-mile ETs, but only 1019 were built.

Steel wheels were standard on 1968 Road Runners.

265

Plymouth ROAD RUNNER

The Road Runner was so successful that it inspired rival manufacturers to offer budget muscle cars of their own. Anyone who drove a Road Runner was soon mesmerized by its incredible performance.

Big-block V8

Inexpensive to build, yet with a few simple tweaks mightily effective, the 6276cc (383ci) V8 was the ideal engine for Plymouth's budget muscle-car. Packing 335bhp and a monster 425lb-ft of torque, it was a street terror even in stock trim.

Torsion-bar front suspension

A typical 1960s Chrysler feature is a torsion-bar front suspension. Twin longitudinal bars provide springing for the front wishbones and give a smoother ride than coil setups. Road Runners have bigger front bars in an attempt to improve handling.

Drum brakes

Most muscle cars are about going fast in a straight line and little else. Stopping the Road Runner could be quite entertaining, with the standard four-wheel drums, so ordering front discs was a wise option.

Hardtop styling

When introduced, the Road Runner was only available in one body-style – a pillared coupe. A hardtop version appeared mid-year and a convertible was introduced in 1969.

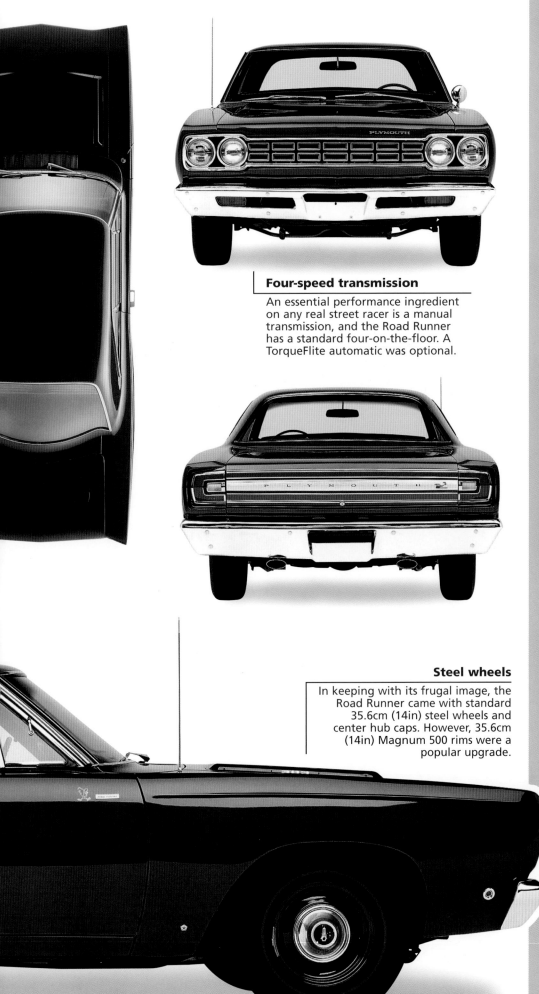

Four-speed transmission

An essential performance ingredient on any real street racer is a manual transmission, and the Road Runner has a standard four-on-the-floor. A TorqueFlite automatic was optional.

Steel wheels

In keeping with its frugal image, the Road Runner came with standard 35.6cm (14in) steel wheels and center hub caps. However, 35.6cm (14in) Magnum 500 rims were a popular upgrade.

Specifications

1968 Plymouth Road Runner

ENGINE

Type: V8

Construction: Cast-iron block and heads

Valve gear: Two valves per cylinder operated by a single camshaft

Bore and stroke: 108mm (4.25in) x 86mm (3.38in)

Displacement: 6276cc (383ci)

Compression ratio: 10.0:1

Induction system: Carter AFB four-barrel downdraft carburettor

Maximum power: 335bhp at 5200rpm

Maximum torque: 425lb-ft at 3400rpm

Top speed: 209km/h (130mph)

0–96km/h (0–60mph): 6.7 sec

TRANSMISSION

Four-speed manual

BODY/CHASSIS

Unitary steel construction with stamped steel body panels

SPECIAL FEATURES

The flat black bonnet centre gave this potent Plymouth a very aggressive look.

RUNNING GEAR

Steering: Recirculating-ball

Front suspension: Unequal-length A-arms with torsion bars, telescopic shock absorbers and anti-roll bar

Rear suspension: Live axle with semi-elliptic leaf springs and telescopic shock absorbers

Brakes: Drums (front and rear)

Wheels: Pressed steel, 35.6cm (14in) dia.

Tires: F70-14

DIMENSIONS

Length: 5.15m (202.7in)

Width: 2.08m (81.7in)

Height: 1.43m (56.3in)

Wheelbase: 295cm (116.0in)

Track: 151cm (59.5in) (front and rear).

Weight: 1542kg (3400lb)

Plymouth **SUPERBIRD**

Developed from the budget Road Runner coupe, the Superbird was designed to defeat Ford's Talladegas in NASCAR superspeedway races. Shortly after Plymouth's powerful rocket appeared, NASCAR changed the rules, and Superbirds were allowed to race only the 1970 season.

'...NASCAR racing warrior.'

'Plymouth built more than 1935 Superbirds as a follow-up to Dodge's less-than-victorious 1969 Daytonas that were designed to slaughter Ford's Talladegas. The strikingly similar looking Superbird proved to be a NASCAR racing warrior. The aluminium wing, flush-mounted rear window, Hemi engine and 45.7cm (18in) metal nose cone all added up to victory in 1970. In race trim at speeds in excess of 305km/h (190mph), the Superbird's nose cone actually added more weight to the front wheels, while the rear wing had to be properly adjusted or the rear tyres would wear prematurely.'

Stock Superbirds had typical Plymouth interiors with only the necessary gauges, console and shifter.

Milestones

1963 Chrysler decides
to take on Ford in NASCAR. As owners of Plymouth and Dodge, they had the 6981cc (426ci) Hemi V8 engine, whose power should have been enough to guarantee supremacy.

1964–68 Power alone
is not enough. On stock car ovals, Ford's supremacy continues because their cars have better aerodynamics.

1969 Dodge Charger
Daytona appears with a rear wing giving downforce to keep the car on the track at 322km/h (200mph) speeds. They win 18 NASCAR races this year – but Ford takes home more than 30.

The Superbirds proved their worth on the superspeedways.

1970 Superbird has
better aerodynamics than the Dodge Charger and wins 21 races (including the Daytona 500) and beating Ford. Not very many people liked its unusual styling, so many were stripped of their wings and nose cones and turned back into Road Runners just so Plymouth could sell them.

1971 NASCAR rules,
designed to keep racing equal, impose a 25 per cent engine volume restriction on rear-winged cars, which spells the end of the Superbird in competition.

UNDER THE SKIN

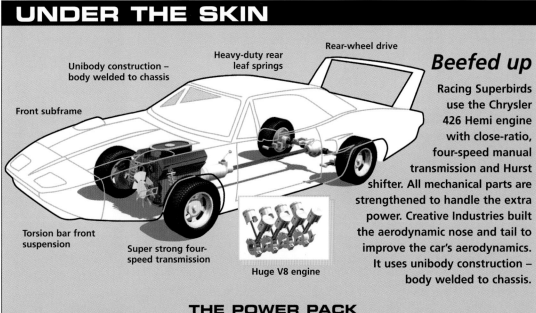

Unibody construction – body welded to chassis

Heavy-duty rear leaf springs

Rear-wheel drive

Front subframe

Torsion bar front suspension

Super strong four-speed transmission

Huge V8 engine

Beefed up

Racing Superbirds use the Chrysler 426 Hemi engine with close-ratio, four-speed manual transmission and Hurst shifter. All mechanical parts are strengthened to handle the extra power. Creative Industries built the aerodynamic nose and tail to improve the car's aerodynamics. It uses unibody construction – body welded to chassis.

THE POWER PACK

More horsepower inch for inch

The Hemi – so called because the combustion chamber (the area where the fuel is actually burned) is hemispherical – was the first mass-produced engine of its type in America. The Hemi head promoted even burning and more room for bigger valves (to get more fuel and air in). It also produced more horsepower per cubic inch than any other design, and forced Chevy and Ford to think about copies. Finally, it was the victim of NASCAR rule changes.

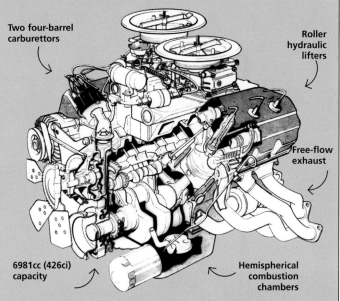

Two four-barrel carburettors

Roller hydraulic lifters

Free-flow exhaust

6981cc (426ci) capacity

Hemispherical combustion chambers

Vinyl Top

Did you ever notice that all Superbirds had vinyl tops? Plymouth was in a hurry to homologate these cars for NASCAR racing. Instead of properly doing the body work around the flush mounted rear window, it just hid the rough bodywork with a vinyl top.

The fender scoops cover a cut out, giving better tyre clearance at high speeds.

Plymouth SUPERBIRD

The Superbird could achieve over 322km/h (200mph) on the race track using the vital downforce generated by the huge rear wing. Even the tamer street version could easily reach 225km/h (140mph).

Rear suspension
Asymmetric rear leaf springs (the front third was stiffer than the rear two-thirds) helped locate the rear axle.

Roll cage
The NASCAR version used a tubular roll cage welded to the frame, which stiffened it tremendously and also protected the driver at 322km/h (200mph).

Four-speed transmission
Heavy-duty four-speed Chrysler model 883 was the strongest transmission available at the time.

Standard steel wheels
Steel wheels are still standard in NASCAR – wider 24.1cm (9.5in) x 38.1cm (15in) are used now, 38.1cm (15in) x 17.8cm (7in) when the Superbird ran. All NASCAR tyres then were bias ply with inner tubes.

Live rear axle
Dana-built rear axle was originally intended for a medium-duty truck. Even in drag racing, the mighty Hemi could break it.

High-mounted rear wing
The rear wing provided downforce at the rear. Its angle was adjustable – too much, and the increased force would shred the tyres.

Front suspension

Front torsion bars resulted in better front suspension than competitors.

Cowl induction

Carburettor intake air was picked up from the high-pressure area at the base of the windshield – called cowl induction.

Aerodynamic nose

The nose was designed to lower drag and increase top speed while adding downforce – it actually put more weight on the front as speed increased.

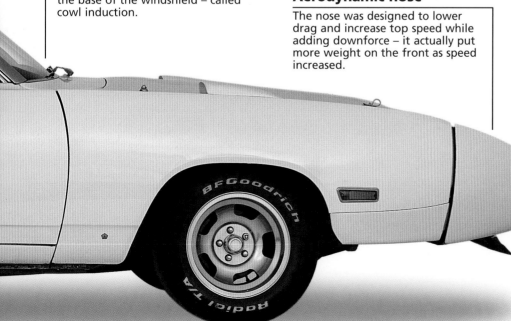

Specifications
1970 Plymouth Superbird

ENGINE

Type: Hemi V8
Construction: Cast-iron block and heads; hemispherical combustion chambers
Valve gear: Two valves per cylinder operated by single block-mounted camshaft
Bore and stroke: 108mm (4.25in) x 95mm (3.74in)
Displacement: 6981cc (426ci)
Compression ratio: 12:1
Induction system: Two four-barrel carbs, aluminium manifold
Maximum power: 425bhp at 5000rpm
Maximum torque: 490lb-ft at 4000rpm
Top speed: 225km/h (140mph)
0–96km/h (0–60mph): 6 sec

TRANSMISSION

Torqueflite three-speed auto plus torque converter or Mopar 883 four-speed manual

BODY/CHASSIS

Steel channel chassis welded to body with bolted front subframe

SPECIAL FEATURES

The rear wing's height means it operates in less-disturbed airflow.

RUNNING GEAR

Steering: Recirculating ball steering, power-assisted on road cars
Front suspension: Double wishbones with torsion bars and telescopic shocks
Rear suspension: Live axle with asymmetric leaf springs and telescopic shocks
Brakes: Vented discs 27.9cm (11in) dia. (front), drums 27.9cm (11in) dia. (rear)
Wheels: Steel disc, 17.8cm (7in) x 38.1cm (15in)
Tyres: Goodyear 7.00/15

DIMENSIONS

Length: 5.54m (218in)
Width: 1.94m (76.4in)
Wheelbase: 2.95m (116in)
Height: 405cm (159.4in) (including rear wing)
Track: 152cm (59.7in) (front), 149cm (58.7in) (rear)
Weight: 1742kg (3841lb)

Pontiac FIREBIRD

The second-generation Firebird is one of Pontiac's most successful cars ever and it remained in production for 11 years. Perhaps the purest and best-performing cars are the early-1970s Firebird Formulas®.

'...plenty of low-end power.'

'While most muscle cars were scrapped by 1972, Pontiac refused to let go. It continued to charge hard with the popular ponycar. Those who wanted attention bought the Trans Am®, but the more sedate-looking Formula shared its power. The Formula has a 6555cc (400ci) V8 under its dual-scooped bonnet. Although power in the 1973 model is down because of the government's strict emissions regulations, this car is still very quick and has plenty of low-end power.'

In 1973, Formulas had plush bucket seats and a sporty centre console.

Milestones

1970 The second-generation
Firebird makes its debut in February. It is longer, lower and wider, with an Endura flexible nose. Four models are available: Firebird, Esprit®, Formula and Trans Am. The latter two are the performance models.

The first-generation Firebird made its debut in February 1967.

1973 The last of the
true muscle Firebirds appear as the 455 Super Duty Formula and the Trans Am.

1974 A facelift
for the second-generation Firebird introduces new front and rear styling to satisfy crash requirements.

The 1979 model was the most popular year, with 211,000 Firebirds being sold.

1979 This is the
last year for the 6555cc (400ci) and 6604cc (403ci) V8s. The 6555cc (400ci) V8 was the more powerful engine and was used with a 4-speed transmission, while the lower performance 6604cc (403ci) V8 was used with an automatic.

UNDER THE SKIN

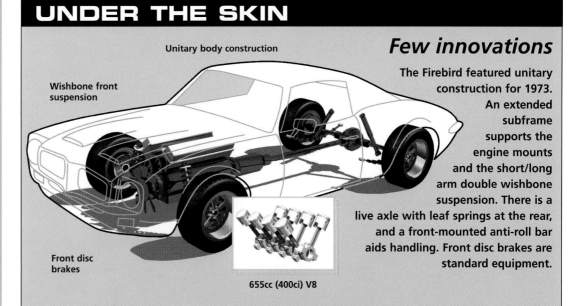

Unitary body construction

Wishbone front suspension

Front disc brakes

655cc (400ci) V8

Few innovations

The Firebird featured unitary construction for 1973. An extended subframe supports the engine mounts and the short/long arm double wishbone suspension. There is a live axle with leaf springs at the rear, and a front-mounted anti-roll bar aids handling. Front disc brakes are standard equipment.

THE POWER PACK

Big and torquey

The second-generation Pontiac Firebird was available with a wide range of engines and power outputs, with everything from a lowly 110bhp, 4097cc (250ci) six to the mighty 7456cc (455ci) V8 with up to 335bhp. In between there was the intermediate 230bhp, 6555cc (400ci) Pontiac V8. The biggest 7456cc (455ci) V8 catered to those who craved real muscle car performance. This brutal engine was only reserved for the outrageous Trans Am models, while a few Formula owners opted for the mighty engine in their cars.

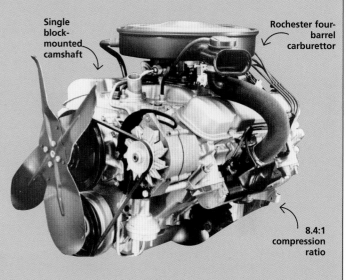

Single block-mounted camshaft

Rochester four-barrel carburettor

8.4:1 compression ratio

Fiery flagship

The flagship of the Firebird line in 1973 was the Trans Am. Apart from spoilers, decals and a shaker bonnet scoop, it is mechanically identical to the 455 Formula. The toughest engine available in 1973 was the 7456cc (455ci) Super Duty, with 310bhp.

1970–1973 Firebirds are the cleanest-looking second-generation models.

Pontiac FIREBIRD

For those who did not have the money to buy the Trans Am but still wanted performance, the Firebird Formula was a good choice. It had the same mechanicals as its more renowned stablemate.

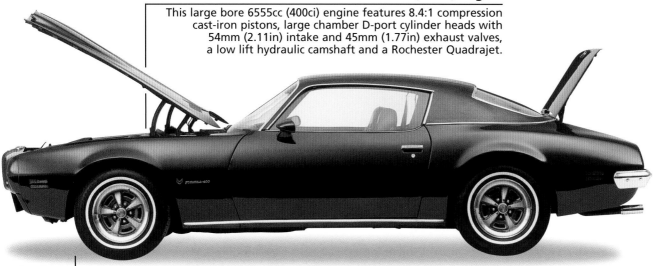

6555cc (400ci) engine

This large bore 6555cc (400ci) engine features 8.4:1 compression cast-iron pistons, large chamber D-port cylinder heads with 54mm (2.11in) intake and 45mm (1.77in) exhaust valves, a low lift hydraulic camshaft and a Rochester Quadrajet.

Steel wheels

Firebirds have steel Pontiac Rally wheels as standard, although special 'honeycomb' wheels were available at extra cost.

Limited-slip differential

Standard equipment with the four-speed manual transmission is the limited-slip differential. It was much easier to offer this as an aid to traction than to re-engineer the Firebird with independent rear suspension.

Separate rear bumper

In contrast to the front color-coded, impact-absorbing Endura nose, there is still a traditional-style chrome bumper at the rear. The last year for this very clean rear-end styling was 1973.

Optional air-conditioning

Unlike its import rivals, even the lowest model of the Firebird could be ordered with air-conditioning as an option.

Impact-absorbing nose

Pontiac was one of the first companies to introduce impact-absorbing bumpers. The Firebird has one of the cleanest nose profiles of any 1973 car.

Specifications

1973 Pontiac Firebird Formula 400

ENGINE

Type: V8

Construction: Cast-iron block and heads

Valve gear: Two valves per cylinder operated by a single block-mounted camshaft, pushrods and rockers

Bore and stroke: 105mm (4.13in) x 95mm (3.74in)

Displacement: 6555cc (400ci)

Compression ratio: 8.4:1

Induction system: Single Rochester 7043263 four-barrel carburettor

Maximum power: 230bhp at 4400rpm

Maximum torque: 177lb-ft at 3200rpm

Top speed: 185km/h (115mph)

0–96km/h (0–60mph): 7 sec

TRANSMISSION

Four-speed manual

BODY/CHASSIS

Steel monocoque with ladder-type front chassis rails and two-door coupe body

SPECIAL FEATURES

Twin bonnet scoops are unique to the high-performance Formula model.

RUNNING GEAR

Steering: Recirculating ball

Front suspension: Double unequal length wishbones, with coil springs, telescopic shocks and anti-roll bar

Rear suspension: Live axle with semi-elliptic leaf springs, telescopic shocks and anti-roll bar

Brakes: Discs, 27.9cm (11in) dia. (front), drums (rear)

Wheels: Steel disc, 17.8cm (7in) x 35.6cm (14in)

Tyres: F70-14

DIMENSIONS

Length: 4.86m (191.5in)

Width: 1.86m (73.4in)

Height: 1.28m (50.4in)

Wheelbase: 275cm (108.1in)

Track: 156cm (61.6in) (front), 156cm (61.6in) (rear)

Weight: 1708kg (3766lb)

Pontiac **FIREBIRD GTA**

By the mid 1970s, the large V8 Firebirds with real power had gone, but in the late 1980s Pontiac reintroduced true high performance to the Firebird with the 5735cc (350ci) GTA (Gran Turismo Americano). By bumping up the power, Pontiac created a machine that was perfect for the performance-deprived 1980s market.

'...a real surge of power.'

'Pontiac modified the suspension with its WS-6 performance handling option of stiffer springs and larger anti-roll bars. The GTA understeers more, giving a reassuring and stable feel. Rocketed through a slalom though, the GTA could easily stay on the heels of a 1980s Porsche. There is also an abundance of raw power that can send the later GTAs to 96km/h (60mph) under 7 seconds while its terminal velocity taps out at 241km/h (150mph).'

The GTA brought the spark back to the Firebird, combining comfort and performance.

Milestones

1982 General Motors redesigns the Chevrolet® Camaro® and Pontiac Firebird with a much shorter wheelbase and sleeker, modern styling. Performance fails to match the looks with only 165bhp on tap.

1555 20th Anniversary Turbo Trans Ams were built in 1989.

1987 The GM corporate 5737cc (350ci) small-block V8 engine is added to the GTA.

In 1991 the Firebird underwent a facelift. This is a Formula model.

1989 Pontiac builds the limited production Turbo Trans Am. It features the same turbo V6 engine found in the Buick Grand National.

1991 The Firebird receives a facelift which includes an aerodynamic nose.

1993 A new-generation Firebird, with 275bhp, is released with an all-new look and drivetrain.

UNDER THE SKIN

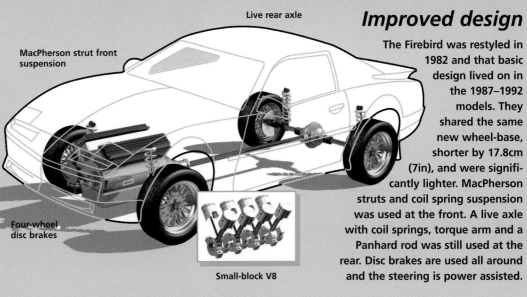

Live rear axle

MacPherson strut front suspension

Four-wheel disc brakes

Small-block V8

Improved design

The Firebird was restyled in 1982 and that basic design lived on in the 1987–1992 models. They shared the same new wheel-base, shorter by 17.8cm (7in), and were significantly lighter. MacPherson struts and coil spring suspension was used at the front. A live axle with coil springs, torque arm and a Panhard rod was still used at the rear. Disc brakes are used all around and the steering is power assisted.

THE POWER PACK

Tuned-port performer

What else could power the fast Firebird but General Motor's legendary small-block V8. It uses a single camshaft, pushrods and rockers to operate two valves per cylinder. Although the short-stroke engine could be made to rev, in 1988 it was tuned for low-rpm torque. Initially, maximum power was only 210bhp at 4400rpm, but torque was an excellent 320lb-ft at 2800rpm. Power was increased substantially when tuned-port fuel injection was introduced. The 20th Anniversary Trans Am was a GTA fitted with the turbo V6 engine from the Buick® GNX™. This was more powerful than the small block with 255bhp.

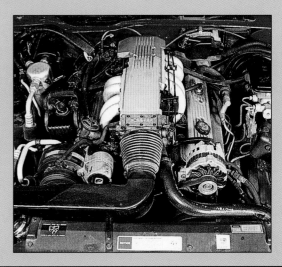

Power boost

The best of the third generation Firebird came once Pontiac had upped the 350-cubic inch V8's output to 240bhp and torque to 340lb-ft. This reduced the 0–96km/h (0–60mph) time by 0.5 second to 6.7 seconds. The turbo models offer even more scintillating performance.

The later Firebirds have more powerful engines and a smoother nose design.

Pontiac FIREBIRD GTA

The extended nose and upswept side skirts that Pontiac gave the later
GTA models were backed up by the performance the original car lacked.
At last, the dramatic looks had the power that they deserved.

Corporate power

It may not have been a true Pontiac engine but the
GM corporate 5735cc (350ci) V8 (basically a small-block
Chevy® engine) was just as useful in the Firebird as it
was in the Camaro. Because the two rival cars were
built on the same floorpan, there was never
a shortage of engines that could be added.

Recirculating ball steering

Despite the GTA's high performance,
Pontiac never saw the need to fit the
more direct rack-and-pinion steering.
It was content with the recirculating
ball with suitable power assistance.

700R-4 equipped

When Pontiac placed the 5735cc (350ci) V8
in the Firebird, it posed a small problem. The
existing five-speed manual transmission could
not handle the higher torque, so a 700R-4
four-speed automatic was fitted.

Bonnet scoops

Although there was enough space to fit the engine without any changes, Pontiac decided to fit bonnet louvres at the front to let more air into the engine compartment.

Live rear axle

Like all Firebirds, this third generation model had a live rear axle. However, with the use of a torque arm, Panhard rod, two lower trailing arms and an anti-roll bar, the GTA was an excellent handling car.

Specifications

1991 Pontiac Firebird GTA

ENGINE

Type: V8

Construction: Cast-iron block and heads

Valve gear: Two valves per cylinder operated by a single block-mounted camshaft via pushrods, hydraulic valve lifters and rockers

Bore and stroke: 102mm (4.0in) x 88mm 93.48in)

Displacement: 5735cc (350ci)

Compression ratio: 9.3:1

Induction system: Tuned port fuel injection

Maximum power: 240bhp at 4400rpm

Maximum torque: 340lb-ft at 3200rpm

Top speed: 241km/h (150mph)

0–96km/h (0–60mph): 6.7 sec

TRANSMISSION

700R-4 four-speed automatic

BODY/CHASSIS

Unitary steel construction with two-door coupe body

SPECIAL FEATURES

Detail changes to the front of the Firebird evolved throughout production.

Later model cars came with airbags fitted as standard equipment.

RUNNING GEAR

Steering: Recirculating ball

Front suspension: Modified MacPherson struts with lower wishbones, coil springs and anti-roll bar

Rear suspension: Live axle, torque arm, Panhard rod, trailing arms, coil springs, telescopic shock absorbers and anti-roll bar

Brakes: Discs, 26.7cm (10.5in) dia. (front), 26.7cm (10.5in) dia. (rear)

Wheels: Alloy, 20.3cm (8in) x 40.6cm (16in)

Tyres: 245/50 VR16

DIMENSIONS

Length: 4.96m (195.1in)

Width: 1.84m (72.4in)

Height: 1.29m (50.4in)

Wheelbase: 257cm (101.1in)

Track: 152cm (60.0in) (front), 155cm (60.9in) (rear)

Weight: 1596kg (3519lb)

Pontiac FIREHAWK

SLP Engineering offered its first Firehawk street car in 1992. The current car, now available in both Formula™ and Trans Am™ format, is the best yet. The uprated suspension gives handling and grip that is matched only by the unequivocal LS1 engine, making the Firehawk a contemporary muscle car.

'...supertuned street machine.'

'SLP shows what clever modifications can do to the handling and power of a typical Trans Am. The Firehawk's variable rate springs give an excellent ride quality despite its low-profile Firestones while its thicker anti-roll bars allow more aggressive cornering. Under the SLP-installed, forced-air induction hood, the engine generates 327bhp thanks to a cat-back exhaust system. This supertuned street machine accelerates to 96km/h (60mph) in 5.1 seconds and has a top speed of 253km/h (157mph).'

The Firehawk's instruments are easy to read and the high bolstered seats give great support.

Milestones

1987 Ex-drag racer Ed Hamburger forms
SLP (Street Legal Performance) Engineering. He negotiates a deal with General Motors to design and make a performance package for the Pontiac Firebird.

The Trans Am is the top-of-the-line factory Firebird with a 305bhp V8.

1992 SLP offers its first
Firehawk street car. It is inspired by the SCCA showroom stock racers.

SLP also offers a package for the Grand Prix® GTP™ called the GTX.

1995 Still using the Formula,
SLP offers the Firehawk in both coupe and convertible styles. Power comes from a 315bhp LT1 engine with a Ram Air induction system.

1998 A new Firehawk,
with 327bhp is previewed, but production does not begin until late in the year.

UNDER THE SKIN

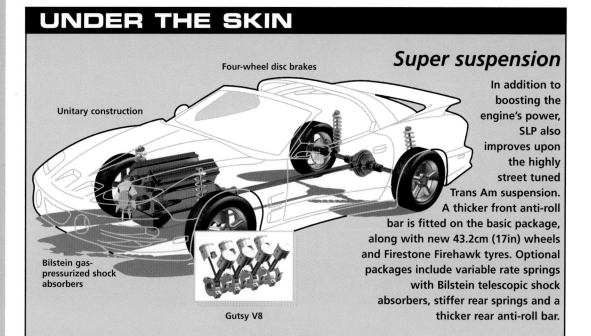

Four-wheel disc brakes

Unitary construction

Bilstein gas-pressurized shock absorbers

Gutsy V8

Super suspension

In addition to boosting the engine's power, SLP also improves upon the highly street tuned Trans Am suspension. A thicker front anti-roll bar is fitted on the basic package, along with new 43.2cm (17in) wheels and Firestone Firehawk tyres. Optional packages include variable rate springs with Bilstein telescopic shock absorbers, stiffer rear springs and a thicker rear anti-roll bar.

THE POWER PACK

Forced-air flyer

Because of the new LS1 engine with its all-alloy construction, cutting edge cylinder heads, a single coil for each cylinder, 10.5:1 compression ratio and composite intake manifold, the Formula and Trans Am have never been faster. As if 305bhp wasn't enough, SLP adds a twin nostrilled, forced-air induction hood and a free flowing cat-back exhaust system. With these hard-core modifications, the Firehawk is able to generate a massive 327bhp.

Sequential multiport fuel injection

Ignition coil for each cylinder

10.5:1 compression ratio

Cast-aluminium block and heads

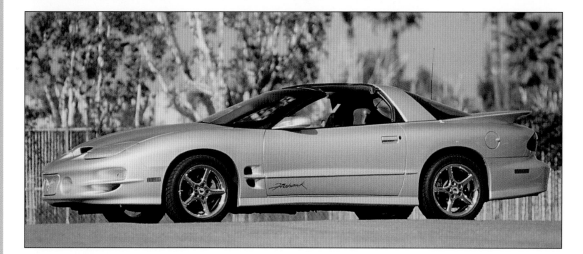

Basic fun

Despite some high-tech features, the Firehawk is a throwback to the old muscle cars of the 1960s. Packing 327bhp and able to run 13-second ¼-miles right out of the box, it is an affordable driving enthusiast's dream, considering its $30,499 sticker price.

As of 1998, the Firehawks can now be based on the Trans Am.

Pontiac FIREHAWK

Exclusivity isn't normally associated with the 1999 Pontiac Trans Am, but if you ordered the top shelf, SLP-modified Firehawk, you would be one of only 500 people with the best-handling Pontiac ever offered.

Heat extractors

In addition to the new forced air hood, SLP designed these heat extractors to draw out hot air from the engine bay.

V8 engine

GM's small-block 5.7l (348ci) V8 is still a classic two-valve pushrod design but shares little with the old LT1. It has a cast-aluminium block and features redesigned cylinder heads, a composite intake manifold and 6-bolt, main-bearing caps.

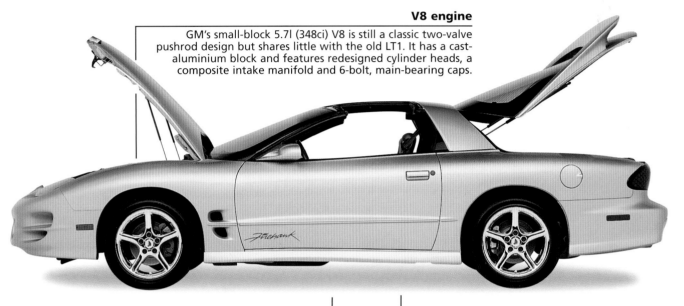

Six-speed transmission

Because of the extra power they make, Firehawks are available with Borg-Warner six-speed transmissions only. If you want an automatic transmission, you'll have to stay with the standard Firebird or Trans Am models.

Bilstein suspension

On the SLP option list, you can specially order the Bilstein Ultra Performance Suspension System. These revalved shocks will keep the Firehawk composed up to .91gs on the skidpad. This option is only available on coupe models.

Optional differential

The standard factory differential can be upgraded with a severe duty Auburn Gear unit. It is available with an AAM cast aluminium cooling cover.

Functional bonnet scoop

Firebirds got a restyled twin nostrilled bonnet for 1998. The SLP forced air induction system is different from the standard Pontiac WS-6 Ram Air hood but works just as effectively.

Performance exhaust

The less restrictive exhaust fitted by SLP helps the engine produce seven extra bhp, but there is very little penalty in extra noise generated.

Specifications

1999 Pontiac Firebird Firehawk

ENGINE

Type: V8

Construction: Aluminium block and heads

Valve gear: Two valves per cylinder operated by a single block-mounted camshaft with pushrods and rocker arms

Bore and stroke: 99mm (3.90in) x 92mm (3.62in)

Displacement: 5.7l (348ci)

Compression ratio: 10.5:1

Induction system: Electronic fuel injection

Maximum power: 327bhp at 5200rpm

Maximum torque: 345lb-ft at 4400rpm

Top speed: 252km/h (157mph)

0–96km/h (0–60mph): 5.7 sec

TRANSMISSION

Borg-Warner T56 six-speed manual

BODY/CHASSIS

Steel unitary chassis with composite two-door coupe body

SPECIAL FEATURES

These chrome plated, five-spoke aluminium wheels are a popular option.

RUNNING GEAR

Steering: Rack-and-pinion

Front suspension: Double wishbones with coil springs, Bilstein telescopic shock absorbers and anti-roll bar

Rear suspension: Live axle with trailing links, control arm, Panhard rod, coil springs, Bilstein telescopic shock absorbers and anti-roll bar

Brakes: Vented discs, 29.9cm (11.8in) dia. (front), 30.2cm (11.9in) dia. (rear)

Wheels: Chrome plated alloy, 22.8cm (9in) x 43.2cm (17in)

Tyres: Firestone Firehawk, 275/40 ZR17

DIMENSIONS

Length: 4.92m (193.8in)

Width: 1.89m (74.5in)

Height: 1.32m (52.0in)

Wheelbase: 257cm (101.1in)

Track: 154cm (60.7in) (front), 153.9cm (60.6in) (rear)

Weight: 1597kg (3520lb)

Pontiac GTO

To circumvent a corporate edict that limited GM's intermediate cars to a maximum engine displacement of 5407cc (330ci), the GTO option package for the Tempest created a new type of vehicle – the muscle car.

'...unlike any other car.'

'With its lightweight body and 348 horses under the bonnet, the 1964 GTO was unlike any other car at the time. Putting the shifter into first and flooring the gas delivers a neck-straining launch off the line. The GTO will cover the ¼-mile in a surprising 14.8 seconds. The heavy duty floorshifter easily handles the engine's huge power and torque output. Handling and braking aren't as powerful, but it's the high levels of torque that define the GTO.'

The GTO has bucket seats, four gauges and a sure-shifting four-speed.

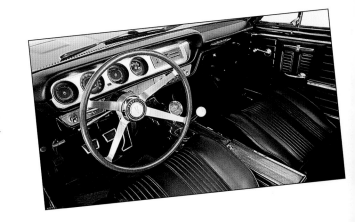

Milestones

1964 For the 1964 model year, Pontiac
begins the muscle car era with the GTO. It comes in three body styles and with a standard 325bhp, 6375cc (389ci) V8.

The 1966 GTO was longer and curvier than earlier models.

1965 Power grows to 335bhp, with an
optional 360bhp engine. A restyle adds vertically-stacked headlights.

The colourful GTO Judge™ was introduced in 1969.

1966 Power is now rated at 335bhp in base
form, and a new 7.6cm (3in) longer model arrives. The GTO is now a separate Pontiac series.

1967 A new 6555cc (400ci) V8 debuts
with 335 or 360bhp.

1968 An all-new GTO makes its debut.

UNDER THE SKIN

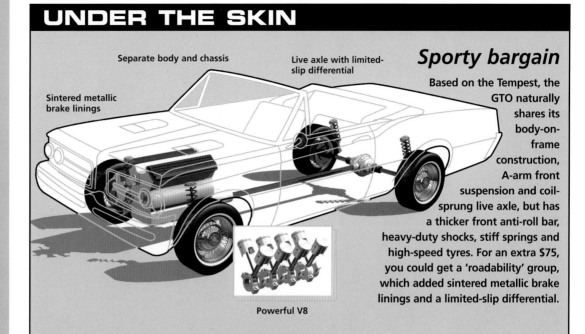

Separate body and chassis

Live axle with limited-slip differential

Sintered metallic brake linings

Powerful V8

Sporty bargain

Based on the Tempest, the GTO naturally shares its body-on-frame construction, A-arm front suspension and coil-sprung live axle, but has a thicker front anti-roll bar, heavy-duty shocks, stiff springs and high-speed tyres. For an extra $75, you could get a 'roadability' group, which added sintered metallic brake linings and a limited-slip differential.

THE POWER PACK

Muscle car genesis

The 6375cc (389ci) V8 is the centrepiece of the GTO package. Even in standard tune with a 10.75:1 compression ratio and a single four-barrel carburettor, it boasted 325bhp. With Tri-Power carburetion, power rose to 348bhp. In the sophomore season, its output rose to 335bhp and 360bhp, respectively. In such a light body, this was exceptionally potent. For 1967, a 6555cc (400ci) engine replaced the 389, with a single four-barrel carburettor (the Tri-power option was dropped midway through 1966).

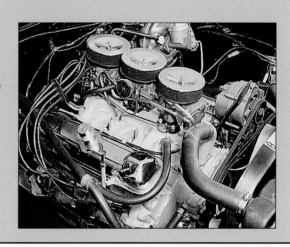

64 flyer

All first-generation GTO models have a special place in collectors' hearts as the first of the muscle car species, especially the original 1964 model. Tri-Power-equipped first-year coupes seem to have a special aura among enthusiasts.

Initial sales were estimated to be around 5000, but 32,450 GTOs were sold.

Pontiac GTO

It was amazing how much torque the GTO had for an essentially stock six-passenger car. Its specification could be tailored to your individual wishes, and it became a legend in its own time.

Choice of transmission

A floorshifted three-speed manual transmission was standard for the GTO, although a heavy-duty three-speed, a Muncie close-ratio four-speed with Hurst linkage and a two-speed automatic were optional.

Big V8 power

It is the powerful V8 engine that gives the GTO its special character – namely its muscle. With up to 348bhp available from the 6375cc (389ci) engine, the GTO could accelerate from 0 to 96km/h (60mph) in under 7 seconds.

Three body styles

You could buy a GTO in any of three body configurations. The most popular was the hardtop coupe (commonly referred to as the Sport Coupe), but there was also a standard coupe and a convertible. Today, the drop-top models are the most collectable.

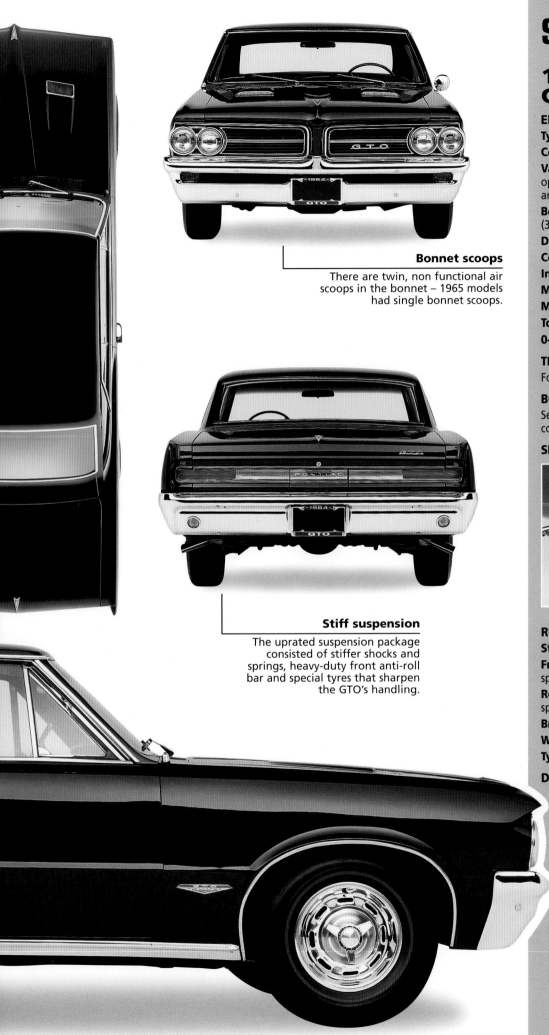

Specifications

1964 Pontiac GTO

ENGINE

Type: V8

Construction: Cast-iron block and heads

Valve gear: Two valves per cylinder operated by a single camshaft via pushrods and rockers

Bore and stroke: 103mm (4.06in) x 95mm (3.75in)

Displacement: 6375cc (389ci)

Compression ratio: 10.75:1

Induction system: Three carburettors

Maximum power: 348bhp at 4900rpm

Maximum torque: 428lb-ft at 3600rpm

Top speed: 193km/h (120mph)

0–96km/h (0–60mph): 6.6 sec

TRANSMISSION

Four-speed manual

BODY/CHASSIS

Separate steel chassis with two-door coupe body

SPECIAL FEATURES

Dual exhaust pipes were a standard feature on the GTO.

RUNNING GEAR

Steering: Recirculating ball

Front suspension: A-arms with coil springs, shock absorbers and anti-roll bars

Rear suspension: Live axle with coil springs and shock absorbers

Brakes: Drums (front and rear)

Wheels: Steel, 35.6cm (14in) dia.

Tyres: 17.7cm (6.95in) x 35.6cm (14in)

DIMENSIONS

Length: 5.16m (203.0in)

Width: 1.86m (73.3in)

Height: 1.37m (54.0in)

Wheelbase: 292cm (115.0in)

Track: 147cm (58.0in) (front and rear)

Weight: 1418kg (3126lb)

Bonnet scoops

There are twin, non functional air scoops in the bonnet – 1965 models had single bonnet scoops.

Stiff suspension

The uprated suspension package consisted of stiffer shocks and springs, heavy-duty front anti-roll bar and special tyres that sharpen the GTO's handling.

Pontiac GTO

Taking a huge engine and putting it into a smaller vehicle was the concept behind the GTO. Pontiac's original muscle car grew larger for 1966 but retained the essential performance ingredients that made it a winner from day one.

'...few cars are cooler.'

'Even today, there are few cars as cool as the 1966 GTO. The front bucket seats may be lacking support by today's standards, but the dash is a delight and the interior tastefully restrained. Once on the road, acceleration is tremendous, and the four-speed shifter is well mated to the 389 V8. However, on damp surfaces wheelspin is almost unavoidable if you're heavy on the pedal. The GTO is no corner-carver and tends to oversteer if you don't take care.'

A two-spoke steering wheel is standard, although a three-spoke one was available.

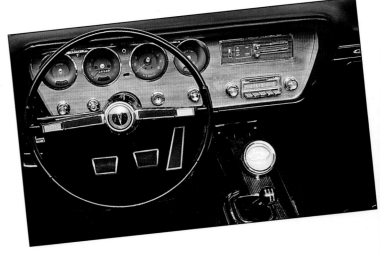

Milestones

1964 A new, larger and more
conventional Tempest® line arrives. The biggest news is the debut of the GTO (Gran Turismo Omologato), with a standard 6375cc (389ci) V8 and sporty touches. 32,450 GTOs are sold in the first year.

The GTO got a crisp restyle for 1965, which included vertical headlights.

1966 The GTO gets a larger, curvier
body, but the basic style and performance remain the same. By this stage, muscle car competition is getting tougher. However, the GTO sets an all-time muscle car production record with 96,946 cars built.

In 1969 Pontiac releases The Judge™ option to strike more interest in perspective buyers.

1967 Pontiac turns its attention to
improving the car. The grill and taillights are altered, and the V8 is bored out to 6555cc (400ci).

UNDER THE SKIN

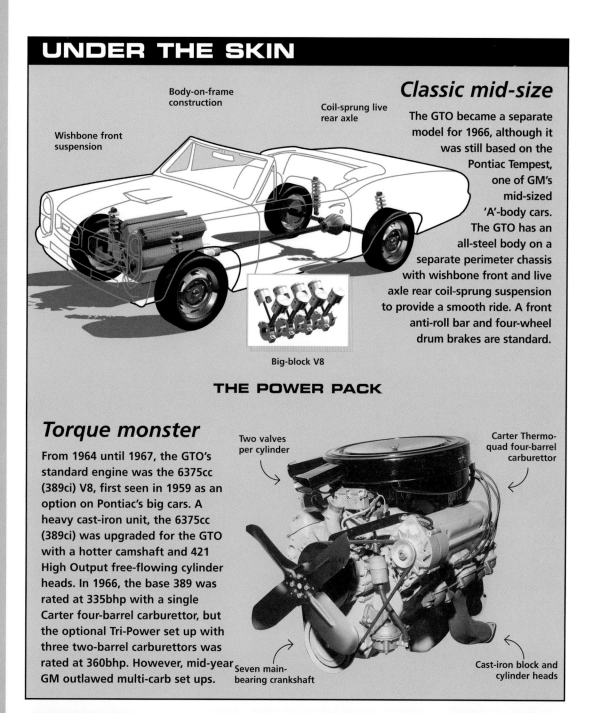

Body-on-frame construction

Wishbone front suspension

Coil-sprung live rear axle

Big-block V8

Classic mid-size

The GTO became a separate model for 1966, although it was still based on the Pontiac Tempest, one of GM's mid-sized 'A'-body cars. The GTO has an all-steel body on a separate perimeter chassis with wishbone front and live axle rear coil-sprung suspension to provide a smooth ride. A front anti-roll bar and four-wheel drum brakes are standard.

THE POWER PACK

Torque monster

From 1964 until 1967, the GTO's standard engine was the 6375cc (389ci) V8, first seen in 1959 as an option on Pontiac's big cars. A heavy cast-iron unit, the 6375cc (389ci) was upgraded for the GTO with a hotter camshaft and 421 High Output free-flowing cylinder heads. In 1966, the base 389 was rated at 335bhp with a single Carter four-barrel carburettor, but the optional Tri-Power set up with three two-barrel carburettors was rated at 360bhp. However, mid-year GM outlawed multi-carb set ups.

Two valves per cylinder

Carter Thermo-quad four-barrel carburettor

Seven main-bearing crankshaft

Cast-iron block and cylinder heads

Loaded Goat

Among muscle car aficionados, the 1966 GTO ranks as an all-time great. Desirable options include Rally I wheels, a four-speed transmission and Tri-Power carb set-up. Add these to a convertible body, and you've got one fantastic summer cruiser.

The 1966 GTO is one of the most desirable muscle cars of all time.

Pontiac GTO

Pontiac set an all-time production record with the 1966 GTO, thanks to the car's combination of outstanding performance, eye-catching looks and attractive pricing.

Ram Air kit
The standard bonnet scoop was purely for decoration, but a dealer-installed Ram Air kit was also available. Quoted horsepower remained unchanged, but fresh air induction would probably add a few additional bhp.

Big-block V8
In 1966, the GTO could be ordered with the 6375cc (389ci) engine in two different states of tune. This car is one of 19,045 ordered with the optional Tri-Power set up, which boosted power output to 360bhp.

Power convertible top
The GTO, if ordered in convertible form, was available with a power top.

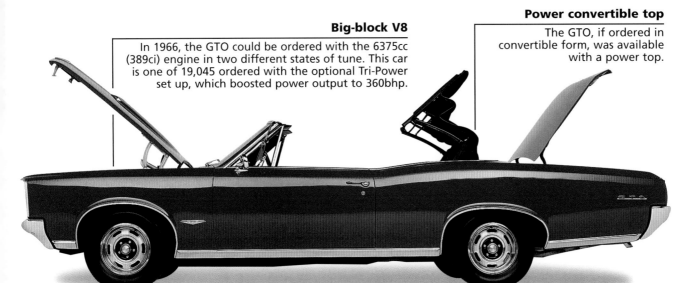

Coil-sprung suspension
Like the other General Motors 'A'-body intermediates of the time, the GTO has coil springs front and rear. This results in a much smoother ride than rival Ford and Chrysler muscle cars.

Four-speed transmission
In order to extract maximum performance from the big-block V8, a four-speed manual was the hot ticket, although a TurboHydramatic automatic was offered.

Promotional licence plate
GTOs quickly became known on the streets and at the race tracks for their unbelievable performance. One of Pontiac's campaign slogans compared the car's power with that of a tiger, hence the 'growling' licence plate.

Restyled body
Still Tempest-based, the GTO grew dimensionally larger for 1966 with a longer body and more flowing lines. It was offered in pillared coupe, hardtop and convertible forms. The hardtop was by far the most popular model.

Fluted taillights

Although base model Tempests and Le Mans have simple rear lights, the GTO has a unique tail end treatment with fluted taillight lenses. These are unique to this model year, as the rear end was revised for 1967.

Optional axle gearing

Since the GTO was after all a muscle car, it had to have considerable torque to get it out ahead of the competition. Naturally, Pontiac offered it with a variety of rear axle ratios, ranging from econo-wise 3.08:1 gears to the tyre-frying 4.33:1s.

Specifications

1966 Pontiac GTO

ENGINE
Type: V8

Construction: Cast-iron block and heads

Valve gear: Two valves per cylinder operated by a single camshaft with pushrods and rockers

Bore and stroke: 102mm (4.06in) x 95mm (3.75in)

Displacement: 6375cc (389ci)

Compression ratio: 10.75:1

Induction system: Three Rochester two-barrel carburettors

Maximum power: 360bhp at 5200rpm

Maximum torque: 424lb-ft at 3600rpm

Top speed: 201km/h (125mph)

0–96km/h (0–60mph): 6.2 sec

TRANSMISSION
Muncie M21 four-speed manual

BODY/CHASSIS
Steel perimeter chassis with separate steel convertible two-door body

SPECIAL FEATURES

Its sinister look is attributed to the vertical headlights and split front grill.

RUNNING GEAR
Steering: Recirculating ball

Front suspension: Unequal length wishbones with coil springs, telescopic shock absorbers and anti-roll bar

Rear suspension: Live axle with coil springs and lower control arms

Brakes: Drums (front and rear)

Wheels: Steel Rally I, 35.6cm (14in) dia.

Tyres: Uniroyal 155/F70 14

DIMENSIONS
Length: 5.05m (199.0in)

Width: 2.03m (79.8in)

Height: 1.39m (54.8in)

Wheelbase: 295cm (116.0in)

Track: 137cm (53.8in) (front), 127cm (50.1in) (rear)

Weight: 1613kg (3555lb)

Pontiac **GTO JUDGE**

Looking to boost sales of its muscle cars, Pontiac created The Judge option package for its 1969 model lineup and made it available on the tyre-incinerating GTO. With its attention-getting paint scheme and outrageous graphics, a Ram Air-powered GTO Judge was a street-wise combination of flamboyance and force.

'...All rise for the GTO Judge.'

'With its legendary Ram Air engines, the GTO is the quintessential muscle car. In 1969, a new option gave this powerful Poncho a new image – all rise for the GTO Judge. The Judge makes a statement even when it stands still. On the move, its true intentions become evident. Push down on the throttle and feel its torque as your body sinks into its bucket seat. Bang second gear and listen to the tyres chirp – now that's power. This honourable hot rod gives a very judicious jaunt.'

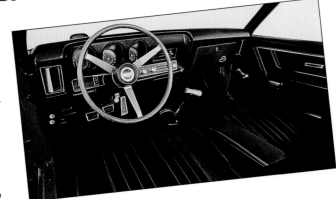

A firm bucket seat, Hurst shifter and a hood mounted tach – what more do you need?

Milestones

1969 Although originally conceived as a single-colour, bare-bones GTO at a low price, the Judge debuts as an option package on the Goat. It is equipped with the standard Ram III or optional Ram Air IV engines. The first 2000 cars are painted Carousel Red, but later variants are available in any factory GTO colour.

This 1968 GTO was one of the first cars to use a plastic Endura front bumper.

1970 GM A-bodies undergo a major restyle, and the GTO has more bulging lower sheet metal, plus new front and rear styling. Power-train choices on the Judge are unchanged, but there are new colours, and spring and suspension settings are altered. Late in the model year, a 7456cc (455ci) V8 becomes available.

The final, 1971 incarnation of the Judge is noticeably different from its predecessors.

1971 The Judge is retired due to a lack of consumer interest.

UNDER THE SKIN

Safe-T-Track differential with 3.55:1 gearing

Body-on-frame construction

All-coil-sprung suspension

Ram Air V8

A-stounding

From 1968, the GTO was built on the 284cm (112in) wheelbase A-body platform. Beneath its stylish sheet metal is a separate-perimeter chassis with an independent front and a live rear-axle suspension. Compared to its Tempest parent, the GTO (and Judge) has stiffer coil springs, a thicker front anti-roll bar and revalved shock absorbers. Options included a limited-slip, Safe-T-Track differential. The Safe-T-Track was standard on cars with the Ram Air IV engines.

THE POWER PACK

Ramming air – III or IV

With outrageous styling, The Judge had to have the power to match. Its standard engine was a 655cc (400ci), Ram Air III, V8. This engine had D-port cylinder heads, a hydraulic camshaft, free-flowing exhaust manifolds and a Rochester Quadrajet 4-barrel carburettor. It made 366bhp. Three is keen, but with four you definitely get more. Owners who wanted to maximize performance ordered their Judge with the barely streetable Ram Air IV 400. It came with forged pistons, round-port cylinder heads and 1.65:1 rocker arms. According to the factory, this engine made only 4 more bhp than the III, but this figure was grossly underrated.

In session

Offered for sale for only three model years, the Judge has long been coveted by collectors. 1969 models boast cleaner styling, and Carousel Red is the definitive colour. Due to high demand, buyers should be aware of GTO Judge imitations.

A Carousel Red Judge with the Ram Air IV is a highly desirable car.

Pontiac GTO JUDGE

Despite taking its name from the popular *Laugh-In* TV show, the Judge was no joke. Fitted with the Ram Air IV, it was one of the most respected muscle cars on the street.

Endura nose

One of the first cars to have energy-absorbing bumpers, the GTO's optional Endura nose could withstand parking lot shunts of up to 6.4km/h (4mph). Hidden headlights were a popular option, but this GTO retains the fixed headlights.

III or IV for the road

Whereas regular GTOs came with a 350bhp 6555cc (400ci) as the standard V8, Judges got the 366bhp Ram Air III. The hot setup, however, was the $389.68 Ram Air IV engine option with a 4-speed transmission. It was endowed with an aluminium intake manifold, 4-bolt mains and, of course, oval-port heads with 67cc (4ci) combustion chambers. Only 34 buyers ordered their GTO Judges with the RA IV/4-speed option.

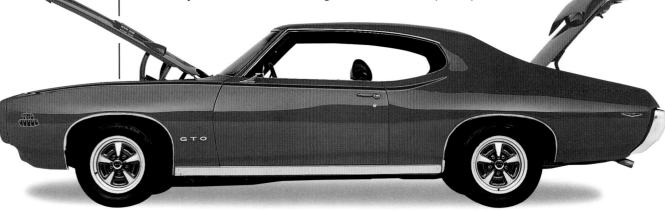

Standard Ram Air IV equipment

If you ordered your GTO with the Ram Air IV engine, you automatically received a heavy-duty cooling system. The standard gear ratio with this engine was a set of 3.90:1s and a Safe-T-Track limited slip differential. If these gears weren't steep enough, a set of 4.33:1s could be specified.

Heavy-duty suspension

Judges came with heavy-duty suspension, which includes stiff springs and shocks. Drum brakes were standard, but front discs were optional – and at a mere $64.25, highly advisable.

Eye-catching paint scheme

By 1969, image was everything in the muscle car stakes. The Judge was launched with one of the loudest schemes around, Carousel Red, set off by blue stripes outlined in yellow and with Judge logos on the front fenders and decklid spoiler.

Specifications

1969 Pontiac GTO Judge

ENGINE

Type: V8

Construction: Cast-iron block and heads

Valve gear: Two valves per cylinder operated by a single camshaft with pushrods and rockers

Bore and stroke: 105mm (4.12in) x 95mm (3.75in)

Displacement: 6555cc (400ci) (R/A III)

Compression ratio: 10.75:1

Induction system: GM Rochester Quadrajet four-barrel carburettor

Maximum power: 366bhp at 5400rpm

Maximum torque: 445lb-ft at 3600rpm

Top speed: 198km/h (123mph)

0–96km/h (0–60mph): 6.2 sec

TRANSMISSION

Muncie M-21 four-speed manual

BODY/CHASSIS

Separate steel chassis with two-door coupe body

SPECIAL FEATURES

'The Judge' decals are prominently displayed all around the car.

The bonnet-mounted tachometer was not only stylish but very useful, too.

RUNNING GEAR

Steering: Recirculating ball

Front suspension: Unequal-length A-arms with coil springs, telescopic shock absorbers and anti-roll bar

Rear suspension: Live axle with coil springs, trailing arms and telescopic shock absorbers

Brakes: Discs (front), drums (rear)

Wheels: Steel Rally II, 35.6cm (14in) dia.

Tyres: Goodyear Polyglas, G-60 14

DIMENSIONS

Length: 4.95m (195.0in)

Width: 1.9m (75.0in)

Height: 132cm (52.0in)

Wheelbase: 284cm (112.0in)

Track: 163cm (64.0in) (front and rear)

Weight: 1589kg (3503lb)

Well-laid-out interior

The second-generation GTO had one of the best interiors of all its peers. All of the gauges were clearly visible, front bucket seats were very supportive and the floor-mounted Hurst shifter never missed a gear.

USA 1968–1972

Pontiac GTO JUDGE

Generally acknowledged as the first factory-built muscle car, the name was borrowed from Ferrari and stood for Gran Turismo Omologato. Now it is one of the top collectible cars of its era.

'...All attitude and performance.'

'While many can argue which muscle car was the fastest, nicest or most powerful, only one can be the first – that's the Pontiac GTO. In 1964, when John Z. DeLorean installed a 6375cc (389ci) V8 in Pontiac's intermediate Tempest cars, he created a legend, not to mention an American automotive trend that would ripple for the next eight years. By 1971, the GTO was all about attitude as well as performance. Styled with the Judge™ option, and powered by a huge 7456cc (455ci) High Output engine with Ram-Air induction, the GTO had the sound and fury of real steel.'

This GTO has the optional bonnet-mounted tachometer that is visible through the windshield.

Milestones

1968 The GTO receives another major restyling. The wheelbase is shortened from 292cm (115in) to 284cm (112in). The new body uses rubber Endura bumpers and hidden headlights are a popular option. Its 6555cc (400ci) V8 retains 360bhp in both the HO and Ram Air versions. Midyear, Pontiac replaces the Ram Air engine with a Ram Air II.

The 1965 GTO was a tough act to follow by 1971.

1969 The Judge is an attempt to revive GTO sales. It features a sharp rear spoiler, stripes and badging. Standard engine is the Ram Air III 400 V8 engine, but for an extra $390 the 370bhp Ram Air IV engine becomes available.

1970 GTOs are again restyled. This is the most refined version yet. The Judge is still available and so is the Ram Air IV engine. A 7456cc (455ci) V8 is also offered, but isn't popular.

1971 Poor sales in 1970 force the Judge option to be dropped after selling 357 hardtops and 17 convertibles. The top engine is a 7456cc (455 ci) V8 with 355bhp.

1972 GTO becomes an option on the Le Mans.

UNDER THE SKIN

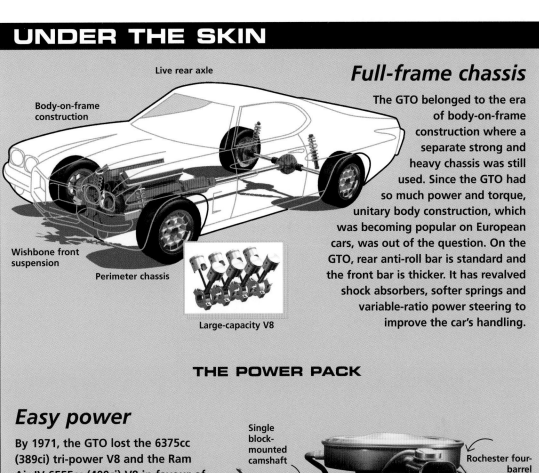

Live rear axle

Body-on-frame construction

Wishbone front suspension

Perimeter chassis

Large-capacity V8

Full-frame chassis

The GTO belonged to the era of body-on-frame construction where a separate strong and heavy chassis was still used. Since the GTO had so much power and torque, unitary body construction, which was becoming popular on European cars, was out of the question. On the GTO, rear anti-roll bar is standard and the front bar is thicker. It has revalved shock absorbers, softer springs and variable-ratio power steering to improve the car's handling.

THE POWER PACK

Easy power

By 1971, the GTO lost the 6375cc (389ci) tri-power V8 and the Ram Air IV 6555cc (400ci) V8 in favour of a less powerful 7456cc (455ci) V8. It has a 105mm (4.15in) bore and 107mm (4.21in) stroke, but tough emissions standards mean the big 7456cc (455ci) makes only 355bhp at 3800rpm and 412lb-ft of torque at 3200rpm. The engine had a small 8.4:1 compression ratio, round-port cylinder heads, a Rochester Quadrajet four-barrel carburettor and low-rise cast iron intake manifold.

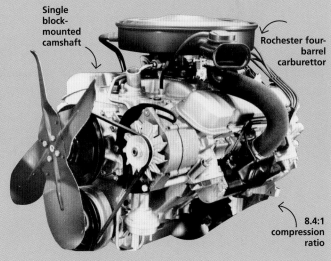

Single block-mounted camshaft

Rochester four-barrel carburettor

8.4:1 compression ratio

Rare Judge

One of the rarest GTOs is the 1971 Judge convertible. Unfortunately, the Judge option was dropped midway through the 1971 model year and only 17 convertibles were built. This pristine Judge is equipped with a High Output 7456cc (455ci) V8.

This rare GTO is one of only 17 Judge convertibles made in 1971.

Pontiac GTO JUDGE

The GTO set the infamous John DeLorean on the road to success at GM and virtually invented the muscle car, giving seemingly ordinary Tempests the performance to embarrass any sports car.

Ram Air

From 1965, all GTOs had an optional Ram Air system. By pulling a knob inside the cabin, hood vents opened and fed the carburettor with fresh, cool air.

High Output 455 V8

By 1971, the biggest and most powerful V8 you could order in the GTO was the High Output 7456cc (455ci) V8 with 355bhp.

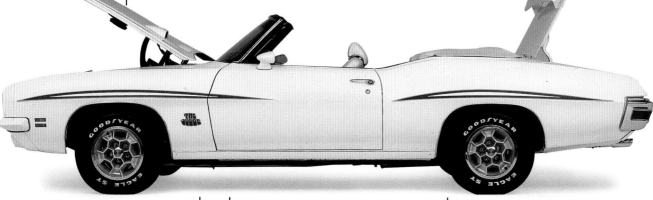

Servo front brakes

While the Le Mans range – which shared much of its hardware with the GTO – had unassisted drum brakes all-round, the GTO models have front discs, giving excellent results.

TH400 Automatic transmission

While the M-22 close-ratio manual four-speed was the racer's choice of transmissions, the TH400 automatic was easier in traffic and just as capable of delivering the power to the rear axles.

Positraction rear axle

Since these cars deliver a lot of power, a positraction rear axle was a popular option. For maximum acceleration, GTOs differentials were available with up to 4.33:1 gearing.

"Judge" graphics

If you wanted to get noticed, the Judge was the car to have. If the huge wing didn't make a loud enough statement, the multi-coloured graphics sure did.

Wishbone front suspension

There are no surprises with the front suspension, which features double wishbones with a thick anti-roll bar, coil springs and revalved shocks.

Wider wheels

To improve cornering and road holding, the GTO has wider wheels than the base Le Mans models. This car carries optional 'Honeycomb' wheels.

Rear anti-roll bar

The rear suspension needed all the help it could get to stop the car's body roll around corners. Its standard rear anti-roll bar greatly improve the way the GTO handles.

Specifications
1971 Pontiac GTO Judge convertible

ENGINE

Type: V8
Construction: Cast-iron block and heads
Valve gear: Two valves per cylinder operated by single block-mounted camshaft via pushrods, rockers and hydraulic lifters
Bore and stroke: 105mm (4.15in) x 107mm (4.21in)
Displacement: 7456cc (455ci)
Compression ratio: 8.4:1
Induction system: Single Rochester four-barrel carburettor
Maximum power: 335bhp at 4800rpm
Maximum torque: 412lb-ft at 3200rpm
Top speed: 206km/h (128mph)
0–96km/h (0–60mph): 6.1 sec

TRANSMISSION

Turbo 400 Hydra-Matic automatic

BODY/CHASSIS

Perimeter chassis with two-door coupe or two-door convertible bodywork

SPECIAL FEATURES

The large vents on the bonnet are for the Ram Air system feeding fresh air to the four-barrel carburettor.

RUNNING GEAR

Steering: Variable-ratio power-assisted recirculating ball
Front suspension: Double wishbones with coil springs, revalved shocks and anti-roll bar
Rear suspension: Live axle with trailing radius arms, upper oblique torque arms, coil springs, revalved shocks and anti-roll bar
Brakes: Discs (front) and drums (rear)
Wheels: Honeycombs 35.6cm (14in) x 17.8cm (7in)
Tyres: G60 x 35.6cm (14in)

DIMENSIONS

Length: 5.2m (205.1in)
Width: 1.95m (76.7in)
Height: 1.32m (52in)
Wheelbase: 284cm (112in)
Track: 155cm (61in) (front), 152cm (60in) (rear)
Weight: 1766kg (3894lb)

Pontiac HURST SSJ

Redesigned for 1969, the Grand Prix became a perennial best-seller during the 1970s. Among the most exclusive and desirable models was the special Hurst SSJ, which was offered for only three model years. With big-block V8 power, it was also a very fast motorway cruiser.

'...peculiar performer.'

'A well laid-out interior with an angled dashboard and good seats makes the Grand Prix a joy to drive on longer road trips. It may have light steering and will lean through hard corners, but the Hurst SSJ was conceived as a fast cruiser – in this role, it excels. With phenomenal torque, the Hurst shifter enables you to get the most out of the 7456cc (455ci) V8. It's not the leanest, or quickest Pontiac muscle car, but the Hurst SSJ just might be the most peculiar performer.'

A curved dash with all instruments facing the driver is a Grand Prix trait.

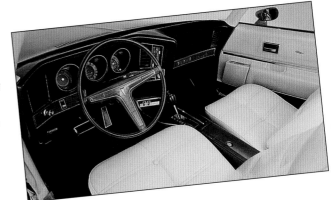

Milestones

1969 A new downsized
Grand Prix arrives, built off the intermediate A-body Tempest chassis. It comes as a two-door hardtop only and with a standard 350bhp, 6555cc (400ci) V8. A 7014cc (428ci) with 370bhp is optional. 112,486 are sold during its first year.

The Monte Carlo was Chevrolet's version of the Grand Prix.

1970 Hurst works its magic
on the Grand Prix, resulting in the SSJ model. It has a Cadillac sunroof and can be built to order. Two exterior colours are offered, Cameo White or Starlight Black, both with gold accents and performance wheels.

With a supercharged V6, the current Grand Prix is as fast as a Hurst SSJ.

1972 Making its third
and final appearance, the Hurst SSJ is offered with 6555cc (400ci) or 7456cc (455ci) V8 power and a long list of options. Production comes to an end this year.

UNDER THE SKIN

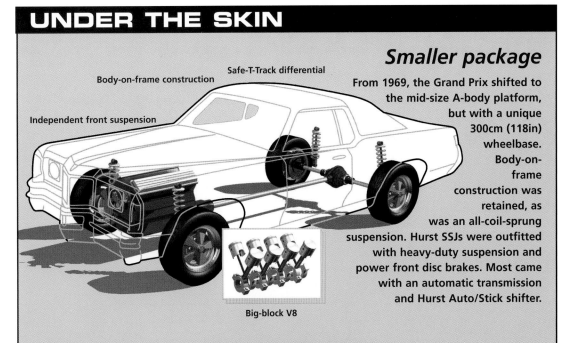

Body-on-frame construction
Safe-T-Track differential
Independent front suspension
Big-block V8

Smaller package
From 1969, the Grand Prix shifted to the mid-size A-body platform, but with a unique 300cm (118in) wheelbase. Body-on-frame construction was retained, as was an all-coil-sprung suspension. Hurst SSJs were outfitted with heavy-duty suspension and power front disc brakes. Most came with an automatic transmission and Hurst Auto/Stick shifter.

THE POWER PACK

Big bore exclusive
From 1969 until 1975, all Grand Prixs relied exclusively on big-bore Pontiac V8s for propulsion. Standard equipment in 1972 was the 6555cc (400ci) D-port unit, rated at 250bhp, breathing through a cast-iron, dual plane intake and four-barrel carburettor. For added power, buyers could order the 7456cc (455ci) mill. Hurst Performance Research modified the engines by blueprinting the internals and installing a more aggressive cam-shaft. The reworked cylinder heads included larger combustion chambers and 54/45mm (2.11/1.77in) valves. Horsepower is underrated at 250bhp with 375lb-ft of torque at a low 2400rpm.

Well equipped
Only around 450 Hurst SSJs were built between 1970 and 1972, making them rare. Desirable options include the 455 engine, Hurst Digital Computer and even a telephone. Performance-wise, these cars are capable of 15-second ETs.

Hurst SSJs were marketed as personal luxury cars with a performance bias.

Pontiac **HURST SSJ**

One of the rarest and most exclusive Detroit personal luxury performers of the 1970s, the Hurst SSJ had to be specially ordered, and although an out-of-house conversion, it was sold through Pontiac dealers with a full warranty.

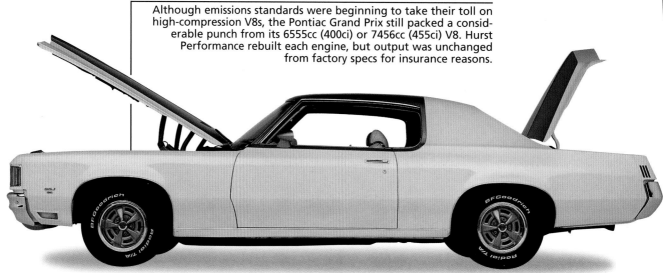

Big-block power
Although emissions standards were beginning to take their toll on high-compression V8s, the Pontiac Grand Prix still packed a considerable punch from its 6555cc (400ci) or 7456cc (455ci) V8. Hurst Performance rebuilt each engine, but output was unchanged from factory specs for insurance reasons.

Unique wheelbase
Although it shared its perimeter chassis with the A-body Tempest/Le Mans, the Grand Prix rode a unique 300cm (118in) wheelbase, freeing up more interior room.

Dual exhaust system
All Grand Prixs up until 1975 came with dual exhaust. With the optional Hurst exhaust system, the 7456cc (455ci) engines would breathe more freely, thanks to larger pipes and low-restriction mufflers.

Vinyl top
Hurst SSJs were offered in two exterior colours: Starlight Black and Cameo White. A half-vinyl roof was standard, although the owner of this one chose to remove it, resulting in a cleaner, more uncluttered appearance.

Stiffer suspension

Hurst SSJs were most often ordered with heavy-duty suspension, which meant stiffer springs and shock absorbers, plus a bigger front anti-roll bar.

Sliding sunroof

A factory-installed item, the sliding steel sunroof was taken from the equally enormous Cadillac Eldorado. It is electrically operated with a switch between the sun visors.

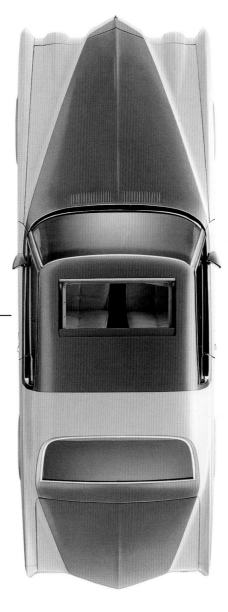

Longest bonnet

When launched for 1969, the new intermediate-size Grand Prix boasted the longest bonnet of any Detroit production car, measuring 1.82m (6ft) in length. This idea was soon copied (notably by the Chevrolet Monte Carlo) and became prevalent on domestic cars during the 1970s.

Specifications

1972 Pontiac Grand Prix Hurst SSJ

ENGINE
Type: V8
Construction: Cast-iron block and heads
Valve gear: Two valves per cylinder operated by pushrods and rockers
Bore and stroke: 105mm (4.15in) x 107mm (4.21in)
Displacement: 7456cc (455ci)
Compression ratio: 8.2:1
Induction system: Rochester Quadrajet four-barrel carburettor
Maximum power: 250bhp at 3600rpm
Maximum torque: 375lb-ft at 2400rpm
Top speed: 201km/h (125mph)
0–96km/h (0–60mph): 8.0 sec

TRANSMISSION
GM TurboHydramatic three-speed automatic

BODY/CHASSIS
Perimeter steel chassis with separate two-door coupe body

SPECIAL FEATURES

European-style door handles add to the upmarket appeal.

RUNNING GEAR
Steering: Recirculating ball
Front suspension: Unequal-length A-arms with coil springs, telescopic shock absorbers and anti-roll bar
Rear suspension: Live axle with coil springs and telescopic shock absorbers
Brakes: Discs (front), drums (rear)
Wheels: Pontiac Rally II, 17.8cm (7in) x 38.1cm (15in)
Tyres: BF Goodrich, GR60 x 38.1cm (15in)

DIMENSIONS
Length: 5.34m (210.2in)
Width: 1.92m (75.7in)
Height: 1.32m (52.1in)
Wheelbase: 300cm (118.0in)
Track: 157cm (62.0in) (front), 152cm (60.0in) (rear)
Weight: 1768kg (3898lb)

Pontiac TRANS AM SD-455

By 1974, only GM could offer anything even vaguely approaching the performance machines of the late 1960s and early 1970s, with the Chevrolet Corvette and the more powerful Pontiac Trans Am SD-455.

'...raucous take-offs.'

'The 1974 Trans Am was strictly "old school" American muscle in the performance and handling departments. Like its predecessors a decade earlier, it was great in a straight line. The massive 7456cc (455ci) engine plays a part in the car's front-heavy handling, although it gives fantastic midrange acceleration. Standard disc brakes up front and a limited-slip differential for raucous take-offs are major plus points.'

There is a comfortable feel to the interior, which is unmistakably 1970s.

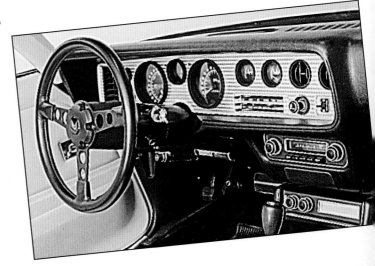

Milestones

1967 Pontiac introduces the Firebird.
It shares its basic shell with the Chevrolet Camaro, which debuted a few months earlier. Both are aimed at the 'pony market' created by the Mustang.

Chevrolet dropped the Camaro in 1975, leaving the Trans Am as GM's only muscle car.

1969 The Trans Am is offered for the first
time as the top-of-the-line performance Firebird. Standard was the Ram Air III, 335bhp 6555cc (400ci) HO engine.

The Trans Am had a bold redesign for 1979.

1974 First major body and engineering restyle
for the Firebird/Trans Am series.

1976 Last year of the Pontiac 7456cc (455ci)
engine, only available in the Trans Am as a limited edition.

UNDER THE SKIN

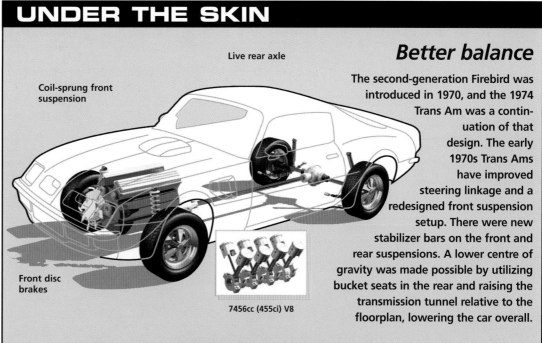

Live rear axle

Coil-sprung front suspension

Front disc brakes

7456cc (455ci) V8

Better balance

The second-generation Firebird was introduced in 1970, and the 1974 Trans Am was a continuation of that design. The early 1970s Trans Ams have improved steering linkage and a redesigned front suspension setup. There were new stabilizer bars on the front and rear suspensions. A lower centre of gravity was made possible by utilizing bucket seats in the rear and raising the transmission tunnel relative to the floorplan, lowering the car overall.

THE POWER PACK

Super-Duty punch

Pontiac's Super Duty 7456cc (455ci) was the last bastion of big-cube power for the performance enthusiast. With a compression ratio of 8.4:1, output was down as the first mandatory emissions controls began to sap power. Nonetheless, the engine still sported all the performance features of the soon-to-be-gone muscle car era. This includes a lot of displacement, four-bolt mains, forged-aluminium pistons and an 800cfm Quadrajet carb. There was even built-in provision for dry-sump lubrication. Earlier 1974 cars make use of the Ram IV camshaft and are capable of 310bhp; later 1974 cars do not and are rated at 290bhp.

Last of its kind

If you wanted a muscle car in 1974, there was only one choice: the Trans Am SD-455. Big-block Camaros had been discontinued and MOPAR, the purveyor of some of the hot muscle car property, had pulled the plug on performance.

For 1974, Pontiac gave the Trans Am new front-end treatment.

Pontiac **TRANS AM SD-455**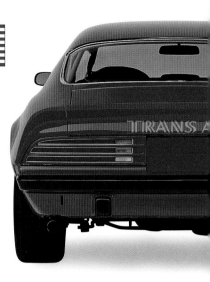

Pontiac Firebirds were offered in four series for 1974: Firebird, Esprit, Formula and Trans Am. The 455-SD engine could be ordered only in the Formula and the Trans Am. Super-Duty equipped Formulas are the rarest.

Special dash

Trans Ams featured a special steering wheel, a faux metal dash and a rally gauge cluster, which included a clock and dash-mounted tachometer. As a sign of the times, a new 'fuel economy' gauge was introduced later in the year.

LSD

Standard on the Trans Am was a limited-slip differential, ensuring minimal wheelspin and consistent launches.

New tyres

For 1974, all General Motors cars had to use steel-belted radials. Hence, the old Firestone Wide-Oval F60-15 bias-belted tyres were replaced with new Firestone 500 F60 x 38.1cm (15in) steel-belted radials.

'Soft' bumpers

New for 1974 was a soft bumper treatment front and rear, utilizing molded urethane foam. These were faced with black rubber front bars to absorb parking bumps.

Scoops galore

Pontiac made sure that the Trans Am looked aggressive and powerful with flared wheel arches and front fender air extractors. The menacing-looking, rear-facing Shaker bonnet scoop finishes off the whole effect with SD-455 decals on the side.

Restyled rear end

The rear-end treatment includes a full-width rear spoiler. Taillights are wider, in a horizontal casing, giving a more integrated appearance.

Specifications
1974 Trans Am SD-455

ENGINE
Type: V8
Construction: Cast-iron cylinder block and cylinder head
Valve gear: Two valves per cylinder
Bore and stroke: 105mm (4.15in) x 107mm (4.21in)
Displacement: 7456cc (455ci)
Compression ratio: 8.4:1
Induction system: 800cfm Quadrajet four-barrel carburettor
Maximum power: 310bhp at 4000rpm
Maximum torque: 390lb-ft at 3600rpm
Top speed: 212km/h (132mph)
0–96km/h (0–60mph): 5.4 sec

TRANSMISSION
Three-speed automatic M40 Turbo Hydramatic

BODY/CHASSIS
Steel unibody construction

SPECIAL FEATURES

The SD-455 logos are seen only on Trans Ams and Formulas.

RUNNING GEAR
Steering: Variable-ratio, ball-nut
Front suspension: A-arms with coil springs and telescopic shock absorbers
Rear suspension: Live rear axle with leaf springs and telescopic shock absorbers
Brakes: Discs (front), drums (rear)
Wheels: Steel, 38.1cm (15in) Rally II
Tyres: F60 x 38.1cm (15in) (raised white letters) Firestone steel belted

DIMENSIONS
Length: 4.98m (196.0in)
Width: 1.86m (73.4in)
Height: 1.28m (50.4in)
Wheelbase: 274cm (108.0in)
Track: 156cm (61.6in) (front), 153cm (60.3in) (rear)
Weight: 1658kg (3655lb)

USA 1978

Pontiac **TRANS AM**

With the outrageous Firebird decal taking centre stage on the bonnet, the 1978 Trans Am naturally lends itself to extreme modifications and competition in quarter-mile racing. Best of all, however, is that this car's suspension setup makes it ideal for autocrossing, too.

'...thunderous roar.'

'The comfortable bucket seats and CD player inside the Trans Am create a relaxing atmosphere. That is, until you turn the ignition! The thunderous roar of the engine is accompanied by a squeal of the tyres as you drop the clutch and leap forward with considerable force. The suspension has been stiffened, and it shows – this car grips and corners without excessive roll. However, push it too hard and the back will come around, putting you in a lurid slide.'

The modified interior of this Trans Am pays great attention to comfort.

Milestones

1969 Pontiac releases its first model to carry the name Trans Am, a Polar White-with-blue-stripes version of the Firebird.

Trans Ams were given a major facelift for the 1978 model year.

1970 The Trans Am becomes a model in its own right.

1974 The first major restyle for the Trans Am sees a new sloping front, which incorporates bumpers conforming to new federal crash legislation.

The last of the 400/403 Trans Ams were built in 1979.

1977 Another nose change sees the adoption of twin headlights.

1982 A new Trans Am with a sleeker body and pop-up headlights replaces the classic shape of the outgoing version.

UNDER THE SKIN

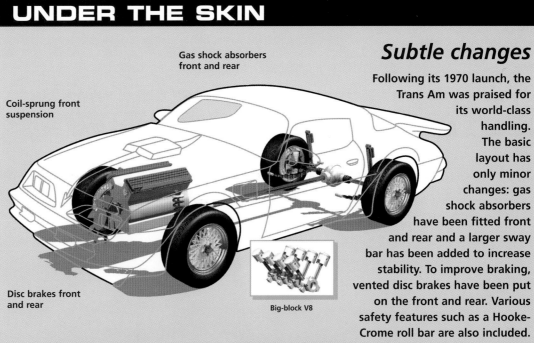

Gas shock absorbers front and rear

Coil-sprung front suspension

Disc brakes front and rear

Big-block V8

Subtle changes

Following its 1970 launch, the Trans Am was praised for its world-class handling. The basic layout has only minor changes: gas shock absorbers have been fitted front and rear and a larger sway bar has been added to increase stability. To improve braking, vented disc brakes have been put on the front and rear. Various safety features such as a Hooke-Crome roll bar are also included.

THE POWER PACK

'7456cc (455ci)' power

Powering this fiery Trans Am is a 7456cc (455ci) from a 1974 Pontiac. The V8 unit, with its cast-iron block and head, has undergone a variety of modifications. An Edelbrock Performer intake manifold has been added along with a 750cfm Quadrajet injector, increasing intake flow. A Crane cam and variable lifters allow the engine to make more power than its stock configuration, a fact seen in the output figures, which see the maximum 350bhp being produced at 4800rpm. Other additions include H.O. Enterprise TRI Y headers and dual Outlaw mufflers. The result is a really responsive motor.

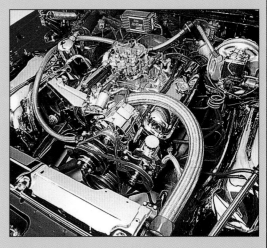

Super quick

In 1978, the most desirable of the Firebird/Trans Am range was the Grand Am Coupe. However, it could not compete with the 350bhp car featured here. Its increased performance makes it one of the most competitive street racers out there.

From the outside, there are a few subtle clues to this Trans Am's performance.

Pontiac TRANS AM

The Trans Am name was perhaps even more important than Pontiac's throughout the 1970s, as it carried the mantle of the firm's only true performance car. It is still synonymous with power today.

V8 engine

In 1974, the 7456cc (455ci) engine was the largest in Pontiac's range. Modifications have enabled it to produce 350bhp.

Safety features

To protect the driver in the event of an accident, Simpson race harnesses and a Hooke chrome roll bar have been fitted. To keep the driver firmly in position, there are also Recaro bucket seats.

Bonnet scoop

Despite the bonnet scoop, this car has no Ram Air system. The scoop is decorative and is sealed, and has no effect on performance.

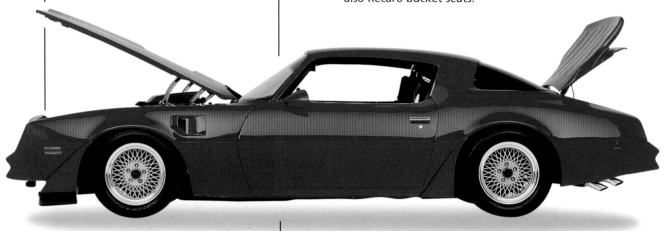

Modified suspension

To enable the chassis to match the performance, the suspension has been uprated. Herb Adams chrome sway bars have been fitted front and rear, and H.O. Enterprises coil and leaf springs have replaced the stock items. In addition to this, KYB gas shocks are used instead of the previous telescopic variety.

Luxurious interior

Despite being built for speed, the owner of this Trans Am has added all the creature comforts, including a CD deck.

Non-stock mirrors

The door mirrors of this Trans Am come from a third-generation Firebird, which was immortalized as KITT in the TV show *Knight Rider*.

Disc brakes

In contrast to its stock equivalent, this Trans Am has vented disc brakes at the rear, providing more consistent braking performance.

Specifications
1978 Pontiac Trans Am

ENGINE
Type: V8

Construction: Cast-iron block and heads

Valve gear: Two valves per cylinder operated by a single block-mounted camshaft with pushrods and rockers

Bore and stroke: 106mm (4.15in) x 107mm (4.21in)

Displacement: 7456cc (455ci)

Compression ratio: 8.0:1

Induction system: Four-barrel Rochester Quadrajet carburettor

Maximum power: 350bhp at 4800rpm

Maximum torque: 360lb-ft at 3300rpm

Top speed: 201km/h (125mph)

0–96km/h (0–60mph): 5.1 sec

TRANSMISSION
TH400 three-speed automatic

BODY/CHASSIS
Steel unitary chassis with steel body panels

SPECIAL FEATURES

The aggressive look of the Trans Am has been augmented by a front spoiler.

RUNNING GEAR
Steering: Rack-and-pinion

Front suspension: Unequal-length A-arms with coil springs and gas shock absorbers

Rear suspension: Live axle with leaf springs and gas shock absorbers

Brakes: Vented discs (front and rear)

Wheels: 40.6cm (16in) x 20.3cm (8in) Enkei polished

Tyres: Goodyear Eagle 255/50ZR16

DIMENSIONS
Length: 4.98m (196.2in)

Width: 1.94m (76.2in)

Height: 1.2m (47.6in)

   Wheelbase: 274cm (108.0in)

   Track: 161cm (63.3in) (front and rear)

   Weight: 1593kg (3511lb)

Pontiac TURBO TRANS AM

Externally it may have looked like the 1979 edition, but with a turbocharged, small-bore engine and an automatic transmission, the 1980 Firebird Trans Am was an entirely different breed. It was, however, still deemed quick enough to pace that year's Indianapolis 500, which it did in style.

'...agile on twisty roads.'

'1980 is often considered the dark time for US performance cars, but you would never know it from driving the Firebird Turbo Trans Am. Although an automatic transmission was mandatory, this Bird still has some bite. The turbo 4933cc (301ci) V8 delivers power like a big bore engine and pulls hard up to 4000rpm, but if you think this car is just a straightline screamer, think again. It is much more agile on twisty roads than can be expected, but oversteer is still easily provoked.'

All Pace Car replicas came with charcoal vinyl and oyster cloth interiors.

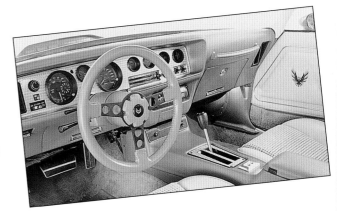

Milestones

1978 After a facelift the previous year, few changes occur for the Firebird Trans Am. The optional 6555cc (400ci) engine gets an extra 20bhp, and a WS6 suspension, including 20.3cm (8in) wide wheels. Larger Fisher T-tops supplement the Hurst Hatches. Pontiac stops building 400 engines but stockpiles them for 1979.

Pontiac released the Silver Anniversary model in 1979.

1980 Firebird Trans Am sales reach an all-time high with 117,109 units sold. A special 10th Anniversary model goes on sale; 7500 of these $10,620 specials are built.

In 1989, a second Firebird Turbo Trans Am paces the Indy 500. It is powered by a turbocharged 3.8l (232ci) V6.

1980 The 400 and 403 V8s are replaced by a turbocharged 301. The Firebird Trans Am is also chosen for Indy 500 pace car duty.

UNDER THE SKIN

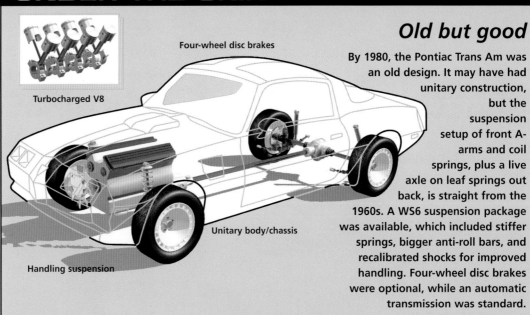

Turbocharged V8

Four-wheel disc brakes

Unitary body/chassis

Handling suspension

Old but good

By 1980, the Pontiac Trans Am was an old design. It may have had unitary construction, but the suspension setup of front A-arms and coil springs, plus a live axle on leaf springs out back, is straight from the 1960s. A WS6 suspension package was available, which included stiffer springs, bigger anti-roll bars, and recalibrated shocks for improved handling. Four-wheel disc brakes were optional, while an automatic transmission was standard.

THE POWER PACK

America's first

With the Pontiac 400 V8s and Oldsmobile 403 V8s having fallen victim to tightening emissions and fuel economy standards, Pontiac needed a solution for its premier performance car. PMD's engineers started with the 4933cc (301ci) V8 (found mostly in station wagons) and bolted a turbocharger onto it. To aid in its reliability, lower 7.5:1 compression pistons, solid-core head gaskets, a reprofiled camshaft and baffled oil pan were specified. Boost on the Garret T3 was limited to 9psi, to enable the engine to run on low-octane gasoline without suffering from detonation.

Indy race car

While collector interests mainly revolve around the older cars, the 1980 model is worth considering. The Pace Car replica (coded X87) came fully loaded, and because only 5700 were built, its value is greater than many other models.

Pace Car replicas are the most collectible 1980 Pontiacs.

Pontiac TURBO TRANS AM

Similar to most cars built in 1980, the Pontiac Firebird Turbo Trans Am wasn't very powerful. However, it did point GM in the right direction for highly successful turbocharged supercars that came on the scene by the end of the decade.

Turbocharged V8

Adding a Garret AiResearch T3 turbocharger to the 4933cc (301ci) V8 boosted power from 140bhp to 210bhp. Some of the changes it required included a sturdier bottom end, stronger rods and pistons, and heavy-duty head gaskets. Amazingly, the turbo motor put out greater torque than the old 6555cc (400ci): 345lb-ft versus 320lb-ft.

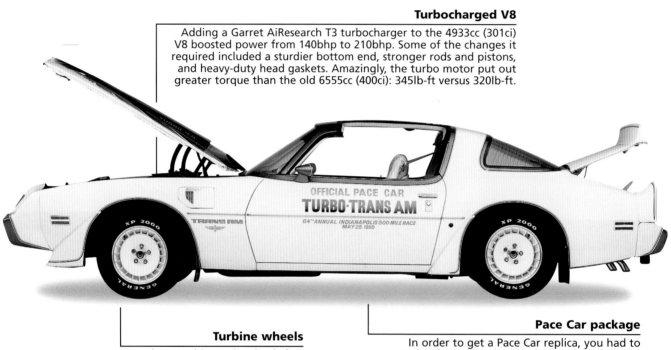

Turbine wheels

These Turbine style wheels first appeared on the 1979 10th Anniversary models and were standard on all 1980 Pace Car replicas. Built by Appliance Industries, they were a Firebird option in 1981.

Pace Car package

In order to get a Pace Car replica, you had to order the X87 package, which included special white and charcoal silver paint, two-tone interior, four-wheel disc brakes, air conditioning, power windows and an AM/FM stereo.

Four-wheel disc brakes

In 1980, only Pontiacs were available with four-wheel disc brakes. Its Mustang and Camaro rivals only offered front discs while still retaining rear drums.

Automatic transmission

Reduced emissions was the priority in 1980, therefore all Pace Car replicas used TH350 automatic transmissions. The 301 turbo engine could not clear California's tougher emissions hurdles and was not certified for sale in the Golden State, even though the cars were built there.

WS6 handling suspension

Introduced in 1978, the WS6 handling package added thicker front and rear anti-roll bars, stiffer springs and shocks, and wider wheels. This setup made the Pace Car replica one of the best cornering cars on sale in the US.

Specifications

1980 Pontiac Firebird Turbo T/A

ENGINE

Type: V8

Construction: Cast-iron block and heads

Valve gear: Two valves per cylinder operated by a single V-mounted camshaft with pushrods and rockers

Bore and stroke: 101mm (4.00in) x 76mm (3.00in)

Displacement: 4933cc (301ci)

Compression ratio: 7.5:1

Induction system: Rochester Quadrajet four-barrel carburettor and Garrett AiResearch T3 turbocharger

Maximum power: 210bhp at 4000rpm

Maximum torque: 345lb-ft at 2000rpm

Top speed: 187km/h (116mph)

0–96km/h (0–60mph): 8.2 sec

TRANSMISSION

TH350 three-speed automatic

BODY/CHASSIS

Unitary steel construction with steel panels

SPECIAL FEATURES

Pace Car door decals came in the boot and were installed by the dealer at the owner's request.

Appliance Industries Turbine wheels were standard on all Pace Car replicas.

RUNNING GEAR

Steering: Recirculating-ball

Front suspension: Unequal-length A-arms with coil springs, telescopic shock absorbers and anti-roll bar

Rear suspension: Live axle with semi-elliptic multi leaf springs, telescopic shock absorbers and anti-roll bar

Brakes: Discs (front and rear)

Wheels: Turbine aluminium, 38.1cm (15in) x 20.3cm (8in)

Tyres: Goodyear Polysteel, P225/70 R15

DIMENSIONS

Length: 4.88m (192.1in)

Width: 1.86m (73.4in)

Height: 1.28m (50.4in)

Wheelbase: 274cm (108.0in)

Track: 156cm (61.6in) (front), 153cm (60.3in) (rear)

Weight: 1666kg (3673lb)

Glossary

A

A-pillar Angled roof supports each side of the front windscreen

ABS Anti-lock braking system

Acceleration Rate of change of velocity, usually expressed as a measure of time over a given distance such as a quarter of a mile, or from rest to a given speed, such as 0–96km/h (0–60mph)

Aerodynamic drag Wind resistance, expressed as a coefficient of drag (Cd); the more streamlined a vehicle, the lower the figure

Aftermarket Accessory fitted to a vehicle after purchase, not always offered by the manufacturer

Air-cooled engine Where ambient air is used to cool the engine, by passing directly over fins on the cylinders and cylinder head

Air dam Device at the front of a car to reduce air flow underneath the vehicle and thus reduce lift at high speeds

Aluminium block Engine cylinder block cast from aluminum, usually with cast iron sleeves or liners for the cylinder bores

Anti-roll bar Transverse rod between left and right suspension at front or rear to reduce body roll

B

B-pillar roof and door frame support behind the driver

bhp Brake horse power, 1 bhp = raising 550 foot-pounds per second; 1 bhp = torque x rpm/5252 with torque measured in foot-pounds

Blown engine or "blower" Engine fitted with a system of forced air induction such as a supercharger or turbocharger

Bucket seat Seat with added support in leg and shoulder area to secure the driver while cornering, used in rally sport

C

C-pillar Side pillar to the rear of the rear seats supporting the roof

Camshaft Engine component which controls the opening and closing of valves via lobes, either directly or indirectly

Carburetor Device for vaporizing fuel and mixing it with air in an exact ratio ready for combustion, via the inlet manifold

Chassis Component to which body, engine, gearbox and suspension are attached

Close ratio Gearbox with closely spaced ratios, used in competition

Clutch Device for controlling the transmission of power from the engine to the gearbox, usually by means of friction materials

Coil spring Helical steel alloy rod used for vehicle suspension

Column change Gearchange lever mounted on the steering column

Con rod Connecting rod that links the piston and the crankshaft, the little end connecting to the piston and the big end connecting to the crankshaft

Cylinder chamber in which piston travels, usually cylindrical in shape

Cylinder head Component which carries the sparkplugs, valves, and sometimes camshafts

D

Differential Arrangement of gears in the drive axle which allows the drive wheel on the outside of a bend to travel faster than the one on the inside

Disc brake System of braking by which friction pads are pressed against a flat, circular metal surface

Double wishbone Method of suspension where each wheel is supported by an upper and lower pivoting triangular framework

Driveshaft Shaft that transmits drive from the differential to the wheel, especially on front wheel drive cars with independent rear suspension

Drivetrain Entire power transmission system from the engine's pistons to its tyres

Dry sump Where lubricating oil is contained in a separate reservoir rather than being held in the crankcase; often used in competition to prevent oil surge/starvation

E

Exhaust Device, usually of metal pipe construction, to conduct spent combustion gases away from the engine

F

Fascia A car's dashboard or instrument panel

Flathead Style of engine where the valves are mounted in the cylinder block, and the cylinder head has a flat surface

Flat twin/flat four Boxer engine configuration where cylinders are horizontally opposed to each other, such as in the VW Beetle

Fluid clutch Clutch using a fluid coupling, flywheel, or torque converter

Forced induction Engine using a turbocharger to pressurize the induction system to force air and hence more fuel, giving more power

Fuel injection Direct metered injection of fuel into the combustion cycle by mechanical or electro-mechanical means, first devised in 1902

G

Gearbox Component of the transmission system that houses a number of gears of different ratios that can be selected either automatically or manually by the driver. Different gears are selected to suit a variety of road speeds throughout the engine's rev range

Gear ratio The revolutions of a driving gear required to turn the driven gear through one revolution, calculated by the number of teeth on the driven gear divided by the number of teeth on the driving gear

Grand tourer Term originally used to describe an open-top luxury car, now typically a high performance coupé

Grill Metal or plastic protection for the radiator, often adopting a particular style or design of an individual manufacturer to make their car recognizable

GT Gran Turismo; Italian term used to describe a high performance luxury sports car or coupé

H

H-pattern Conventional gear selection layout where first and third gear are furthest from the driver and second and fourth are nearest

Helical gears Gear wheel with its teeth set oblique to the gear axis which mates with another shaft with its teeth at the same angle

Hemi engine An engine with a hemispherical combustion chamber

Hydrolastic suspension System of suspension where compressible fluids act as springs, with interconnections between wheels to aid levelling

I

Independent suspension System of suspension where all wheels move up and down independently of each other, thus having no effect on the other wheels and aiding stability

Intercooler Device to cool supercharged or turbocharged air before it enters the engine to increase density and power

K

Kamm tail Type of rear body design developed by W. Kamm, where the rear end of the car tapers sharply over the rear window and is then cut vertically to improve aerodynamics

L

Ladder frame Tradition form of chassis with two constructional rails running front to rear with lateral members adding rigidity

Limited slip differential Device to control the difference in speed between left and right driveshafts so both wheels turn at similar speeds. Fitted to reduce the likelihood of wheelspinning on slippery surfaces

M

Manifold Pipe system used for gathering or dispersal of gas or liquids

Mid-engine Vehicle with its engine mounted just behind the driver and significantly ahead of the rear axle to provide even weight distribution, thus giving the car better handling characteristics

Monobloc An engine with all its cylinders cast in one piece

Monocoque Body design where the bodyshell carries the structural strength without conventional chassis rails (see "unitary construction")

O

Overdrive Additional higher ratio gear(s), usually on the third or fourth gear selected automatically by the driver

R

Rack and pinion System of gearing used in a steering box with a toothed rail driven laterally by a pinion on the end of the steering column

Radiator Device for dissipating heat, generally from the engine coolant

Rocker arms Pivoting arm translating rotational movement of the camshaft into linear movement of the valves

Roll bar Strong, usually curved bar either internally or eternally across a vehicle's roof then secured to the floor or chassis to provide protection in the event of the car turning over. Used on some open-top sportcars

Running gear General description of a vehicle's underbody mechanicals, including the suspension, steering, brakes, and drivetrain

S

Semi-elliptic spring Leaf spring suspension used on the rear axle of older cars in which the spring conforms to a specific mathematical shape

Semi-independent suspension System on a front-wheel drive car where the wheels are located by trailing links and a torsioned crossmember

Sequential gearbox Gear selection layout in which the selection is made by a linear movement rather than in the conventional H-pattern, used on some sportscars and rally cars

Servo assistance Servo powered by a vacuum, air, hydraulics, or electrically to aid the driver to give a powerful output from minimal input. Typically used on brakes, steering and clutch

Shock absorber Hydraulic device, part of the suspension system typically mounted between the wheel and the chassis to prevent unwanted movement, to increase safety and aid comfort. More correctly known as 'damper'

Spark plug Device for igniting combustion gases via the arcing of current between two electrodes

Spoiler Device fitted to the front of the car, low to the ground, to reduce air flow under the car and increase down-force, thus improving roadholding at higher speeds

Straight 6, 8 An engine with six or eight cylinders in a single row

Supercharger Mechanically-driven air pump used to force air into the combustion cycle, improving performance

T

Tachometer device for measuring rotational speed (revs per minute, rpm) of an engine

Torque The rotational twisting force exerted by the crankshaft

Traction control Electronic system of controlling the amount of power to a given wheel to reduce wheelspin

Transmission General term for the final drive, clutch and gearbox.

Transverse engine Engine type where the crankshaft lies parallel to the axle

Turbocharger Air pump for use in forced induction engines. Similar to a supercharger but driven at very high speed by exhaust gases, rather than mechanically to increase power output

U

Unibody Monocoque construction in which the floorpan, chassis and body are welded together to form one single structure

Unitary construction Monocoque bodyshell structurally rigid enough not to require a separate chassis

Unit construction Engine in which the powerplant and transmission are together as one, integrated unit

V

Venturi principle Basis upon which carburetors work: gas flowing through a narrow opening creates a partial vacuum

W

Wheelbase The measured distance between the front and rear wheel spindles

Index